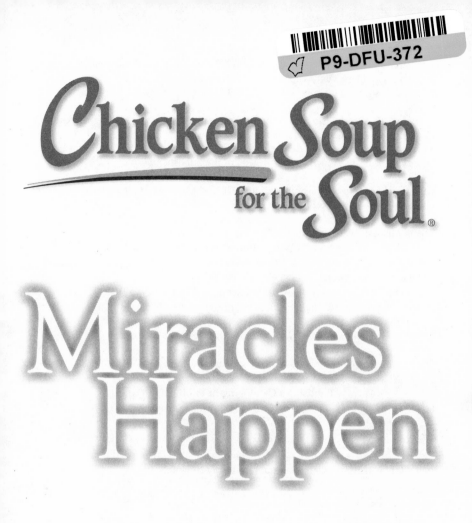

Chicken Soup
for the Soul.

Miracles
Happen

Chicken Soup for the Soul: Miracles Happen
101 Inspirational Stories about Hope, Answered Prayers, and Divine Intervention
Jack Canfield, Mark Victor Hansen, Amy Newmark
Published by Chicken Soup for the Soul Publishing, LLC www.chickensoup.com

The publisher gratefully acknowledges the many publishers and individuals who granted Chicken Soup for the Soul permission to reprint the cited material.

Front cover photo courtesy of iStockPhoto.com/gheo (© gheo).
Back cover photo courtesy of iStockPhoto.com/DNY59 (© DNY59).
Interior photo courtesy of iStockPhoto.com/zoomstudio (© zoomstudio).

Cover and Interior Design & Layout by Brian Taylor, Pneuma Books, LLC

Distributed to the booktrade by Simon & Schuster. SAN: 200-2442

Publisher's Cataloging-in-Publication Data
(Prepared by The Donohue Group)

Chicken soup for the soul : miracles happen : 101 inspirational stories
   about hope, answered prayers, and divine intervention / [compiled by]
   Jack Canfield, Mark Victor Hansen, [and] Amy Newmark.

      p. ; cm.

   ISBN: 978-1-61159-932-9

   1. Miracles--Literary collections. 2. Miracles--Anecdotes. 3. Hope--Literary collections. 4. Hope--Anecdotes. 5. Prayer--Literary collections. 6. Prayer--Anecdotes. 7. Anecdotes. I. Canfield, Jack, 1944- II. Hansen, Mark Victor. III. Newmark, Amy. IV. Title: Miracles happen : 101 inspirational stories about hope, answered prayers, and divine intervention

PN6071.M54 C452 2014
810.8/02/038202117   2013954433

PRINTED IN THE UNITED STATES OF AMERICA
on acid∞free paper

24 23 22 21 20 19 18 17 16 15 14   02 03 04 05 06 07 08 09 10 11

Chicken Soup for the Soul

Miracles Happen

101 Inspirational Stories about Hope, Answered Prayers, and Divine Intervention

Jack Canfield
Mark Victor Hansen
Amy Newmark

Chicken Soup for the Soul Publishing, LLC
Cos Cob, CT

www.chickensoup.com

Contents

❶
~Miraculous Connections~

❷
~Power of Prayer~

❸
~The Doctor Is In~

❹
~Dreams and Premonitions~

❺
~Divine Appointment~

❻

~Guardian Angels~

❼

~Divine Intervention~

❽
~Messages from Heaven~

❾
~Angels Among Us~

❿
~Love that Doesn't Die~

⑪
~Everyday Miracles~

⑫
~Count Your Blessings~

Chapter 1

Miracles Happen

Miraculous Connections

Miracle at the Maple Street Jam

Angels deliver Fate to our doorstep—and anywhere else it is needed.
~Jessi Lane Adams

I wasn't looking forward to Christmas. The past year had been a downer. I hadn't counted on missing my mother so much. Often, I'd driven by her apartment building on my nursing rounds, thinking I would run in for a quick coffee. Then I would remember—no more coffee perking, no cookies, no Swedish coffee cake, no Mom.

She left too soon. One day, she wound up in emergency for a "little sore on my leg," as she put it. Within twelve days, she was dead from a widespread infection that couldn't be stopped. The tough lady I knew was no match for necrotizing fasciitis.

I ached for her. She seldom left my mind. The day she died, I started writing songs. That was a year and three hundred songs ago. Memories of her live in everything I write.

We sang her to Heaven in the hospital room with "Angels Watch O'er Me," a song I penned while I mopped her fevered brow. How could I drum up Christmas spirit this year? I didn't think I could.

"Hi, Gloria! Coming out tonight?" It was one of my band mates.

I had forgotten. Wednesday—jam night. Bluegrassers from the town gathered for a night of music, or "jamming," coffee and treats at the community hall on Maple Street. It was usually a fun time for me.

"Nah—I've got a lot of paperwork, and it's going to take me a while," I said.

Paperwork? Where'd that come from? I had no paperwork. Actually, I wanted to put up my little Christmas village. I had bought some new pieces, and my granddaughter would be looking for it.

"Aw, come on. It's the last one before Christmas."

Jeez, she got whiny sometimes. Couldn't she tell I just wanted to have my own little pity party tonight?

"Besides, it's your turn to pick up Isabelle," my band mate said.

Isabelle. I couldn't disappoint her. I loved this woman. She was an elderly blind lady we met at a concert a few years back. Attended everything we put on. She was our best ambassador—and she made fantastic hermit cookies.

Isabelle had no family that we knew of, and couldn't drive, so she depended on the Bluegrass Guild members to bring her to the jams. She sang and played guitar too.

"I'll phone her and pick her up," I said.

Maybe the jam would pull me out of this funk. Grabbing my mandolin and my autoharp, I headed out. The Christmas village would have to wait.

The aroma of coffee greeted me, and made me miss my mother again. People rose to help Isabelle to her seat.

"Coffee, Isabelle?" someone asked her.

"No, maybe later," she answered. "Let's sing. Key of G, 'Blue Ridge Mountain Blues.'" It sure didn't take her long to unpack and tune up.

When coffee time rolled around, I hated to stop. It was one of those rare nights when everyone was clicking. The music was top notch, everyone playing his or her best.

As we prepared to go back to jamming, a stranger came in, carrying a guitar. She looked a bit lost, so I went over to greet her. I remembered my first time there, same feeling.

"Come on in—I'm Gloria. Have a seat. Still lots of coffee."

"Thanks. I'm just in town for a conference tomorrow at your hospital. I saw the jam notice in the paper. Mind if I join you? I'm Violet, by the way."

"Not at all. We're just getting ready to start up again. Love to hear you play, Violet." Her pale face was lined and tired, eyes sad. This woman had a story.

I worked at the hospital. I knew the conference had something to do with development of a new treatment centre. Maybe she was a presenter.

"Oh, I'm not that good. I just like playing along," Violet said. "Mmm. This coffee's good."

With that, she sat down across from Isabelle and me, as the banjo signaled the beginning of "Katy Daley."

Violet played a mean guitar, but she seemed distracted by Isabelle. It was not unusual. People stared at Isabelle when they first saw her. Her eyes were continually wandering upwards. She sometimes wore dark glasses, but tonight she had chosen not to.

I finished "Dream of a Miner's Child" with harmony and backup from my band mates. Isabelle stood up. In a soft voice, she began singing "Silent Night." We played along in the background, but I noticed that Violet had put her guitar down to search for something. Probably a Kleenex, because tears streamed down her face. The old carol must have hit the same nerve as me, especially as sung by Isabelle, hauntingly beautiful. Music moved some people that way.

As the carol ended, Violet got up and walked over. She took Isabelle's hand. The room fell silent. People gaped, including me.

"Mom?"

"Violet? Is that you? My girl?" The two fell into each other's arms, sobbing openly.

By the end of the evening, we were treated to a duet from Violet and Isabelle, and a heartrending story of how and why they had drifted apart. Violet was on the road, speaking to organizations about her life as a former drug addict.

Isabelle didn't say too much. She did tell us she always prayed Violet was all right.

It was the best jam ever, and I am glad I didn't miss it. My mother was still on my mind, but the events of the evening did much to dull the sorrow I had felt earlier.

The music was good, Isabelle's cookies were delicious, and we were witnesses to a miraculous reunion on Maple Street. To this day, I think angels had something to do with it.

~Gloria Jean Hansen

Nighttime Mothering

*The tie which links mother and child is of such
pure and immaculate strength as to be never violated.*
~Washington Irving

A cry in the night. Whimpering turns to desperate screams. I hear it, but I don't really want to hear it. It is dark and cold, and my bed is warm and soft.

I throw my feet over the side of the bed, as I grab my cell phone and give it a tap to light my way down the hall. The screaming sounds like death. Gruesome images flash in my mind. Broken limbs? Anaphylactic reaction? Chest pounding, I rush to the door and open it.

My silhouette is recognized in the doorway and the screaming instantly stops.

Once again, I cradle my child's head against my heart in the wee hours. I rock gently to soothe my tear-soaked baby back to sleep. My bare feet touch the cold, hardwood floors in rhythmic movement. My back starts to ache and my arms quiver from the strain, but I don't stop moving until I am sure it is safe to put him down, so that he does not notice he is no longer in my embrace.

I am tired.

As I make my way back to bed for the third time this night, images of my own mother fill my mind. She was there for me when I cried out in the night, too.

There was a time when I was sixteen and angry with my mother.

She and I had not been on speaking terms for a while, even though she didn't know it. She had abandoned me. She did not show up for my school events, she didn't know my friends' names, and she didn't care if I came home at two o'clock in the morning. She had a new infant to wake her in the night, and her new husband. I was left to cry it out on my own. So, I lied to her that night. "Going to the movies, Mom."

Instead, I got into a 1978 yellow Peugeot, packed with teenaged girls and Olde English 800, and headed up a long abandoned logging road that ran alongside a cliff, hanging over the Snake River. The forty-minute switchback ride up the hill promised a kegger party at the top.

Our chauffeur was sixteen years old. A girl named Dorothy. She had just gotten her driver's license. She beamed at every twist and turn the road made, like she was playing the latest Atari game. But she wasn't at all familiar with navigating on slippery gravel. Sometimes our back tires didn't go straight as our front tires turned a harsh corner.

Our car fell off a cliff. The only cedar left on the clear-cut logging road twenty feet down caught it.

The fall threw my friend, Jana, from the car and her arm was pinned under the left front tire, broken, but keeping her from falling to her death. The children that remained in the car with me, although mildly injured, were covered in my blood. My face and torso slammed through the dash and front windshield. I shattered the glass with my cheekbones and rib cage.

Screams in the night for our mothers.

Out of a dead sleep, in the darkness, a ringing. My mother reached out to the sound, startled, as her feet hit the cold floor for the third time that night; but this time, it wasn't the scream of her infant. The voice on the other end of the phone said, "Your daughter Jennifer is in the ER. Hurry, we don't know if she will make it." My mother rushed out of the house, forgetting all details of the phone call. Gruesome images flashed through her mind as she drove.

Because I had lied to my mother and told her I was going to the movies, she went to the wrong ER demanding to see her baby girl who wasn't there. Confused, she went to another ER, and yet another, until she found me.

She was too late. I had already left my broken body behind to become one with the light. Surrounded in a warm glow that comforted me in a divine embrace, I felt no pain, just love.

I looked down on my naked body lying on a gurney. I watched a frantic emergency room doctor and three nurses pump an air bag on my face and do chest compressions while a blaring EKG flatlined. There was panic in the room.

Just then my mother burst through the ER double doors, exhausted, yelling, "My baby, my baby!" In an instant, my breath was back with a painful force, and I cried out for my mother.

She stayed by my side for days, picking the glass out of my face with tweezers for hours, feeding me ice chips, and telling me that everything would be okay, only slipping out of the room when I didn't realize that I was no longer in her embrace.

The night comes. Mothers get up and go to their children. My babies cry out for me and I cry out for my mother. It never stops being important. But it is more than that. Sometimes it feels like life and death and mothers help us choose life.

~Jennifer Knickerbocker

The Beeping
of a Miracle

When you're a nurse you know that every day you will touch a life
or a life will touch yours.
~Author Unknown

I stuck my head into the driver's window to find a woman slumped forward and lifeless. She was not breathing. Then I noticed flames bursting from under the hood. I summoned the closest man to assist me, and together we pulled the woman from the burning car. We then laid her on the asphalt a safe distance from the flames. She still was not responding, but thankfully the movement had been enough to open her airway and she was now breathing.

I would begin nursing school later that week, and the realization of my inexperience in facing a crisis began to overwhelm me. I gratefully turned my very first patient over to the emergency crew when their helicopter landed. She was soon on her way to the hospital. An officer at the scene approached me for my account of the situation. I told him, "I begin nursing school later this week, but I was not ready for this."

After my nerves settled, my spirit began to soar. I knew I wanted to help others in their time of greatest need.

Once settled into my training, nursing became my passion. I remained truly passionate for many years after. However, as time passed, the reality of doing more with less took a toll on my enthusiasm. I felt as though the needs of my patients were simply tasks to complete by the end of a shift. My love for hospital nursing seemed to be fading.

Taking an assistant manager position on the hospital's medical unit was a welcomed break from the physically and mentally heavy workload of bedside nursing. My new duties consisted of checking on patients. I was often present for the nurses shift report every morning, and would choose which patients might need a little extra attention. Basically, though, I decided whom I would round on.

One morning, the night nurse gave the particularly sad report of a patient, Ms. Brandon, who came in via the emergency department during the early dawn hours. An unfortunate victim of an accident, she suffered irreversible damage to her right arm and required amputation. Sadly, the patient had lost the use of her legs from an accident many years prior. Now, she would have to function with the use of only one limb. Despite hearing her sad case, I fully intended to avoid Ms. Brandon's room during my morning rounds. That was, until I heard the beeping of an unattended IV pump. Any good nurse knows a beeping machine must be attended to.

I caught the sound of a soft whimper as I entered room 403. The patient lying there was Ms. Brandon, a woman in her early fifties. Her grotesquely disfigured arm was propped on a pillow to her right. I paused and asked if she was okay. While wiping the tears from her eyes with her unaffected hand, she replied, "I will be okay. I don't have to worry about losing my arm, because I know God is going to take care of me."

While looking straight at me she said, "Did you know a nurse saved my life?" She quickly explained further. "I mean after my first accident fifteen years ago, a nurse pulled me from my burning car. She helped me until the helicopter arrived to take me to the hospital. My family tried for a long time to find the nurse without any luck."

My heart fluttered. "Were you driving a black Monte Carlo?" I asked. She innocently responded, "No, it was maroon." Then the atmosphere in the dim room became surreal, and I realized that of course a dark maroon car could have looked black to me.

"Do you want to meet the nurse?" I asked.

"Yes! I have always wanted to meet that nurse!" she gushed.

"Ms. Brandon, I am that nurse," I said as I offered my hand.

Before I could say another word, she burst into tears again. This time they were tears of joy. I explained I had tried to find her for weeks after the accident and feared she was dead.

My encounter with Ms. Brandon that day was a miracle for both of us. She was blessed to know that God was still with her despite her recent misfortune, and would keep her close. I, on the other hand, felt a renewed sense of wonder and excitement for my beloved profession. Since then, I know my nursing career is a serendipitous adventure, and miracles can happen when you least expect it!

~Suzie Farthing, RN

The Angel Tree

Outside the open window
The morning air is all awash with angels.
~Richard Purdy Wilbur

"I want you to build a healing center." I heard the words in my spirit while confined to bed after a major car accident that affected my bones, organs, and brain function — my diagnosis was pages long. My bedroom smelled of liniment, and a jumble of prescription bottles cluttered my nightstand. Scheduled meetings with corporate presidents and business owners who sought my financial advice were replaced with medical appointments.

I was thirty-six years old with a grim prognosis — inoperable, deteriorating. The orthopedic doctor ripped a prescription from his pad and handed it to me saying, "Learn to live with the pain." My family physician cautioned me against the prescribed codeine. "You'll be a drug addict." I tossed the painkillers.

At night, when Edward, my husband of sixteen years, slept, I eased myself to the floor and rolled side to side with the excruciating pain. I knew Jesus Christ worked miracles. I immersed myself in God's scriptural healing promises.

After three months of inability, I heard, "…build a healing center and from all over the world people will come. Without advertisement, they'll arrive at your door." I responded without hesitation, "Yes, Lord." The improbability never occurred to me. Edward came home and I told him what I'd heard. A man of faith, Edward believed, but where would we build the center? We both feared it might be in a remote place like China.

We asked the Lord in prayer. He said, "Don't worry." The land had been set aside for the healing center from the beginning of time, and we couldn't mess it up. He said we could ask Him when we were ready to know the location. Meanwhile, God assured us that the angels were there, watching over the land. He said that as Edward and I prayed together each night, the land was growing more beautiful and our hearts were growing more beautiful as well.

Weeks passed and we were ready to know. I opened the Bible and read, "Wade across the stream… wade across the stream… it was now a river I could not cross… a river impossible to cross… Do you see son of man?" (Ezekiel 47)

I clearly understood. "Yes, Lord," I said. "It's Wading River." The community of Wading River was about fifteen miles from us, but a world away. We didn't know much about it. After Edward agreed, I phoned Carol, a crackerjack businesswoman. After my accident, Carol expressed a willingness to help me in any way. Without disclosing anything about our experiences or mentioning a healing center, I asked her to do some footwork regarding land in Wading River.

"Annette, did you know I grew up in Wading River?" she replied. "Did you know years ago I'd bought and sold plots of land in Wading River?"

I didn't know any of that. Carol said she'd inquire. She called two weeks later after looking at property.

"One piece was across from a cemetery, that won't do. Another is off the main road, a snow removal problem. There is one property I recommend."

Edward and I went to see the property. Birdsong filled the air. A black walnut spread its branches over a tangle of tall grass and wild raspberry canes. Grape vines and wisteria climbed the oaks and maples at the perimeter. To the left stood a historic Cape Cod covered with cedar shake with white-trimmed windows. The moment we stepped on the land, the soles of my feet tingled. I squeezed Edward's arm, and his quick smile told me he felt something special, too.

Robin, the Realtor, directed us, Edward supported me, and we joined her beneath a majestic tree with a girth of six feet and a spreading crown that reached one hundred feet from the ground to the azure sky. The tree was cloaked in a pleasing pattern of pale gray and green. The trunk shed its colored bark in many places, revealing a creamy white underlayer. Drifts of bark lay on the ground and some large exfoliated strips formed tubular curls.

"This house was built in the 1700s for a couple who were getting married," Robin said. "Friends came from England for the wedding and brought the seeds for this tree. The story goes that England's cities were ugly in the 1700s." I nodded agreement. Edward's firm was based in England and our British friends toasted each other with a line from a 1700s Robert Burns' poem, "Long may your chimney smoke." Written during the Industrial Revolution, it referred to the unsightly black coal smoke that stained all the buildings.

Robin warmed to her story. "The angels asked God if they could beautify the city. God asked if they had a plan. They said, 'Yes! We would like to plant trees throughout London.' God gave His approval. And in their gratitude, the angels washed the trees every day. That's why this tree sheds its bark." She spread her arms in a dramatic flourish saying, "Angels are here watching over the land!"

Our eyes widened. Robin reacted to our strange looks saying, "I'm not crazy! I just heard that story tonight." What! She had no idea why we were looking at the land. She had heard that story just in time to tell us so we would know this was the place for our house of healing.

Later, I spoke with Carol.

"Annette, let's look back on that night I went to the Realtor's office," she said. "Robin told me there was little available. Another agent walked in. She held a map of land she had just listed. You've put a binder on that property."

We bought the Wading River land. Every week Edward drove us to pray on the property. Sometimes Edward set up a tent and people would gather. Over the years people came from Nigeria, Argentina, Australia, Pakistan, Switzerland, from all over the world to pray on the land. My condition, which doctors said would deteriorate, began to improve. I was no longer bedridden, no longer had seizures. My progress was unnatural; it was supernatural. Edward and I prayed, "Our God shall provide all our needs." I began to drive again and then to study counseling. After twenty years of prayer, we built the house as our international base for healing.

Today, I hear a splash in the waterfall pool, golden sides of a fish glint in the sunlight. Church bells play "Amazing Grace" on the corner. A breeze catches the sea's salt fragrance and swirls through Wading River trees that bow and make a sound we call clapping their hands. Each window looks out on exquisite views, but my favorite faces west. Bathed in the setting sun's rays stands The Angel Tree. Fresh curls of bark pile up on the lawn each day. Because the angels are here, taking care of the land.

~Annette M. Eckart

Heartfelt Gift

The measure of a life, after all, is not its duration, but its donation.
~Corrie Ten Boom

Easter was always my favorite holiday. The weather started warming up, flowers were blooming, and the Easter Bunny was so much fun. But most importantly, it is a day to remember the resurrection of Christ.

Every year I would pick out special things to fill my children's Easter baskets—the usual candy as well as other fun items. As they grew older I continued to fill their baskets just as I did when they were younger. When asked how long I would continue this, I responded, "Until I am no longer here to do it for you."

Three years ago Easter Sunday started with giving our seventeen-year-old son his basket and seeing the joy on his face as he looked through it. We then went to church and had our Easter dinner.

That was the last normal moment in my life. I lost my son to a tragic accident that very day.

He was taken to the nearby hospital. Doctors did all they could, but my son showed no brain activity and I was told he would not pull through. They asked if we would consider donating his organs to Gift of Life.

I never thought twice about being an organ donor myself. But when asked to donate my seventeen-year-old son's organs, my emotions went everywhere. If they took his organs, it would be real and

I did not want it to be real. Finally, I was able to pull it together and agreed to donate his organs.

Now Gift of Life had a lot of work ahead of them in finding perfect matches for my son's organs. But almost immediately they came back with a perfect match for his heart—a sixteen-year-old girl who lived in another state. Even though Gift of Life normally stays within our own region, this match was too good to pass up, so they went out of state. Over the next twenty-four-plus hours, Gift of Life kept us updated as to where our son's other organs were going. A few times throughout this process they told us his liver or another organ would most likely go to someone, but then changed due to further tissue testing. But from the very beginning, the heart never changed. It would go to the sixteen-year-old girl in another state.

The following afternoon, a close friend of my family told my sister she believed she knew who and where my son's heart was going. Her friend's prayer request had gone out in a nearby town for her sixteen-year-old niece, who was about to receive a heart she had been waiting for. A phone call to the aunt of this child pretty much confirmed her niece was the one receiving my son's heart.

I felt that my guardian angel, or maybe my parents, who I had already lost, brought me this confidential information. It helped me so much to understand that even though I lost my son, he was saving a girl who had been sick since she was eight years old. After that, I had no doubt whatsoever that I had made the right decision to donate my son's organs.

Gift of Life never broke their confidentiality agreement but since we had all figured it out ourselves, I was able to meet this girl, along with her family, a year after my son's death. We have all grown close. It is remarkable how much our families have in common. And since we knew the whole story, and we agreed to give up the confidentiality, Gift of Life eventually did confirm that this was the child who received my son's heart.

~Lisa Benkert

A Tragic, But Miraculous Summer

Seeing, hearing, feeling, are miracles,
and each part and tag of me is a miracle.
~Walt Whitman

I was doing a carpentry project that summer four years ago. Inspecting leftover wood piled in a field, I accidently disturbed a wasp nest. Wearing jeans, I didn't realize a wasp had stung me just above my right knee. I was not allergic to wasp stings, and went on with the day not thinking anything about it. Two hours later, while in the work shed, I began to feel nauseated and had a terrible pain in my leg. I left the shed and went to the main house to tell the owner I had to leave. The wasp sting pain would not stop, and I went home to lie down for a while.

After resting for a few hours, the pain only got worse, so my wife Catherine took me to the hospital. In the emergency room, the doctor looked at the wasp sting and said he's seen stings like mine throughout the summer. It was no big deal. He gave me Benadryl for the reaction and Demerol for the pain. He said the pain would go away, and released me. The only worrying sign that the doctor saw was a purple bruise developing near the sting site. And it was a far bigger deal than either we or the doctor thought.

The severe pain continued throughout the night and worsened by early morning. My son, Cameron, rushed me back to the hospital.

By the time we reached the hospital, I was going into septic shock. At home, Catherine called the hospital to find out my condition. At the time, they told her I was okay, but were keeping me for observation to find out why I went into septic shock.

Several hours later, a nurse called Catherine and told her that my organs had begun to shut down. I was put in the ICU. A hole about the size of a doorknob had opened on the right side of my leg, just above my knee. They asked Catherine if I had arrived in the emergency room with my leg in that condition. Catherine replied, "The reason why he returned to the emergency room was because the pain from the wasp sting would not stop. When he left home, it was still just a purple pin dot. He came in earlier and the first doctor just looked at it and prescribed Benadryl and Demerol. He did not fully examine what else could be causing the extraordinary pain he was having."

What were they observing? Didn't my vital signs show something seriously wrong? Why hadn't they taken my clothes off to examine my whole body? They only discovered my deteriorating leg after I was transferred into ICU. The condition of my leg was deteriorating rapidly, as was my whole body. These questions cannot be answered.

Richard G. Martin, Jr., M.D., F.A.C.S. General Surgery/Breast Cancer Surgery, had just come out of surgery. Because of his expertise and experience, one of my examining doctors asked him to assess the situation. He had seen several cases similar to mine and immediately said, "This man is very sick; he needs to be transferred to a disease specialist right away." He called three hospitals: Vanderbilt in Nashville, Erlanger in Chattanooga, and Saint Thomas, also in Nashville. I was now in critical condition.

After the doctors stabilized my situation, I was flown to Saint Thomas Hospital by Life Force, an air medical transport team. At Saint Thomas, they rushed me immediately into surgery. At this hospital I was, eventually, diagnosed with group A streptococcal toxic shock syndrome. I had developed several serious infections. I had also contracted rare flesh-eating bacteria in my right leg, and it was now entering the upper part of my body.

The bacteria eventually infected several other parts of my body. I had respiratory failure, acute kidney failure, blood clots, tissue rotting and bowel failure. So much of my body was failing that only a specialist would understand.

Things were not going well. The doctors told my wife and four children that I had very little chance of survival. The family gathered at the hospital, waiting to hear the worst. The doctor returned to battle the odds, trying to save my life. I was told later these were very tense moments. Most of the medical team said I would probably not make it. The surgeon came to inform my wife. Catherine asked if there was anything more they could do. He said that if they amputated my leg at the hip and removed part of the bacteria that had entered just above the hip it would stop the spreading. She replied, "Do what you must do."

I had never been that sick in my life. Had the original doctor diagnosed my severe pain correctly from the beginning, maybe my leg might have been saved. The investigative medical doctors concluded that no one will ever know what caused this extraordinary illness. As one doctor said, "He is lucky to be alive." Another said, "His survival is a miracle of God."

Approximately a year and a half later, I personally met Dr. Martin at the Fairfield Glade. I did not know who he was until he introduced himself. He had been sitting on a bench watching his son play basketball. I had also come to watch my son play basketball. The bench was large, so I asked if I could join him. He looked at me in amazement and said, "You don't know me, do you?"

"Sorry sir, but should I?" I replied.

"I am Dr. Richard Martin. I know who you are, and I know all about your case." He then told me of his involvement in my situation. After our intense conversation, his wife came from the pool area to where we sat. He was about to introduce us, but she already knew who I was.

"Did he tell you what he did?" she asked me.

"Yes."

"His insistence that you be transferred may have saved your life," she said.

She then left and headed to the changing room.

Dr. Martin and I sat talking for quite some time while we watched our sons play. We talked about many other unrelated things. When he was leaving, I asked for his business card. I didn't ever want to forget this man.

~Jay Fox

The Chance Encounter

Coincidence is God's way of remaining anonymous.
~Albert Einstein

This past summer I sat next to a lovely eighty-something-year-old widow on a subway ride to my mom's place in Brooklyn. We had an inspiring conversation. I then asked her name. It was Beverly, which happened to be my mother-in-law's name as well as the name of my brother's mother-in-law.

I asked where in Brooklyn she lived. "By the Botanical Gardens," she said. Turns out Beverly lived one block from where I grew up! She asked where my mom now lived. "Trump Village," I said. That was where she had lived for thirty years!

I told her my mom also spends five months each year in Florida. "Where in Florida?" Beverly asked. I told her Pembroke Pines. Beverly also spends her winters every year in Pembroke Pines!

"Where in Pembroke Pines?" she asked. Turns out that my mom and Beverly both live in the same sprawling retirement community during the winter—Century Village!

So today, my mom and her caregiver, June, sat by the pool at her place in Florida. A woman came up to them, thinking my mom was someone else entirely. "Oh, I'm so sorry," she said, somewhat embarrassed. "I haven't seen you around here before. Are you new here?"

June explained that my mom has spent many winters there but lives in Brooklyn the rest of the year. "Where in Brooklyn?" the woman asked. When told Trump Village, the woman's eyes bulged.

"By any chance, does she have a son named Gary?"

June was dumbfounded. "Yes, how in the world did you know that?" she asked.

The woman couldn't stop laughing.

"I sat next to him on a subway ride in New York City last summer!"

June's mouth agape, she exclaimed, "Oh my! Is your name Beverly, by any chance?" The woman nodded. June was flabbergasted. "Gary had told me that story about your conversation on the train that day! He said he was sure we would somehow run into each other! Oh my God!"

Yep. That's all I could say when June told me about what happened. Oh my God.

~Gary Stein

The Wig

Miracles come in moments. Be ready and willing.
~Wayne Dyer

Our hiking group met at Starbucks at 8 a.m. that Sunday in Scottsdale. We were headed to Tonto National Forest in the Salome Creek Wilderness, northeast of Theodore Roosevelt Lake. Our hiking leader, Richard Allen, estimated it would take two hours to get to the trailhead. We had twenty hikers and six vehicles. My husband Dick and I drove alone so we could leave if we wanted without inconveniencing anyone else.

It was a beautiful drive through the Arizona desert that mid-March morning. Recent rains had brought green to the sagebrush and other shrubs and grasses. There was a profusion of gold and purple wildflowers, starting at the road and running right up the sides of the mountains.

We drove past the town of Punkin Center, where my former piano teacher had moved about twelve years before to live near her daughter. I told Dick that on the way back I would like to stop and look her up, if it wasn't too late in the day. He asked, "How would you find her?"

Even though I was having trouble remembering my piano teacher's name, I just knew I would. I knew she was an older woman and I recalled that she wore a large brown wig that reminded me of a beehive. I answered, "Oh, it would be easy because Punkin Center is so small, and her daughter owned a store there." Punkin Center, originally founded in 1945 as a weather station, is part of the Tonto Basin area.

I remembered being upset when she announced she was moving after I had taken piano lessons from her for several years. Not only was I fond of her, but also knew I would have trouble finding another piano teacher who would accommodate my crazy work hours as a lawyer. And I was right. When she moved, it was basically the end of my piano instruction.

Now we left Route 85, a few miles before Roosevelt Lake, taking a dirt road cut-off that would lead us around the northern end of the lake to the trailhead. Just after exiting the main highway, we came to a large "Road Closed" barrier. We cautiously went around it.

A short distance ahead, we saw the problem — the road crossed a wash, which had water running through it two feet deep. Richard Allen was concerned that deeper water was ahead from recent rains. He suggested we abandon plans to hike the Salome Creek Wilderness area and go to Four Peaks instead, another nearby wilderness area.

When we got to the Four Peaks area, the mountains still had snow in the upper elevations. We agreed to drive to the trailhead, but if we ran into snow, we would eat our lunches and head home.

The dirt road to the Four Peaks trailhead was one lane, twisting and turning up the rugged mountain. While Dick drove, I looked off the steep cliff on my right to the desert foothills below. The rapid change in altitude made me dizzy. After a particularly hair-raising bend, I announced I couldn't take any more.

Dick got the van turned around at a cutout, and headed back down the mountain. We pulled off at a viewpoint, ate our sandwiches and started home, stopping for gas along the highway.

As we came to Punkin Center, I said, "Let's stop and say hello to my teacher."

Dick pulled off the highway to take the bypass through town, saying in a puzzled tone, "I don't know where to look." Since it was Sunday, the post office and most stores were closed. But as we drove down the road through a hodgepodge of buildings, off to our left I saw a trading post up on a slight rise, set back fifty yards from the road, just before a large embankment blocked my view.

I said somewhat nonchalantly, "Oh, that must have been my teacher's daughter's store we just passed. I spotted my piano teacher's wig."

Dick uttered a large "Huh?" but he backed up and pulled the van up the rise to the front of the store.

I jumped out. It was my piano teacher. She had just closed the trading post for the day and was walking to her home about sixty yards away.

She immediately recognized us and invited us in to see her very nice manufactured house. She served mango juice and cookies, and we got caught up on what had happened in the years since she had moved from Phoenix. She had taught one of my sons piano too, and I had the pleasure of telling her he was now married with two young daughters.

As we visited, I finally remembered her name: Helene Todd. How I knew that I would find Helene if we went to Punkin Center in search of her that day is a mystery. A sequence of synchronized steps arrived at this harmonious conclusion.

It was only because Helene had left the trading post exactly when she did, and we arrived exactly when we did, that I saw her. If we had arrived a few minutes earlier because we hadn't stopped for gas, she still would have been inside the trading post when we drove by.

If we had driven by a few seconds later, I would not have seen her because she already would have walked behind the embankment that blocked the view from the road.

I had no way of knowing the trading post was the store owned by her daughter until I saw Helene walking away from it. Just driving by, it did not even appear to be open, as no cars were parked in front. Since I could not remember her name, I could not have asked passersby if they knew her.

And I would not have realized that the woman I saw from the road, in the second before my view was blocked, was my former teacher, either—except for the wig! You couldn't miss the wig!

Helene did tell us she was ninety-one, and slightly hard of hearing, but otherwise was fine.

When we got home, Dick sent Richard Allen an e-mail about what had happened. He replied the next morning:

Dear Dick and Brenda:

I'm glad things worked out okay for you. Actually, that bend was the worst place in the road. It got better after that. From the top, you can see Phoenix in the distance. I got the message that you had stopped. Thanks for being such good sports about all the changes of plans, etc. Nice that you could run into the teacher—maybe it was meant to be!

Richard

Yes, maybe it was meant to be. I can always go on another hike, but I might never have seen my piano teacher again if we had continued to the Four Peaks trailhead. She passed away two years later, and seeing her that day was indeed a pleasant, nostalgic experience.

As we travel the highway of life with incidents seemingly taking place at random, small miracles happen in a way we cannot explain.

~Brenda Warneka

The Miracle Mare

There is something about the outside of a horse that is good
for the inside of a man.
~Winston Churchill

On a cool fall day in 2010 I had the pleasure of meeting an elderly mare who would change my life and the lives of many others in profound ways. We had moved our original company, Spring Reins of Hope, to a farm in central New Jersey within the heart of Hunterdon County. Shortly after, we started a sister company, Spring Reins of Life, a nonprofit to help raise funds for equine assisted psychotherapy (EAP). We offer EAP to at-risk youth, veterans with PTSD, and bereaved children.

When I met Straw—a twenty-two-year-old Quarter Horse with some physical disabilities and deformities, I, like most people, couldn't help but feel sorry for her and wonder how she managed to get around and live a productive life. Somewhere around 2008 Straw had been involved in a bad accident (we presume a trailer/transportation debacle). She broke both of her front legs and her neck in two places. X-rays showed fusion of Straw's right ankle, fusion of the C4-C6 vertebrae, and a shattered left knee, which healed crooked and bowed. If Straw lies down to roll or rest on her right side, she has the ability to pop back up on her own. If, however, she loses her balance or slips onto her left side, she is grounded (unable to get up on her own).

At first glance, most horse people gasp and wonder how this horse was not put down after such a horrific injury. I wondered that myself. Straw's first career was as a champion-producing broodmare. In fact, I have learned that she is somewhat like "royalty" within her breed. Plainly after these injuries she would not be having any more babies.

As time went on I realized that Straw might really enjoy being a teacher and a healer in the EAP arena. We brought in a specialty farrier and an equine dental expert to ensure her stability and balance so that she could safely be loose in the arena with clients. The EAGALA Model of EAP does not permit any riding/mounted work, but clients interact heavily with the horses from the ground.

As we started integrating Straw into our work and the herd of equine therapists, it became quite clear that she was the one teaching us, not the other way around! I personally have learned so much and have grown in my own heart as a result of knowing this horse. And that pales in comparison to what I have witnessed her do with the clients who come to Spring Reins of Life, dealing with so much trauma and heavy scars from their lives.

In minutes and without saying a word, Straw teaches at-risk and gang youth the meaning of compassion and empathy. She shows PTSD veterans that while you may feel, look, or even be broken, you do not have to live broken. Straw provides a way for grieving children to feel peace. She does all of these things with ease just by simply being herself.

Straw makes no excuses and therefore does not accept any either. We all, staff and clients alike, have learned quickly that pity is a four-letter word in her book. Countless times someone will go to lead her and say or think, "Take it easy now, be careful now," only to feel themselves pulled off as she turns up the pace as if she's saying, "Worry about yourself, I'm just fine and going over there." Giving up is not an option in Straw's world—go around, go over, go through, go under, take a break, but do NOT give up!

Several of the veterans that come to the farm for EAP are hospitalized for PTSD when they first visit, and sadly, we are notified some are "on suicide watch." One group had a soldier who had completed several tours of duty in Iraq. I saw such torment in his young blue eyes. He was quiet and kept to himself. That day Straw seemed to pick this young man out of the group. Later on, he began to talk. And talk. About his farm growing up, his horse, his donkey, his divorce, and the color of the grass, etc. We later learned that he had hardly spoken in nearly six months. Seeing what Straw had overcome was like turning the key in the ignition; it revived him.

Another Iraq veteran had severe shakes from anxiety and we were working on a leading exercise so he could experience being in control of something, even if something changed while he was in control. When we asked this young man to change pace as he led Straw, he became anxious and upset. He said there was no way he would ask her to go any faster and abruptly stopped. She stopped promptly by his side. Relief washed over his face as he petted Straw, realizing that to stop was a change and that she stood right there in support of his choice. Later he saw her trotting with another veteran and asked me, "That mare with the legs, she really, really is okay, isn't she?" I let him answer his own question, for Straw and for himself.

I look at Straw now and think back to when I first met her. She looks so different to me now. I see true strength. I see survival. I see wisdom and compassion. I see love and beauty. Straw is a living miracle that provides a pathway for others to find their own miracles.

~Christianna Capra

New Direction

*You have to take risks. We will only understand the miracle of life fully when
we allow the unexpected to happen.*
~Paulo Coelho

ired, I thought as I navigated my car through the late morning traffic. I can't believe I just got fired.

Even though I saw the conflict escalating and expected
I wouldn't be at that job much longer, I was truly surprised
when I showed up at work that Thursday morning and was told my
services were no longer required. I didn't think the politics had gotten that bad, and I had been sure I'd be able to find another position
and quit first. I was wrong.

Now I had a mortgage, a car payment, credit card debts, and
living expenses, and no job.

My house felt strange when I arrived home and entered the
workday stillness. I put down my purse and thought, now what?

I'd been combing the Help Wanted section of the newspaper for
a couple of months already, applying for anything that seemed like a
good fit for my skills and experience. Nothing had materialized.

By Friday afternoon I began to wonder if maybe I was going
about this all wrong. Being without a job was frightening, certainly,
but it was also somewhat freeing. These were desperate times, and
desperate times sometimes mean drastic action. I'd felt like I was in
the wrong place doing the wrong thing for a while now, but with my
financial obligations I couldn't justify quitting my job to pursue my

dreams. Maybe now I could consider a change in direction. Maybe now I could consider a new career path, one a little more fulfilling than sitting in a cubicle all day, tracking numbers in a spreadsheet and making sure they all added up. Maybe now I could further my studies, and do what I really wanted to do.

By Saturday I was completely confused. I needed a paycheck. Dreams were for people with money, and I didn't have any. I could expand my job search outside my field and hope for the best, but that was all I could afford to do. I had responsibilities.

On Sunday I stashed my worries for the day and drove to a large convention center forty-five minutes away. My denomination was celebrating a significant anniversary in my state, and was doing it up big. My church had recruited me to help distribute communion to approximately ten thousand people, so I did my part and worshiped in the largest gathering I'd ever seen. It was hard for me to pray in such a venue—I was used to the smaller, more intimate space of my home congregation—but I prayed anyway: Please, Lord. Show me the way you want me to go.

After worship I wandered around the vendor hall. Various ministry organizations, publishing houses, charitable foundations, congregations, and schools were advertising themselves to passersby. I stopped at a few tables, vaguely curious whether a job opportunity was hiding behind any of the tri-fold displays. None was.

I worked my way through the hall, row by row, until I was finally near the exit. There I found a table advertising a prominent graduate school about an hour east of my home. The slightly gray, middle-aged gentleman standing at the table got my attention and began chatting with me.

"Enjoying the festivities?" he asked me.

I told him I was, and he asked if I'd been raised in this denomination.

"No," I said. "I just joined my church about two years ago."

"Where were you attending before that?"

Without intending to, I laid out my whole convoluted faith journey, including my break from my childhood church, my stints with atheism and agnosticism, and the two other traditions I'd visited before settling on this one. "I wasn't looking for the perfect church," I told him. "Just one where I'm comfortable serving God, without always feeling like I'm doing it wrong."

He asked me about my profession and my undergraduate degree, then a few minutes later he informed me, "I think you'd make a great pastor. Have you ever considered going into ministry?"

In fact I'd been having this conversation with my own pastor for several months; I was even taking a couple of courses at a nearby seminary, just to see how it felt. I loved the coursework and, as much as the idea frightened me, I had to admit that I felt somewhat drawn to ministry.

"I'm the Dean of Admissions," he said. "Based on what you've told me, I'd like to offer you a full merit scholarship for our Masters in Divinity program. The scholarship will cover your entire tuition for the duration of the program. We'll also give you a small stipend for books and fees. I can't make it official until I get back to my office next week, but what do you say?"

What could I say? If he'd made this offer one week earlier, I'd have turned him down immediately, citing my financial obligations and the necessity of my keeping my job. But now, with no job and a willingness to think creatively about my finances—maybe this was the answer to my prayers.

I gave him my contact information and went home. A few days later I got an official letter reiterating the offer he'd made at the convention center. I looked up some student loan information and discovered I could borrow enough money to pay for my living expenses—if I was able to sell my house and live in student housing.

I called the dean and asked about student housing. A room was available in a shared house two miles from the school; it was mine if I wanted it.

I contacted a Realtor. My house sold five days after being listed, just a hair under my asking price. I accepted the offer, put most of my belongings in storage, and began my new life as a full-time seminary student, ordination-track, that September.

God had set me in a new direction, one I never would have taken if I hadn't been fired from my job that Thursday.

~Karen Goltz

Chapter 2
Miracles Happen

Power of Prayer

Out of the Pit

Darkness cannot put out the Light. It can only make God brighter.
~Author Unknown

"If I give it everything I've got, maybe I can still free myself," I thought. I'd been saving the last of my energy for a final push, and now was the time. It had to be. I'd been stuck in the depths of a cave for hours, and my hope was fading fast. If I didn't get out soon, I wasn't going to. I clenched my jaw, strained my muscles, and used every ounce of energy left in my body in that final struggle. Everything I had was locked in combat against the limestone that had been my prison for nearly a day. My body groped and searched in the dark for a way that I could contort my body to free myself from the cold grip of the stone. I shouted in anger. No one heard. That's when I collapsed in defeat on the cold hard floor of the cave. And my hope died.

More than twenty hours earlier, my friend Emma and I had stood at the entrance to the cave. We had laughed and joked as I climbed down the steep mouth and she followed. Six of us had gone on that camping trip, but after a full day of spelunking, the others had gone back to camp to eat. Emma and I decided to explore one more cave.

The mud of the cave floor was soft and sticky as we snaked our way through the winding tunnel. The air was musty and heavy. As the passage twisted through the earth, it shrunk. Then, suddenly, after a tight squeeze, I emerged into a larger room.

"Once you make it past this narrow spot you can almost stand,"

I told Emma, as I stretched out my arms and legs and enjoyed the ample space.

"Alright, I'm almost th… " Emma's sentence was cut short. I turned around.

"Are you alright?" I asked. All I could see was her face, and her eyes were full of fear.

"I don't think so," she said. "I'm stuck."

Emma and I tried everything we could to free her, but it became apparent we needed help. Help that I couldn't go find because Emma was stuck between me and the cave mouth. That's why we were so relieved when we heard voices behind us. A beam of light shot down the tunnel.

"What's going on here?" rang a young man's voice.

"We need help," I shouted. "She's stuck."

"I've got two buddies with me," he said. "They can go find a park ranger, but I'll stay here and see if I can help from this side."

The next several hours were long and arduous. Even with the stranger's help, we weren't able to budge Emma. Eventually a park ranger came down. The fire department was on its way, but a rescue would take time. I gave Emma my shirt to cover her cold legs and tried to keep her calm.

Almost five hours after we had entered the cave, the rescue team arrived. Our rescuer slowly chiseled away the ancient cave wall, and then worked with Emma to dislodge her. "Let's get you out of here," the firefighter told her as he gave a sigh of relief. They wriggled their way out of the cave, and I followed behind.

As we worked our way out of the cave, I became hung up in a tight spot.

"Are you okay?" Emma asked.

"Yeah, I just need to take a breather, my chest is stuck," I said.

"We'll get her out of here and then come back to check on you," a fireman assured me.

Emma looked at me one last time. Then her face faded into shadow, and I was alone.

As I tried to free my chest from the rock, I found that I was making things worse. No matter what I did or how I moved, the rock squeezed tighter. The summer before, I had worked shoveling concrete. Rock that moved. I wished I could move this stone. When the fireman returned to the passage, he tried to talk me through the obstacles in this macabre game of *Twister*. I ended up wedged deeper in the crevice. I was exhausted, cold, hungry, and terrified.

The next sixteen hours were agony. Soon after my entrapment, the fireman explained that they could chisel away very little of the cave wall for fear of collapsing the cavern. Instead, the rescue team tried everything from arm power to ropes and harnesses to pull me from the cave's grip. They brought oxygen tanks and lanterns. A woman read me a note from my parents, who were now waiting at the mouth of the cave. I wondered if I would see them again.

After dozens of attempts, the rescue team moved me several inches. Enough that I could see there might be a possibility of my escape. However, I could also see that for this to happen, I would need to move my body into exactly the right position. It was also going to take extreme physical force and effort. Strength I didn't know if I had anymore. I hadn't eaten in more than twenty-four hours. I hadn't slept in forty-eight.

With the guidance of the rescue team, I stretched and strained against the cave walls. I tried every angle. I used every muscle. Several times I felt I was close, but each time I fell back into the crevice. Each time I grew more exhausted. Eventually the rescuers needed to switch shifts, and I was alone again, saving my energy for that one final push. And I did push. Alone in the cave I put everything I had into my final struggle.

Nothing happened.

Now, instead of hoping for rescue, I hoped for a swift end.

I hadn't cried for years, but alone in the darkness I wept. I cried out to God for mercy. I called out for God to hear me. Then I realized something. My strength was entirely gone, but God's was not. Until now, I had wanted to free myself with own strength. With my human strength. I knew now that this wasn't possible. If I were going to get out of this cave alive, it would be only through the strength of the

Lord. So I prayed. Not that I would have the strength to free myself. But that God would free me with His strength. And with that prayer I pushed one more time. But I didn't feel myself move my muscles. I felt myself being moved. With no struggle, my body moved exactly where it needed to go.

I was extracted from the stone.

When the rescuers returned to the passage they were astonished to see me sitting on the edge of the crevice. They helped me the rest of the way.

One woman asked me, "How did you get yourself out?"

"I didn't, I replied.

And as I emerged from the maw of the cave, I knew two things. Human strength wanes. God's does not.

~Logan Eliasen

Miracles in Uniform

When a man is at his wits' end it is not a cowardly thing to pray,
it is the only way he can get in touch with Reality.
~Oswald Chambers

I graduated from college in August 2001. A month later, the tragic events of 9/11 unfolded and changed my life forever. Before college, I had been an enlisted man in the Army. In the wake of the attacks, I felt the need to serve once again; however, that didn't happen right away.

I'd worked at a grocery store for over eight years but, foolishly, quit six months prior to graduation with the rationale that I'd have little trouble finding new employment upon graduation. I'd saved enough money to make ends meet as long as nothing went wrong. Unfortunately, within two weeks of quitting my job, the transmission blew in my car. It was all downhill from there.

I was blessed to have friends who were also small business owners and there to help during my time of need. I got pretty good at cleaning carpets and digging trenches for irrigation systems.

It helped, but it wasn't enough.

The Army kept telling me I would ship out in just a couple of weeks, so I wasn't able to get a real job.

My credit got so bad that I got turned down for a paper route.

Like I said, times were tough.

Along this dark journey, I'd often find myself in prayer, simply asking the Lord to help me make it. At the time, I thought it meant

I was asking Him to relieve me of the challenges in my life. In hindsight, He did exactly what I asked of Him. One day at a time, He helped me make it.

I finally reported to Officer Candidate School (OCS) at Fort Benning, Georgia, one year to the date after 9/11. As my luck would have it, I was assigned to Alpha Company, notoriously known as "Alphatraz," for a grueling fourteen weeks of training. I'm not exactly sure when, where, or how, but sometime early on I injured my right knee. What initially began as mild discomfort eventually became unbearable, excruciating pain.

Not only did I have intense pain in my knee, but it would also buckle several times throughout the day, which often sent me tumbling to the ground. Steps were the worst.

This went on for several weeks.

I was hesitant about going on sick call, because an extended profile, which restricts physical activity, would cause me to miss training and likely be recycled to another company. Those who do not complete OCS are reassigned to positions and units based on the needs of the Army.

The culminating event of my ordeal took place during the early hours of a chilly morning as we started what was to be a relatively short road march, fully equipped with rucksacks and training weapons, known as rubber ducks, in hand.

Within a matter of minutes, I was using the rubber duck as a crutch as tears streamed down my face. I gave it all I had but was eventually forced to abandon the road march and take refuge in the truck following our formation.

Make no mistake, the pain was immense, but the tears had more to do with the trials and tribulations I'd endured over the past year combined with a real sense of hopelessness.

Not only had the past year been filled with hardships, but so had much of my life.

I'm a lifelong stutterer.

My parents divorced when I was two. My father was a diabetic, lost his vision, and died when I was just eight years old.

We didn't have a lot. I grew up with nothing. Like many folks, I'd worked full-time while going through college, excluding those last six months.

Nothing had come easy, and all my eggs were in this basket.

By the time I got to sick call that morning, the swelling was immense and my knee was about three times its normal size.

I was given an initial ten-day profile and would indeed be recycled. I was devastated. I lost all hope.

I prayed that night. I mean, I really prayed.

For me, praying, most of the time, is as routine as brushing my teeth, turning off the light, and closing my eyes. It is just another step before going to sleep.

This night was different. It was really different.

I felt connected in a way I had only experienced on one other occasion. I asked the Lord to help me get through this difficult situation. I asked him for courage, strength, and perseverance but never asked to be healed. The tears were flowing as I eventually fell asleep.

As usual, the lights were abruptly turned on the next morning at "zero dark 30." Upon first call each day, we had only five minutes to be standing outside in formation ready to start the day.

As I readied myself to jump down from the top bunk, I grimaced while anticipating the agonizing pain that would soon follow. However, much to my surprise, I stuck that landing like Mary Lou Retton at the '84 Summer Olympics.

There was no pain. Zero. Nil. Nada. Nothing. The swelling had disappeared, too.

I was overwhelmed at the miracle before my very eyes but wasn't completely convinced, so I maintained my profile for the remainder of that day.

I experienced no setbacks, so I returned to sick call the next morning and asked the doctor to rescind my profile. He accommodated my request.

I graduated from Officer Candidate School and was sworn in as a Second Lieutenant in the United States Army on January 10, 2003. I went on to serve three tours of duty in Iraq where I experienced even more miracles in uniform, ones that can only be attributed to divine intervention.

I drove past an improvised explosive device that failed to explode.

A rocket-propelled grenade skipped across the hood of my vehicle.

A mortar landed approximately fifty feet from where I was standing without detonating.

The day I raised my right hand and stated the oath of office is undoubtedly the proudest moment of my life. I know without a shadow of a doubt that it never would've happened without the blessing of a miracle that fateful morning at Ft. Benning.

Prayer got me to OCS, but a miracle inspired by the power of prayer got me through OCS and has allowed me to serve admirably as a commissioned officer for the past decade.

I am a walking, talking true testament to the power of prayer and the existence of miracles. Believe.

~Jody Fuller

Off the Hook

Prayer does not change God, but it changes him who prays.
~Søren Kierkegaard

"You're my best friend," Marcie told me, lifting the red book in her hands. "I'm worried about you. You have got to quit smoking!" She held the self-help book out to me and said, "This book really helped my husband quit. Maybe it'll work for you too."

I sighed. My husband and children had been nagging me for years and now my dearest friend was stepping up to remind me as well. I had been smoking since I was fifteen. Over the years I had tried numerous times to quit—aversion therapy, hypnosis and many attempts at going cold turkey—but the cravings were so intense and my willpower so weak, I would be miserable and only last a week or two before giving in. Second, I had struggled with chronic depression for many years and each attempt to quit smoking would trigger an episode, exacerbating my feelings of hopelessness and despair.

"Thanks, Marce," I said, taking the book with what I hoped would pass for a grateful smile. "I'm kind of busy lately but I'll get to it as soon as I can." After she left, I took the book and set it dutifully on the coffee table where it sat, radiating guilt vibes at me. "Leave me alone," I muttered. "I'm happy smoking. I don't want to quit."

But I wasn't happy smoking, and I did want to quit. I hated knowing I was addicted to something as stupid as lighting a cylinder of leaves and sucking toxic smoke into my lungs. I knew I was playing Russian roulette with cancer.

I covered the book with a magazine, grabbed my cigarettes and went outside.

Months passed. I shuffled the book from one end of the coffee table to the other, studiously ignoring the bright red cover that said *Hooked But Not Helpless*. Each time Marcie asked if I'd read the book, I'd mutter, "Soon."

One day, in the midst of a devastating bout of depression—sadness and despair so deep that rising from bed in the morning seemed like a mountain too high to climb—I felt strangely compelled to pick it up. In resignation, I started to read. At least I'll be able to give it back to Marcie, I thought, and get it off my coffee table.

Hours later, I finished the book. Its premise for overcoming smoking addiction had been simple but innovative, teaching the reader how to change thinking patterns about smoking, and including good strategies for dealing with feelings of deprivation. Sitting back, I found myself experiencing an unfamiliar feeling… hope.

On the heels of that feeling came an unquestionable knowledge: God wanted me to quit. I put my head in my hands and groaned.

"No way, God!" The very idea made me mad. "I can't do it. You know I can't!"

But the feeling persisted. And it wouldn't leave me alone. Finally, I threw the book down on the table and, I'm embarrassed to say, issued a very irreverent ultimatum: "Apparently you want me to quit smoking, even though you know I'm drowning in depression down here. Well, I think it's completely unfair of you to even suggest it, but here's the deal: I'll try—but I'm telling you this—if I do, You have to do it all. I mean every bit of it. If I have one craving, I'm giving in and smoking."

God, His usual, enigmatic self, didn't say a word.

I got up, put my pack of cigarettes into a drawer and resigned myself to the misery of deprivation.

The rest of the day passed. The family came home and we ate dinner, watched TV and went to bed. Morning came and we all arose and went about our routines. My husband went off to work, the kids left for school and I busied myself with cleaning, laundry and my usual chores. Throughout the day, I kept having the strange feeling that I was forgetting something. I'd stop what I was doing, think, scratch my head, then when nothing came to mind, shrug and go about my work. It took about two days of this before I realized… I wasn't smoking! Not only wasn't I smoking, I had totally forgotten about it! Shocked and wary, I searched my mind for any of the cigarette cravings that had ruled my life for so long. Nothing. I had absolutely no interest in smoking.

That was twenty years ago. I have never had a craving and have never missed smoking. It is as if I had never smoked. Not a day goes by that I'm not awestruck at the magnitude of this miracle, and filled with gratitude — I'm off the hook! Thirty-five years of bondage, broken in a moment by an irreverent, even faithless prayer. And I understand now that our Father listens to and answers His children's supplications no matter what emotional state we are in when we call out.

So the next time you feel like you're all alone in the world and God's too busy or disinterested to listen to little you and your problems, He isn't. Pray anyway. What do you have to lose?

~Tina Wagner Mattern

14

Yellowstone or Bust

Faith is not belief without proof, but trust without reservation.
~Elton Trueblood

It was a beautiful morning to tour Yellowstone National Park. Our family had traveled from Illinois, planning our detour through Yellowstone on the way to visit our son in Idaho. We had decided to travel the northern route, hoping to enjoy splendid scenery. We had traveled all night and arrived at Yellowstone early that morning.

We were just in awe of the beauty of the park. As we maneuvered a sharp turn at the top of one of the high mountains, my husband suddenly exclaimed, "Oh, no, the car is losing power!"

Our hearts fell. However, just around the curve was a place we could pull off the road. Gliding to a stop, my husband and I and our three children tumbled out of the car in dismay. We stretched our legs, wondering what to do next.

My husband always carried tools when we traveled; however, they are always packed first and are in the back of the fully packed trunk.

"Okay, everyone help unload the trunk. I have to get to my tools," my husband said.

The children groaned as they headed for the back of the car. Everything in the trunk had to be removed to reach the tools. So we all helped set our personal belongings in neat piles.

After extracting his tools, my husband raised the hood of the car and began assessing the problem. He adjusted things here and there and would have one of us try to start the car again, all without much success. The sun was getting higher and things were warming up. The children were tiring of exploring that one area and beginning to feel hot and grouchy.

Finally he announced, "Well, I have tried everything I know how to do, so we will just have to flag someone down and get a ride for help."

Our youngest daughter had a suggestion. "We could pray," she said.

Stunned for a moment, my husband and I looked at each other. I know he had been praying silently and I certainly had been, but we had not thought to have a family prayer.

My husband quickly said, "Okay, gather around. Sarah, since it was your idea, why don't you offer the prayer?"

She gave a wonderful prayer, asking our Heavenly Father to help the car to start so we could have a good day and reach our destination safely. And she prayed that we would not have any more trouble on our trip. A warm feeling, that had nothing to do with the sun or heat, enveloped our family.

As we all joined in on the "Amen," we turned back to the car, gathered up the tools and put them back in the toolbox. Everyone helped repack the trunk, with the toolbox back in its place at the very far corner.

"Okay," I said. "Let's get going."

Everyone climbed into place in the car and fastened their seatbelts without any complaints. With confidence, my husband turned the key and the engine roared! We were on our way once again.

A few minutes later, as we descended the mountain, I suddenly realized what had just happened. Our Heavenly Father had truly answered a child's prayer and a miracle had occurred. We stopped to pause and give thanks to our Heavenly Father.

We continued on our vacation without any more problems, returning safely to Illinois, as she had asked.

~Shirley M. Oakes

15

Daddy's Light

Faith is like electricity. You can't see it, but you can see the light.
~Author Unknown

My dad had been battling cancer for five years and surviving that long largely because of the positive attitude born of his newfound faith. Living on the opposite end of the continent, it was hard for me to travel to see him. But when the doctors recommended hospice I knew I needed to pay him a visit. When I arrived it was obvious that my stepmother, Barb, was exhausted from caring for him. So when my younger sister, Renee, came into town, we explained that we wanted her to take a day and rest.

"The two of us can handle Daddy's care while you go home a sleep for a while. Otherwise we'll be taking care of you," Renee told her. After Barb painstakingly helped her husband of forty-three years to a chair, she agreed to take us up on our offer.

Daddy sat up for a while, but he obviously was in a lot of pain. Just before lunch he wanted to lie down. Ren and I walked him across the room to his bed. After fluffing pillows and rearranging covers until we felt that he was as comfortable as we could possibly make him, we headed toward the couches at the far side of the hospice room to catch up while Daddy slept.

Renee didn't hear him but I did. Clutching his covers until his knuckles were white with pain, he whispered, "I hate this."

I walked back to my dad's bedside with Ren following me, asking what was wrong and what was going on. Without explaining to her, I took my hurting father by the hand and said all I knew to say, "Daddy, I'm so sorry you hurt. I'm so sorry you are in this pain." Then I did what my faith had taught me to do when I didn't know what to do—I prayed. Holding his hand I prayed out loud, "Lord, you know your son hurts and you told us that we could come to you and you would give us rest. Let him rest in your arms of peace right now."

Fervently lost in prayer, I felt a sense of peace come over me. Then I felt a gentle tap on my shoulder. It was Ren. She was standing on the other side of the Daddy's bed holding his other hand.

Just as I opened my eyes, I saw a brilliant ray of light radiating between us and resting gently on my dad. His brow, furrowed from the pain, now relaxed as he slept, serenely enveloped in the glow. The light still shining, Ren began to pray out loud for my dad. When she finished, I started again. I don't know how long we stood there. Time seemed to stand still during that sacred moment.

A knock at the door interrupted us. It was a longtime family friend who had come by to check on my dad. I ushered him to the sitting area of the hospice room so that my dad could sleep. Ren joined us and we informed him of my dad's current condition.

He didn't stay long and the minute he walked out the door, Ren jumped up in her delightful, dramatic style that I had come to love over the years. "Can you believe that light?" she asked. "I'm so glad you were here, Lin, because no one would believe me. I'm not sure I would believe me!"

"I'm glad you were here too," I said.

Just then Ren's husband, Bill, joined us. She rushed to tell him our story. From the way he rolled his eyes, I could tell he wasn't buying a bit of it. Bill makes his living as an airplane pilot, and is not taken by the emotions of the moment. Turning on his heels, he walked over to the window next to the bed where my dad lay sleeping. He returned to the sitting area wide-eyed and slack-jawed.

"Ya'll, there's a building in front of that window," Bill reported, shaking his head.

"I know," I said to my skeptical brother-in-law. "You can't say it was just the sun shining through the window, and explain this away as some natural occurrence." Bill seemed to let this soak in.

My stepmom returned from a day of much needed rest, accompanied by my twin sister. We left Bill to watch my dad, and we crossed the hall to the kitchen where wonderful church folks brought meals for the hospice families each week. We ate quickly in case my dad woke up and needed something, but as we did, Ren recounted our story about our prayer and the light. "This radiance was bright yellow," she said. "And glowing."

"It enveloped the room," I chimed in.

As we both struggled for an adequate description, we stated at the same time, "It had substance."

When my dad needed God's comfort the most, the Lord was there. His presence brought light and rest to my hurting father, and that brought peace to the rest of us.

~Linda Newton

Fear of Fire

Believers, look up—take courage. The angels are nearer than you think.
~Billy Graham

As a child I had an irrational fear of fire, and I had night-mares about our home burning down. I have always believed this was the result of an oven fire at our home when I was small. I couldn't have been more than three, but I vividly remember screaming with terror as I saw flames coming out of that oven.

Our small town had only a volunteer fire department. Back then the only way to summon firefighters to the station was by setting off a loud siren. How I hated the sound of it! Even as I got older I would wind up in my parents' bed when it sounded at night. It was a great relief to me when the city stopped using it in the late 1980s, designating it for use only in the event of a disaster.

As I entered my teenage years, my fears about fire subsided and that siren remained silent. But on a summer day in 1992, those fears came racing back.

I had gone to run errands with my family that day, temporar-ily closing the office of the small motel my parents had owned and operated all my life. We locked up and left our dog in charge for a few hours. Upon our return we were horrified to see the lot full of fire trucks, and firefighters descending ladders in the front of the building. A lamp cord had shorted out, igniting a fire that swept through the front office and living quarters, leaving serious damage.

Thankfully the firefighters arrived in time to rescue our dog, but the office was a total loss.

I immediately blamed myself for what had happened. I had agreed to stay behind and mind the office that day, but at the last minute decided to go along. I can remember hugging my father and sobbing, apologizing for allowing it to happen. In his loving, gentle way, he put his hands on my face and smiled, telling me that it wasn't my fault and he was just thankful I wasn't there, where I might have been hurt or killed. The rest of the day was filled with chaos as family members and friends arrived to offer help and we began surveying the damage.

I don't recall a great deal about what went on, but I do vividly recall the moment that changed everything. As I stood at a distance from the door and watched what was happening, I saw a firefighter enter the office through a side door. Almost as if my eyes had switched into slow motion mode, I watched through a sooty window as he trudged through the office. At that moment I felt the same fear that had crippled me as a child.

I spent the rest of that summer afraid. I was nineteen years old and wouldn't leave my parents. I could hardly sleep, and when I did my dreams were filled with fires. I shook with terror at the sound of every ambulance or police car. I had to drop out of my college classes. I got up several times every night to make sure the house wasn't on fire. I was a complete mess. I couldn't even function normally, and it was sucking the life out of me. I attended counseling for PTSD, but it didn't seem to help.

I was at the end of the proverbial rope one August night when it all changed — again.

I lay in bed in the wee hours of the night, scared and crying as usual. My eyes could not stay open, but the moment I fell asleep the fire alarm inside my mind would sound. I would wake to make sure I was ready to run if a fire started. I was physically, mentally, and emotionally exhausted. I got up and sat down at my vanity table. The reflection I saw in the mirror was pathetic. I looked sick and old.

I put my face in my hands and began sobbing uncontrollably. I could not continue living this way, but didn't know what to do. In desperation I cried out, "God, please help me!" I cried a while longer, then slowly raised my head once more.

As I looked, again, at my reflection in the mirror, I caught sight of something over my left shoulder. It was a sort of white mist, almost like smoke, and it seemed to dance just behind me. I wiped my eyes, certain it was the product of too many tears and an overactive imagination. But as I looked beyond my shoulder, it was still there, thicker and even more visible than before. It mesmerized me, and I watched intently as it hovered over me. Suddenly it shifted and entered my body like lightning. At that moment I felt the unmistakable sensation of hands touching my shoulders.

I sat upright, frozen in disbelief as I felt the pressure on my shoulders intensify and a sensation of deep warmth flow from my head to my toes. I took a deep breath and the moment passed. In my own fear and doubt, I arose and made a hasty exit. I spent the rest of the night out on the couch, where I slept better than I had in two months. In sharing my experience with my mother the next morning, she surmised that an angel had visited me.

As the next few weeks passed, something amazing happened—I got my life back. I slept normally, resumed my classes, began socializing again, and no longer plagued by nightmares or afraid of sirens. In fact, just a month later, I started work as a dispatcher for our local police and fire department. I was on duty the day our city held its annual Emergency Services Appreciation Day, when a day of activities ended with a loud parade of sirens from various emergency vehicles. As part of the festivities, organizers decided to fire up the old volunteer siren, done by pulling a lever inside the police station. I was thrilled to be the one to pull that lever, that day and for years to come. I did so each time with a smile, remembering the little girl who had once been so afraid of it.

That was over twenty years ago, and I have never forgotten that night or that amazing encounter. I was recently hired as a dispatcher in another city, where setting off sirens is part of my daily routine. My co-workers hate the sound of it, but I get a real charge when I hear the volunteer siren begin to whine—and there isn't a single time it does that I don't remember my angel.

~Linda Nichols

17

Unbelief at the Crossroads

Are you wrinkled with burden? Come to God for a faith lift.
~Author Unknown

The day started like any other. Our two young children went off to their private Christian day school, and my pastor husband went to run several errands. I looked forward to having a day to catch up on housework and craft projects. But then, at 10 a.m., I got the phone call that would send us on a two-year journey of learning.

My husband Gordon hadn't seen the out-of-control car screeching toward him. The impact sent Gordon and our aging station wagon into the other lane of traffic. Thankfully, no one had any broken bones and all the passengers walked away from the accident. Only the two cars were damaged beyond repair.

But Gordon suffered an internal injury—his lower back was severely strained. The doctor reported that he would always walk with a limp and never jog again. That was not good news to a young, active, father. We had learned to cope with a variety of life's struggles, and settled in to accept this diagnosis.

Days turned into weeks and weeks turned into many months. Life was pretty normal, with one exception—Gordon was in constant pain. We accepted the fact that this accident had changed our lives forever. That fall, several family friends made it a point to visit us. Both ladies were enthusiastic and full of reports from church meetings they had just attended. They talked of learning about the love of our Heavenly Father and His desire to heal us. After hearing of Gordon's accident and his ongoing struggle with chronic pain, they insisted he should make the trip across the country to attend these services.

Our understanding of God was solid—or so we thought. Our teaching and belief did not include healings. Months passed and we had no desire to attend these so-called healing meetings. However, the next spring we found ourselves on a family road trip. We had taken up the invitation to visit our enthusiastic friend, but our plan didn't include attending one of these meetings.

We arrived at our friend's house just in time to go to the evening service. We tried every excuse possible. We were too tired. We had just driven across the country. We wanted to stay home and rest. But their prompting was not nearly as strong as the prompting we felt from the Lord to attend that evening.

We entered a large auditorium, filled with 1,000 people of every nationality. People from around the world had heard of these meetings and came to experience the presence of God in a fresh way. The problem was that we weren't sure we wanted to experience anything new. We were happy with the way we were serving our God.

The worship that evening was quiet and respectful. We had expected wild and loud. As we looked around us, we saw happy people. Many were praying. Others worshipped God in a very private way. What we had feared wasn't so bad after all. We allowed ourselves to join in and receive. Forgetting about ourselves, we started to feel the presence of God in our midst.

The preacher had finished and the worship team started singing. The invitation came for anyone who had physical pain to go forward to receive prayer. This was our critical moment. Everything in us cried for us to retreat.

Nevertheless, we decided to step out by faith and receive prayer. We were scared. I was first to position myself in line for prayer. My healing was spiritual. Gordon wasn't far behind me in the prayer line.

We found ourselves surrounded by hundreds of others who came for healing and prayer. But at that moment, we stood alone in the presence of God. Time stilled. Sounds and voices of those around us subsided. Instead of fear and doubt, we felt surrounded by a holy peace. Hands were laid on us, petitions and blessings prayed over us. Then those who ministered that evening moved on.

Gordon left the meeting that night totally healed. No more back pain. The internal, unseen pain no longer existed. Doctors could no longer find torn ligaments and tendons. We had just experienced a miracle. No, in fact, we experienced many miracles that night. We had moved past our boundaries and allowed God to perform His perfect plan for our lives. Never again would we believe that God no long healed, that He isn't still in the miracle business.

~Connie Hyde Thurber

18

Freeze

God is with you always. Simply turn your face to Him.
~Kirpal Singh

h no! The moment the latch clicked, I knew I was in trouble. While owning a charter-fishing bed and breakfast business in Seldovia, Alaska often meant problems, nothing we had ever dealt with had been this frightening.

In 1986, in response to my urging, my husband Dave resigned from a job he disliked to do what he loved most—fish. We sold our home and most of our possessions, had a boat built and, having no income, and no insurance moved with our two children to a location accessible only by boat or by plane. Dave's fishing business met with almost instant success. Clients soon learned to trust his knowledge of the sea and the sturdy craft he captained. Dave also knew where to find halibut, Alaska's most sought-after fish. A stay-at-home mom, I cooked hearty meals and did whatever else was needed to keep our growing list of clients comfortable.

A few years into the business, we added freezing of halibut for our customers. When our two small freezers proved inadequate, we purchased a used 8' x 16' walk-in freezer from The Seldovia Native Association. That the older-model freezer had never been equipped with a safety door worried me not because its hinges were bad and the door required an extra shove in order to shut tight. I would go in and pull the door closed without letting it latch, so as not to waste electricity.

One spring, before opening our business for another season, we added foam insulation to the aging freezer. Dave tore its rotting door apart, reinsulated it and installed new hinges.

"This is going to be so nice," I said, trying the latch, noting how smoothly the door worked.

We turned the freezer on the day before our first clients arrived. The next morning, following a hearty breakfast of pecan pancakes and reindeer sausage, I walked down to the boat with our clients and kissed my husband goodbye. Returning to the house, I cleaned up the kitchen and hurried out to the freezer to make sure all was ready for the fish Dave was sure to bring in. I stepped inside the freezer, turned on the light and pulled the door gently behind me as usual.

It latched! I had just shut myself in the freezer!

Maybe the door didn't shut very tight.

Did I mention that I am an optimist? I pushed with both hands. Nothing.

Backing up, I ran at the door, shoving hard against it with my shoulder. The door refused to budge. Repeated slamming forced me to face reality. The temperature inside the freezer registered well below zero. Dressed for summer, I wore no gloves, no hat, not even a jacket to help keep me warm.

No one knew I was in there. Was I going to freeze to death?

Grabbing onto one of the heavy metal carts we use for packaging fish, I rammed it against the door, then backed up and rammed it again. My efforts proved futile. The new insulation no doubt muffled whatever sound I might make. Besides, our closest neighbors lived too far away to hear.

Pushing the cart away, I bowed my head and prayed aloud, "Lord, I know you love me. If I die, I know I will go to Heaven. But what is my husband going to do without me? We have all these charter trips planned. He will come and he won't know where I am. Lord, I don't know how I'm going to get out of this freezer. There is no way I can survive until five o'clock."

Ice crystals brushed my cheeks as I closed my eyes. "God, you are my hope. If I ever needed a miracle, I need one now. If I can't get out of this freezer, I'm coming to Heaven. I'm not afraid to die."

Icy fingers of cold gripped my body. I shivered uncontrollably. How long did it take for one to freeze to death?

A gentle urging broke through the chill: Try the door one more time.

No problem. For as long as I could breathe I would keep pushing on that door.

Rather than back up and make a run for it. I placed both hands flat against the door and pushed. The door opened!

Stepping out into the warm sunshine, I began to cry. Raising my arms, feeling it's heavenly warmth, I praised God and thanked him for saving my life. I then went in the house, grabbed the phone, and called in an order for equipment that would enable us to open the door from inside.

Sunday at church as I relayed my experience, a man who had worked for The Seldovia's Native Association and had used the freezer for many years said, "Peggy, there is no way you can get out of that freezer from inside. That door cannot be opened from inside."

"I know," I said. "If God had not opened that door I would not be here today. It was a miracle from God and I thank Him!"

~Peggy A. Cloninger

A Heart that Won't Stop

Who so loves, believes the impossible.
~Elizabeth Barrett Browning

L abor definitely got its name appropriately. After many hours of this strenuous work, the nurse finally said it was time to push, and the doctor was on her way. A short time later, my physician came into the room and immediately called for assistance. I quickly realized something was not right as an army of nurses and other doctors stormed into the room. They told me I might need an emergency caesarean section. Thankfully he came on his own, a beautiful, four-pound, eight-ounce baby boy; but he wasn't crying.

Repeatedly, I asked the doctor what was wrong and why he wasn't crying. The pediatric neonatologist, neurologist and cardiologist whisked him from the room. No letting my husband cut the umbilical cord. No placing him on my chest for pictures. They simply took him away before I even got to see him.

The nurses kept assuring me everything would be fine. The doctors were working with him and I would have news soon. I was finally informed my baby's Apgar scores were 0 at birth and 2 at five minutes, which meant he was blue, had no pulse, no response to stimulation, no activity and was not breathing. After a while, they let us see him. He was so tiny and had wires attached everywhere. No "what to expect" book had prepared me for this situation. I was told my baby had brain damage, high acidosis, low blood pressure, and his lungs were not working properly. They didn't give him much hope.

About eighteen hours after birth, a nurse in the neonatal intensive care unit saw Spencer having a seizure. They gave him medication to try to stop the seizure and it sent him into respiratory and cardiac arrest. As they worked on him, they called my husband and me down to the NICU. After six shots of epinephrine to try to regulate his heart and breathing, six vials of fluid pulled from around his heart and manual CPR for over thirty minutes, the doctors gave up. They informed my husband and me that if we wanted to hold our son before he died, we needed to give them permission to stop working on him. My son had extremely low blood pressure and his heart was beating fewer than twenty times per minute.

They wrapped my newborn baby in a soft blue blanket and hat that covered everything but his little face, trying to hide the fact he was already turning gray. They said this was my opportunity to hold my baby for the first and last time. I hadn't held him since he'd been born and now I had to say hello and goodbye.

They placed my husband and me in a room off the NICU and left us with our pastor to spend the last moments of my new son's life. Not knowing what else to do, we began to pray. We prayed for God's will to be done and whatever that will was, we would be strong enough to accept and face it together. We prayed the desire of our heart be given to us, which was for our son to live, but also acknowledged we weren't in control, and whatever happened could and would be used for good.

The doctor kept coming into the room to check on us. Each time he would pull down the blanket and place a stethoscope on Spencer's little chest to see if his heart had stopped beating so he could call an official time of death. The nurses had already filled out a death certificate and informed our family and friends in the waiting room that our son had passed away. Phone calls were made to more of our family, friends, and church.

The third time the doctor came into the room to check his heart, I knew something was different. He quickly pulled the stethoscope away and took Spencer from my arms. I cried out, "Please don't take my baby from me, I don't care if his heart has stopped beating. I just want to hold him a little longer."

But the doctor replied, "I'm not taking him because his heart has stopped, sweetie. I'm taking him because his heart has started. It's back over 100 beats per minute and we need to see what is happening."

As the doctor met the nurse at the door, she asked for time of death.

"This baby isn't dead," the doctor said. "He is alive."

We experienced a miracle that day.

We spent about two more weeks at the hospital where they ran every test imaginable on our baby. They just couldn't explain how a baby that one day showed brain and lung damage, couldn't breathe on his own, and had an irregular heartbeat was now perfectly healthy. But we knew. What happened to our son was not in the medical realm, it was in the spiritual realm.

They released us after ten days with instructions to follow up with a developmental neuropsychologist to assess how Spencer might progress in the future. After meeting with that doctor we were told our son had an "area of insult" on the left lateral hemisphere of his brain in the place that controlled speech and motor skills. The injury looked consistent with a possible stroke at birth. He most likely would never be able to walk or talk—another situation for which we weren't prepared.

Again, we prayed. We also started occupational, physical and speech therapy.

With a lot of hard work and prayer, by age three Spencer could not only walk, he could run, play ball and talk. Sometimes I thought he would never be quiet, but I knew in my heart it was because God answers some prayers abundantly.

To be given life every day is a miracle. But sometimes there is a little more drama, and that is when God shows us just how great He is.

~Amy Wyatt

Chapter 3

Miracles Happen

The Doctor Is In

20

New Kind of Faith

Let God's promises shine on your problems.
~Corrie Ten Boom

I laid still and listened for my husband's car. Since the disks in my back had herniated two months earlier, I'd been in bed. Now I could discern the sound of his car from others.

Normally, I'd be half wild to have him come home. Being bedridden was lonely. But today was different. It wasn't the end of the day and Lonny wasn't coming home with our two little boys. It was the middle of the afternoon and Lonny was coming home from work because I'd called him.

I believed that I'd heard from God.

"Stand and walk," is what I thought I'd heard the Lord whisper to the quiet part of my soul.

Now I waited, heart hammering in my chest, and wondered if I'd gone mad.

My back had been my Achilles tendon for a long time. I'd had surgery several years before, and I was used to some struggle and pain. But this time was different. The pain was much worse, with sciatic pain shooting down my leg. Also, I was five months pregnant, and surgery, at this point, wasn't an option. "We'll do a clean-up job after the baby is born," my neurosurgeon said. But that was four months away. I couldn't imagine recovering from back surgery while recovering from a C-section. And how could I lift and care for a newborn when my core was stitched together like a Raggedy Ann doll?

The two little sons I already had kept me running pretty fast, so in the past I had dreamed about taking an afternoon nap. But now that I was bedridden, I longed to run with those boys. My heart broke for the walks we were missing, picnics in the park, swinging in our back yard. I even longed to wash and fold their T-shirts, to make peanut butter sandwiches, and to do even the most menial task for my family. I'd have given gold to wipe a smudgy counter clean. I wanted my life back.

Now the best time of my day was evening—when my three men came home.

"Mom, are you up there?" my six-year-old called every night. I'd hear his footsteps on the stairs.

"Where else would I be?" It was a game we played. "In the garden?"

"No," he'd holler.

"Swimming in the lake?"

"No," he'd shout. "There you are," he'd say and burst into the bedroom, his blond hair tousled. He'd smell of sweet fresh air. "I knew you'd be right here."

It was our daily ritual. Lonny and our other son would perch on the bed and conversation would run fast and free. But dinnertime would come too soon, and they'd gather around the table downstairs. They'd set up a baby monitor, so I could join their table talk too, but it wasn't the same.

The days rolled into weeks and the weeks shifted to months.

I wriggled my toes under my flannel sheet. I felt anxious. It wouldn't take long for my husband to come home.

The only good thing about being bedridden was the opportunity to read God's Word. Every afternoon, I pulled my Bible from the bedside table. I'd prop it on the high stand of my belly and dig right in. Before my back issue, finding time for this had been a struggle. But now it was just me and the Lord, and opening His Word was hearing His voice.

Many of the passages I'd read before. But with the quiet house and nothing to tug at my mind or heart, it was as though I was reading my Bible for the first time. When I read that the Lord promised to never leave me, I felt it in my spirit. When He told me to not be afraid, the sharp points of fear would pull away like retracted claws.

And one afternoon, when the sun was high and the air was still, He told me to stand and walk.

I'd been reading the gospel of John when I came to the passage about a lame man. He didn't know who Jesus was and he'd put his hope in supposed healing qualities of a pool. But Jesus sought him out and asked him if he wanted to get well. Then He told the man to get up, pick up his mat, and walk!

Get up! Walk!

The words felt like a command to me. Like the Lord whispering to my very own soul.

It was personal.

Powerful.

And it scared me to death.

So I called my husband. And instead of deeming me a mad woman, his words were kind.

"If the Lord told you to stand, then I'm going to come home."

The sun threw gold bars over my bed quilt while I waited. I ran my fingers into the light. Could this really happen? Was I imagining things? Did God still heal this way?

Before long Lonny's work boots sounded in the stairwell. A moment later, he stood in the bedroom doorway.

"Are you ready?" he asked. "If you're ready, let's hold hands and pray."

I wasn't sure what I was ready for. My hands began to shake. But Lonny kneeled on the floor beside my bed. And he cupped his hands around mine. Tight.

"Lord, if you've spoken to Shawnelle, if You intend for her to stand and walk, I ask that you be with us now."

My arms looped around Lonny's neck. His arms wrapped around my back. The baby rolled and kicked in the basin of my belly.

And I sat.

I turned and moved my legs over the side of the bed.

My feet hit the floor.

And I stood.

"You okay?" Lonny asked. I couldn't read his eyes. Surprise? Wonder? I wasn't sure. But something in my heart broke and I was warm from head to toe.

"Steps," I said. "I want to take steps."

Lonny kept his arm around me, and for the first time in months, my feet moved across the floor. Baby steps. Just two of them.

But it was walking just the same.

"I'd better rest," I said. My head felt foggy and thick. Lonny walked me back to the bed, helped me in, and then curled around me. We closed our eyes and didn't talk. At least not to each other. I'm sure we were both thanking the Lord.

Those two steps were the beginning of my miracle. The next day, I took a few more. Soon I'd walked down the stairs. Within the week, I'd resumed care of my family.

And three months later, I walked to the nursery to peer at my newborn son.

That impending surgery? It never happened.

I believe all those disks were pushed right into place.

My back was made solid and firm. Steady and supporting and sure.

Just like my new kind of faith.

~Shawnelle Eliasen

21

Abbie's Serene Smile

Peace on the outside comes from knowing God on the inside.
~Author Unknown

"We've done all we can and... Sarah, we don't think she'll survive the night," my daughter's neurosurgeon told me.

I froze.

The team created for my four-year-old Abigail, sat across from me, showered and well rested, fresh. They each had on dry-clean-only business attire under their ironed white doctor coats. I glanced at the pajama pants I had pulled on this morning—one of three pairs I'd brought. They were stiff from washing them the night before with hand soap in the small hospital sink and hanging them on the shower rod to dry. I was wearing my husband Ian's T-shirt. It was two sizes too big but still smelled like his Axe body wash. I ran my hands through my greasy hair and spun my wedding ring on my slightly thinner finger, as I stared at the images of Abbie's brain above the doctors. I felt defeated and scared, but looked down to meet each team member's gaze, then boldly said, "I won't accept that. Find someone that will save her."

I walked out of the conference room and back to the unit where my baby's lifeless body lay. I paused in her doorway and prayed, "Dear God, please don't take her." Gada, her nurse, occupied the recliner that had been my bed for weeks. She was reading Abbie the book she had earned for the spinal tap she didn't know she'd had a week ago.

Gada handed me the book. "She didn't wake up," she said. "I'm sorry." I nodded and waited for the door to click shut before I reached for the phone. I was relieved when Ian answered. I explained that Abbie had developed aseptic spinal meningitis. "She needs a shunt but they don't think she would survive the surgery. All she does is stare." After a moment of silence, he reminded me it was a three-hour drive and he was on his way. I didn't tell him to drive carefully; I knew he wouldn't.

Abbie's room was still, nothing but the steady beat of monitors tracking her every breath. I sat on the edge of her bed, picked up her limp hand and reminded myself that I would not cry. "I'm not ready to let her go," I said. I closed my eyes and thought about how we got to this point.

Three months prior, I took Abbie to the children's hospital in Pittsburgh because she had a migraine and 105-degree fever for three days; something was wrong. I could still hear myself explaining over and over that she was walking with a wide base, like she was try-ing not to fall. The doctor diagnosed her with mono and told me I could take her home to rest. I initially accepted the diagnosis, but by the time I received her release papers, I knew something more was wrong. I insisted on additional testing. Abbie was admitted; four days and every test they could think of later, she was diagnosed with an infection at the base of her brain and severe Chiari malformation.

We met with Pittsburgh's neurosurgery team and they told us that the bottom of Abbie's cerebellum had grown out the bottom of her skull and was fusing to her spinal cord. They explained that, in her case, it restricted blood flow to her brain and that until surgery was performed, she couldn't run and play, that she needed to lie still. They described it to us like this: Abbie's spinal cord was a straw; at the point where the Chiari was located, it shrunk to the diameter of a coffee stirrer. She could have a stroke or worse, they said, fall asleep one night and just not wake up. We took her home and interviewed a few neurosurgeons, deciding that Dr. Raffel of Nationwide Children's Hospital in Columbus, Ohio was the best man for the job. The date for surgery was set.

"Surgery was a success. The Chiari was very tight but back where it is supposed to be. Once she is settled in the ICU, a nurse will take you to her," Dr Raffel stated, and I fought back the urge to hug him.

When we walked into the ICU room, my heart sank; she was asleep, an IV in each hand and one in her main artery. The next day she moved to the neurology unit. Ian headed home to help with our other two kids, Jacob and Mackenzie, and return to work. Two days later, it was time to reduce the morphine and get Abbie up. As the nurse and I helped her sit without straining her neck, her eyes rolled back. Her body went limp and started to shake as she fell back to the bed. I felt like everything was in slow motion. I was afraid to blink while I watched the nurses check my baby girl's vitals. The downhill slope had begun. With each day she got weaker; she stayed asleep with no interest in anything. Five days turned into five weeks.

Minutes after Ian walked into Abbie's room, Dr. Raffel joined us. The three of us sat in silence until Dr Raffel said, "I made a few calls. My mentor suggested I give her this." He held up a vial. "He said that twenty-seven years ago he saw scans similar to Abbie's. All he had was this and massive steroids."

Ian and I reached for the authorization form and watched as Gada added this vial of medication to Abbie's IV cocktail. I'm not sure if any of us slept that night but in the morning Abbie's vital signs improved. Every hour, medication went into her IV. Two days later Abbie sat. She smiled and said, "Hey Mum, when did you get here?" Then she asked for a brownie. Ian headed home and the meds continued. Abbie improved. A week later, Dr. Raffel loaded her up with meds before they unhooked her IV and Abbie waved bye to the line of staff that had come to see her off. That three-hour drive felt like five; we wanted to get home and I needed to hug the kids I hadn't seen in almost six weeks.

Three days later, I was reading my kids their bedtime story when Abbie stopped me and said, "Mum? Where did Jesus go?" I smiled and said, "Jesus never goes anywhere. He lives in your heart. He is always with you." She pointed to the ceiling on her left and said, "But he was right there, and now he's gone." I was stunned silent for a minute. Then I asked, "Well, he is still with you. Is that what you have been looking at… Jesus?" She smiled big and said, "Oh yes. He kept saying, you will be okay my child."

Today, Abbie is a strong, healthy eight-year-old. She has a serene smile and peaceful way about her that only someone touched by God can have. I know that Jesus held my little girl when I couldn't.

~Sarah Mitchell

Luminous

God enters by a private door into each individual.
~Ralph Waldo Emerson

The *Merriam-Webster Dictionary* defines a miracle as "An extraordinary event manifesting divine intervention in human affairs." I have no doubt that I experienced a miracle.

I began attending services at an African evangelical church because some women who heard me sing at a multi-cultural festival suggested that I'd really enjoy their music. I had reservations. As a child, I experienced religious abuse and corruption that left me suspicious.

Paradoxically, I'm passionate about gospel music, and have no issues with the words of most songs. They're pure, loving and uplifting. I've even given gospel music concerts. When I was the leader of a popular club band, I usually ended the night by singing "Swing Low, Sweet Chariot," and asked the audience to drink responsibly and drive safely.

As I've sung with African-Canadian and African-American groups, I had expectations of what this church would be like. A strong director leading people with beautiful voices in soul-stirring gospel music. A passionate sermon. I had an idea what "going to church" was about. Or thought I did.

I did not expect services that lasted three to six hours, mainly consisting of dance and song. Or the phenomenon of "speaking in tongues." I listened, watched and sang along as people danced and then fell on their knees, praying. Some rolled on the floor and shook. I was moved and uneasy at the same time. It turned out that the churches I'd previously attended were quite moderate.

Church members welcomed me, and asked why I had pulled up a padded chair. Were the pews not comfortable? I explained that I'd survived assault and torture sessions that left me with a spinal crush injury, fractures and ruptured disks. I had mornings where walking was difficult. My left shoulder joint had formed into a viciously sharp point that jabbed into the muscle when I raised my arm, and the ligament between my shoulder and elbow was permanently stretched. I had about fifty percent use of my arm.

My ability to play guitar, piano, carry items and some days, even dress myself, was limited. A small amount of pressure "over the limit" caused my shoulder to dislocate, scaring onlookers and necessitating assistance. Sleep was traumatically interrupted any time I rolled to the left. I was in constant pain. My condition was inoperable. I also had chronic anemia, in a form that no mineral supplementation helped. I was exhausted from years of my body being unable to maintain a healthy level of red blood cells. I'd been to Emergency several times. I felt hopeless.

One churchwoman took charge. In the middle of the service, she stood behind me and wrapped her arms around me. Loudly, she began to pray. She asked Jesus to heal my battered body and relieve my pain. The music, prayers and dancing around me lifted me to a higher level. Other people joined in her personal prayer for me. When the altar call came, I approached, singing along and weeping with the beautiful "Softly and Tenderly."

Church members prayed in this manner for me twice more.

I still felt qualms about joining a religion, and pulled away. Such phrases as "washed in the blood of the lamb" sounded violent and off-putting to me. Wasn't Jesus supposed to be gentle? Church political views were a significant bone of contention.

Shortly after this experience, I had my semiannual medical checkup. I always dreaded the doctor relating my test results, as they invariably showed my body deteriorating further. "Inoperable" is also a depressing thing to hear.

My doctor's eyes gleamed as she pulled her chair next to mine. For the only time in the five years I've known her, we sat side by side, knees brushing. She pointed out my test results with excitement. "Your blood count is perfect," she said, tapping my chart.

"Do you mean the numbers have gone up?" I asked.

"No, I mean they're in the perfect range. Your blood is perfect. This is astonishing. Now here's the other thing," she said, and pointed to my new CAT scan results. My shoulder and arm were also perfect. Even the stretched ligament, for which medical science has no repair, had healed. One of my three spinal fractures had knitted.

"It was the faith healing!" I blurted. I outlined my church experience. My normally cynical mind didn't have an iota of doubt.

My doctor said that whatever it was, it was amazing.

"It's a miracle," I said.

She smiled and got up to leave. "Whatever it is, enjoy it."

I drove home feeling elated and confused. How could this happen as the result of a few visits to a church simply for the music—and which I no longer attended?

In my bedroom, I spontaneously dropped to my knees in the pose my mother had taught me as a child. I bowed my head and asked in wonder, "Jesus, how did you do that?"

I felt a warm, benevolent presence surround me. A deep male voice said, "I washed your blood with mine."

As I kneeled with eyes closed, I had a vision of Him crucified. His blood fell directly on me, and became luminous. The glowing red substance, half blood, half light, entered my veins and circulated throughout my body. It healed where I was ready to heal. I saw its relationship to the healing with Universal Light I'd learned from my grandmother, which I'd also rejected for a time.

I was still afraid to raise my left arm. I'd once experienced an embarrassing public scene. Disability can be lonely. While in the pool doing my routine therapy, I saw a group of people playing ball and forgot myself. For a moment, I was whole. I tried to volley the ball. Pain doubled me over, screaming.

Lifeguards, pool patrons and a doctor gathered around me. To this day, I remember it vividly. The humiliation was nearly as bad as the pain.

I went back to church one more time. Hesitantly, I started to raise my left arm in the gesture of praise I'd seen others perform. At shoulder height, I hesitated again, then gritted my teeth and raised my arm straight up. No pain. In fact, it felt great. I waved my hand.

"That's what your arm is for," I heard in my ear.

Jesus appeared to me again soon after. I was in crisis with my housing situation; nasty landlords who entered my home without notice. My PTSD symptoms were over the moon. He stood in the doorway of my bedroom with crossed arms. His linebacker shoulders filled the space. His large brown eyes were filled with compassion. "You are safe," He said emphatically. "I'm here."

I knew He was talking about not only the present situation, but my past.

I still live with considerable pain. But having the full use of my arm and no longer suffering with anemia has eased my stress considerably. I can ride a bike for a few minutes, a cherished activity my physiotherapist had forbidden.

When I'm ready, when I feel I can remain unstressed by church politics and doctrine, I'll go back and ask for help to produce more miracles.

~R. Stone

Not Mine, But Yours

When we put our cares in His hands, He puts His peace in our hearts.
~Author Unknown

I listened to my sweet daughters giggling and squealing in the back yard as they played with our gentle Border Collie, Daisy. It was a beautiful Saturday evening. The next day was Mother's Day. As I stood at the kitchen sink washing the dishes, watching the girls through the window, I marveled at how blessed I was with our family.

Our daughters, four and two years old, were truly miracles. We had tried to conceive for four years before I got pregnant with our older daughter. Our younger daughter came two years later after a miscarriage and months of infertility treatments. This Mother's Day, like every Mother's Day for the past four years, found me full of gratitude.

I was loading the dishwasher when the squeals in the back yard turned to screams. My neighbor burst through our front door.

"She's been bit! She's bleeding!" my neighbor, Rachel, yelled, running straight to the back door, opening it just in time for us to see my older daughter and her bloody face.

"The dogs were playing with each other through the fence, and she stuck her face in the opening and our dog bit her!" my neighbor explained.

We had played with Scout—the neighbor's dog—countless times, so I knew this was not a malicious act. But my child looked as though she'd been mauled.

I scooped her up and grabbed the keys to the minivan, my husband racing from the back to the house to join us. Rachel scooped up my visibly shaken and obviously frightened younger daughter; she would keep her until my mom could arrive.

As we sped to the emergency room, I kept a dishtowel pressed to my child's beautiful face. I saw a scratch mark at her hairline just over her right eye and a scratch mark on the left side of her round little chin. I feared for her eyes and her nose and her infectious little smile. I prayed that the damage under the bloody towel would be minimal.

The emergency room staff cleaned her up quickly and gently. Her eyes, thankfully, escaped any damage other than scratches on her eyelid. Her nose had deep tracks through it, but they would heal easily with antibiotic cream. Her lip, however, had a half-inch gap that formed an upside down V just under her nose. Her smile would be marred if they couldn't line up her vermillion border, or lip line, exactly.

The emergency room doctor opted to give her a medicine that would put her out completely for about fifteen minutes. That would be just enough time to stitch the vermillion border perfectly.

But there was a catch: One in every 1,000 patients administered this drug never woke up, staying in a permanent coma. The doctor assured us that he'd administered it probably a thousand times and each time, the patient woke up fifteen minutes later without fail.

We trusted the doctor, signed the consent and the nurse administered the shot. Amidst a cry of protest, our baby's body went slack, and the team swiftly positioned her lip line and gave her five stitches.

The doctor left the room and said he'd return in fifteen minutes to dismiss us.

We watched the clock.

Fifteen minutes later, our child still slept.

Thirty minutes later, a nurse came to sit with us, and our child still slept.

An hour later, the team was back in the room. They drew blood for tests, hooked my slumbering child to oxygen and a heart monitor. And still she slept.

Two hours passed. Three hours passed. Four hours passed.

Without saying a word, my husband and I comforted each other. Not wanting to utter the truth we were facing: Our child might be that one in 1,000.

Six hours passed, and I mourned the fact that it was now officially Mother's Day and I was sitting at the hospital bed of my child who wouldn't wake up. My beautiful daughter who would have perfectly repaired lips but might never smile again. I wept, but silently; I had convinced myself she was just sleeping.

The night slowly ticked on and the nurse kept vigil with us as we all stroked my daughter's wavy auburn hair and her soft hands, and rubbed her tiny chubby feet.

Exhausted and mentally spent, the words of "I Surrender All" began quietly singing through my mind.

"All to Him, I freely give."

If my child, my baby, my life, were to be in a coma for the rest of her life, I'd rather give her up to a fuller life with Him.

"I will ever love and trust Him. I surrender all."

And then I uttered the only words I had spoken since my first-born had fallen asleep: "She's Yours."

As if still in the moment eight hours ago when the nurse, now well into her second shift, had given her the shot, my daughter sat straight up in bed and announced in a rather angry tone, "I don't want that shot!"

The doctor and other personnel came into the room. After an observation period and some more testing, during which my child ask for waffles and wanted to go home and play with her dog, she was dismissed twelve hours after first being admitted.

My body was physically exhausted, but my heart was very much awake as I celebrated that Mother's Day with both of my beautifully smiling daughters. I surrendered and was given a miracle.

~Heather Davis

Boston Miracles

For with God nothing shall be impossible.
~Luke 1:37 (KJV)

Our lives turned upside down in 2005. Following a routine pre-football physical and screening heart scan, our fifteen-year-old son, Blake, was diagnosed with pulmonary arterial hypertension (PAH). After receiving the results of Blake's scan, our pediatrician, Dr. Sally Goza, referred Blake to a pediatric cardiologist, who helped coordinate more tests than we could count. Blake's cardiologist referred him to a pediatric pulmonary specialist, who became Blake's medical coordinator.

Pulmonary hypertension is a rare lung condition that causes the blood pressure to increase in the pulmonary artery, which in turn damages the small blood vessels in the lungs. Normal mean pulmonary artery pressure is 14 mm HG at rest. In PH patients, it is greater than 25 mm Hg at rest, and 30 mm Hg during exercise. Blake's was 35 to 40 mm Hg resting. We were told that Blake's life expectancy was somewhere between four and ten years. Sometime later, after scores more tests, we were told that Blake's case was aggressive, and we were looking at a prognosis of closer to four years. Blake remembers hearing that living to twenty-five would have been considered a good outcome for him.

We soldiered on. My husband, Ed, and I rejected all negative pronouncements. We have witnessed too many healing miracles that had no medical explanations. We knew without a doubt that doctors don't know everything, and cannot predict the future.

Our family, church family, and friends continued to pray for Blake's miraculous healing. We put Blake's name on various church and online prayer lists, whose members circle the globe.

As we settled into our post-diagnosis routine, we regained some of our equilibrium. We tried to live as normally as possible. All the while, doing research, studying new treatment options, and planning our lives around heart scans, blood work, diagnostic tests, and consultations with various doctors and specialists.

My husband and I closely monitored Blake's health and vital signs. Sometimes, he seemed totally fine. He would have a couple of months with no symptoms and good heart scan reports. Then, without warning, Blake would get dizzy at football practice and feel like he was going to pass out or be sick. His scans showed increased pressures.

We rode a roller coaster of ups and downs in Blake's condition for over a year and a half. Against the current wisdom of the time, Blake's doctors believed that sports and exercise could possibly help improve his lung function, so we allowed Blake to play football. We wanted Blake's life to be as normal as possible, while avoiding unnecessary risks that might make his pulmonary hypertension worse.

On July 12, 2007, after consulting with our longtime cardiologist friend, Steve Clements, we took his advice to go to Harvard's Boston Children's Hospital, where they were equipped to administer heart catheterizations during exercise. The first day's scan confirmed increased pressure in Blake's pulmonary arteries, as had previous scans. The team expected the catheterization the following day to confirm the scan results.

The next day, several doctors and aides struggled to stabilize the device equipped with bicycle pedals, as our strong 6'1", 163-pound son pedaled with the heart catheter in place. The miraculous report afterward stated, "Hemodynamics were completely normal at rest… (and) his pulmonary artery mean was 20 mm Hg, indicating a completely normal response to exercise." To summarize, there was no evidence of damage from prior elevated pulmonary artery pressure, and such pressure was gone. The doctor told us that Blake's heart was completely healthy. Furthermore, he "did not recommend any further testing or follow up on a cardiac basis."

We celebrated Blake's Boston Miracle the next day at Fenway in box seats purchased for face value. We were told by several Bostonians that getting those tickets for a sold-out game at Fenway was another miracle! That worked for us! Experiencing the Green Monster, enjoying the manual scoring, cheering the Red Sox as they beat the Toronto Blue Jays 9-4, and singing "Sweet Caroline" and "Dirty Water" with an exuberant Boston crowd, all felt miraculous to us. We thank God for every miraculous Boston moment!

~Jamie White Wyatt

They Don't Belong to Us

I've seen and met angels wearing the disguise of ordinary people living ordinary lives.
~Tracy Chapman

Dustin had always idolized the idea of being a drifter. My youngest son was nineteen and roaming the Western U.S. with friends. He frequently disappeared off the grid for months at a time before reappearing again. I worried about him and prayed that he was well.

One night, I came home from work and almost immediately received a call from a hospital in Santa Cruz, California. My son had been in an accident.

"You must come immediately," the doctor told me.

He stated that Dustin had been drinking with friends. Rather than take the pedestrian bridge from the Santa Cruz Boardwalk to town, they decided to take a shortcut on the train trestle. The trestle was about forty feet over the Santa Cruz River, which was several feet deep and contaminated.

As the boys crossed the bridge, Dustin suddenly disappeared. His friends realized he had fallen into the water. In a panic, they ran to the end of the bridge and searched for him in the river. A retired nurse, Wilma, heard their frantic cries as she rode by on her bicycle.

Hearing their fear and desperation, she slid down the hillside to help them.

They searched for about fifteen minutes before finally finding his body. He was not breathing and Wilma immediately checked him. No heartbeat. She could smell the alcohol. She later told me that she was hesitant to perform CPR because the contaminated river was known to harbor diseases. He had been underwater for so long that she doubted it would make a difference, but she decided to do it anyway.

Wilma worked on him until the EMTs arrived. They took over CPR and started his heart again. Dustin was transported to the Dominican Hospital and immediately admitted to the ICU. He had no brain activity and was put on life support with a machine breathing for him. One hour later, they located me in Washington State.

As I spoke to the doctor and he told me Dustin's slim chance of surviving, flashes of Dustin played in my mind. My husband was deployed in Iraq and all of my family lived out of state. The doctor didn't know if Dustin would make it through the night. I told him I would fly out as soon as I could.

I thought of Dustin and his wandering ways. He was a bohemian, supporting himself by his wits and guitar skills. He often played for money and scavenged for food, but he loved exploring. He often called and told me about the fascinating people he met on the road. Traveling around the country was romantic for him. I, on the other hand, always felt fearful for him. Did he have enough to eat? Where was he sleeping? Was he safe? His accident on the bridge confirmed my greatest fears. And now I was going to California to decide what would happen to him.

I dropped to the floor and wept. Wept for grandchildren I would never know, wept for not having hugged him more, wept for yelling at him. I wept that I would never see him at his wedding or hear his voice again. The reality of a forty-foot fall into five feet of water and being submerged for fifteen minutes was too much for me.

As I sobbed, I suddenly felt more peaceful. I would take care of this and take care of him. I called my boss, Al, and told him what had happened. I calmly said that I would fly out in the morning and would be in touch. I did not know when I would return. Al, a retired Air Force man, immediately offered support, as he knew Dustin's father was deployed. Did I need a ride to the airport? Did I have someone to be with me? Was there anything that he could do? I thanked him and told him I had already started arrangements and notified the Red Cross to get Doug back.

I flew out at six in the morning and arrived in California. I quickly ran through the airport and drove to the hospital, sixty miles away. I walked into the ICU and told the nurse who I was. She immediately took me to my son. Dustin was intubated and under a cryotherapy sheet. They had lowered his body temperature in an attempt to save him. His monitors showed no brain activity. He was ashen and so very cold.

As I sat at his side, I touched him. I touched his arms and his legs and his face. I gave thanks that I was with him. Nothing the doctors told me was sinking in, and they finally left. As I sat in the open bay, a cleaning lady came in. She asked if I spoke Spanish, and I nodded. Then she asked if this was my son, and I tearfully said he was. As she tidied his area, she smiled and said, "You know, they don't belong to us, our children. They belong to God. He lets us keep them for a little while but eventually they have to go back to Him. He is going to be okay. You will, too." She emptied the trash and quietly left.

As I wiped my tears, I realized she was right. For all the doctors had told me, not one word offered me any peace of mind. They spoke of parts of the brain, comas, nursing homes and slim chances. This woman spoke volumes with her simple words.

I sat for a little while longer and went to find the doctors again. When I did, I asked them to remove Dustin from the life support machine. They were horrified. "You just got here," they said. I calmly told them I had made my decision. They asked me to wait for my husband. I calmly told them that I would not. I told them Dustin was existing, not living. He would not want this, nor would his father. After several discussions, they honored my request and took him off the machine.

Two days later, Doug and I were still in Santa Cruz, at our hotel. We received a phone call from the hospital. Had we seen Dustin? No, he was not with us. Security eventually found him, skateboarding outside with his friends. He had decided the hospital room was a bit restrictive and escaped, after polishing off every crumb of his lunch.

You see, Dustin began breathing after he was taken off the machine. Later that day he woke up and said hello to me. He stunned the doctors by getting up and standing, a mere sixteen hours after I arrived in California. After some initial short-term memory loss, he quickly regained all function and an impressive appetite. He was released four days later.

Other than a slight tremor, Dustin continues to rock out on his guitar and dabbles with the banjo. He has no recollection of the accident. He works at a body shop as a detailer. We keep in touch with Wilma, who delights in knowing Dustin is well and walking around. Dustin has a girlfriend and no longer travels. I suspect he's starting to settle down.

The miracle of Dustin's accident continues to resonate with everyone touched by it. The impossible can happen, and it happened to us. Most of all, I learned comfort can come from the most remarkably humble people whom we may only meet for a few minutes yet magically strengthen us for a lifetime.

~Teresa DeLeon-Cook

Breath of Life

Don't look for God in the sky; look within your own body.
~Osho

I kept my head down as I crawled away from the burning motor home. I could not see ahead of me because of the billowing black smoke and the intense heat. I must be in Hell, I thought. And I could see the liquid pour off my arms and legs. At the time I did not know it was my skin melting from the heat. With each breath, the burning pain pierced my throat.

That was 1993. It wasn't until seven years later that I started having a breathing problem. With each gasp for breath the wheezing sounds increased. After seeing many doctors and several trips to the emergency room, the diagnosis was asthma. Inhalers became a way of life for me.

Then another seven years later, in 2007, my breathing became so bad that doctors put a scope down my throat and found my trachea was only five percent open. A normal trachea is the size of a quarter, but mine was smaller than a dime. I went to a specialist doctor at Cedars-Sinai where I had laser bronchoscope surgery. They removed a percentage of the scar tissue created by the fire fourteen years before. The wheezing began again ten months later. Every May for the past six years I have had this surgery so that I can breathe one more year.

This year would be my seventh year, and in the Bible seven means complete. All through this journey the number seven was significant. This year, my scar tissue was growing more rapidly than usual. People could hear me before they saw me, and I was afraid that I would need the surgery before May. I needed a miracle!

Our missionary son came home from Haiti to visit. He said his good friend was coming over and bringing two ladies from Kenya to pray over him and the orphanage. The five of us sat in my living room sharing all the wonders of God and how nothing was impossible. They did not know me, but could hear the struggle I had with each breath. One quietly asked if they could pray over me before they prayed for my son. I believe in the power of prayer and said, "Of course, I would love that." Each of them put a hand on my throat and one on my stomach, and started praying. They asked the Lord to send me a brand new trachea. I coughed and with the next breath all I could hear was silence.

As I lay in my bed that night thanking God for His miracle, I kept thinking how many times I had been prayed over. All the other prayers asked for God to heal my trachea and take away the scar tissue. Now I had a new trachea! After so many years, wheezing had become my new normal. So it took a few weeks to get used to the sound of quiet.

I waited until April to see my doctor and once again have the scope put down my throat. He mentioned several times how good I sounded. I said, with a big smile, "Thank you." As he checked my throat, he said, "You look so much better." I noticed on the monitor that the pale yellow scar tissue had been replaced by a healthy pink. He looked puzzled as he took out the scope. I told him the miracle story, and said, "Can I hear you say miracle?" He hugged me and whispered, "Miracle."

I wake up every morning and thank God for one more breath to share His story with so many others. I am a speaker, and was always asked to speak when my breathing was at its worst. My breathing became my testimony.

We will celebrate my twentieth burniversary next month, and I will rejoice with singing and dancing. I am completely healed, thank you God.

~Susan Lugli

The Miracle of Faith

Miracles happen to those who believe in them.
~Bernard Berenson

We sat at the kitchen table watching the snow cover the bird feeder, flake by falling flake. Soon the cardinals' brilliant red plumage contrasted with the snow-clad trees and the white-covered seeds. The chickadees' dark backs turned light, matching their white bellies, and the woodpecker's beak scattered snow as he pecked at the peanut butter and suet cake.

My husband picked up my hands, turning them over in his. The calluses caused by a lifetime of hard work were gone now, leaving his hands almost as soft as mine.

"You know that it's about time. As much as I hate to talk about it, we gotta discuss it," he said.

"I know."

"Seriously, we do have to discuss the future."

"I know, but we still have time."

He'd been off his chemotherapy treatments for three months. He didn't want to subject his body to any more poison pumped into his veins, like it had been for the past three years.

"You know what the doctor said. The cancer would spread when we stopped the treatments. It's been three months and four days. As I see it, it's time to make some plans."

I toyed with my spoon, making circles in my coffee. "I'm not convinced of that. I predict you're going to be surprised when you get the results of the scans tomorrow."

"What makes you say that?"

"Maybe I know something you don't. I have it on a higher authority that we are going to take that vacation we planned for the spring."

"Honey, you got to face it. It's early March. Our trip isn't until June. According to the doctors I won't have that much time."

"I know all that, Glen, but I have faith."

"There you go again with that faith talk." He squeezed my hand. "Hon, I wish I could believe, but I just can't."

I was forced to step out on my faith. I had to share with him or it would do no good to have faith. I had a strong impression God was telling me that our time had not yet come. We had another trip—our annual trip with our daughters. "Please dear God," I prayed silently, "I hope I have not misinterpreted the answer You gave me."

With renewed assurance, I spoke my heart. "Then I'll have enough faith for both of us. I'll go a bit further and say I promise you we'll go to Gulf Shores again this spring. The girls have their hearts set on it, and I have prayed you'd be around a while longer." I tried to laugh. "You know I can't reach the top of that feeder. I gotta have someone around to do my chores."

Tears welled in his eyes. "I wish I could always be here for you."

"You will be." I struggled to keep from crying. I never let him see me cry. I would—when it was time for us to have that talk he kept referring to, yet that time was not now.

His doctors had diagnosed him with lung cancer and given him only five weeks to live. That was three years ago. Since then we'd traveled south to the Bahamas and north to Canada, covering most of the states between, coming home for him to take a round of chemotherapy and spend time with our family.

Glen sat quietly with his head down. "We'll talk later, but soon you're going to have to face it."

"I know."

The next day our daughters, Rachel and Beth, met us at the

Kentuckiana Cancer Institute. As we waited for the doctor, they tried to hide their fear behind cheerful façades by joking around with their dad. One of them sat on one knee and the other plopped down on the other, ignoring the fact they were both in their twenties.

"Look, Daddy, you got hair!" Rachel tried to gather a bit of fuzz between her fingertips. "I can almost pinch an inch."

Beth slapped Rachel's hand away. "Let my daddy's bald head alone. I like it that way." They bumped heads as they simultaneously kissed their daddy's hairless head.

"I'm about to stand up and dump both of you children if you don't behave yourselves." He pretended to rise and they almost slid onto the floor. "You two had better go on home and start planning. Spring's just around the corner." I saw the veil of panic pass over their faces and I knew what they were thinking, but Glen surprised us. "We're gonna have us one good time in that RV come spring. We're going to Gulf Shores."

Before the discussion went further, the door opened and the doctor walked into the room. He glanced at the files in his hand. A quizzical smile spread across his face. "Mr. Kinsey, I have no explanation, no medical reasons, but the cancer is gone. You, my friend, are cancer-free. I don't know how or why."

"I do," Glen responded. "My family's been praying."

We each hugged each other and cried. There were no words for what we felt.

We had our vacation at the beautiful Gulf Shores and rambled around the Florida Panhandle before returning home. It was a miraculous vacation we shall never forget. I had my husband, and my children had their father for two more years before it was finally the right time for that dreaded talk. I thank God for His miracle that extended my husband's life, and I thank Him even more so for the greatest miracle of all — that my husband believed.

I sit at the kitchen table watching the snow cover the bird feeder, flake by falling flake. Soon the cardinals' brilliant red plumage will contrast with the snow-clad trees as they scratch in the white-covered seeds. The chickadees' dark backs will turn light, matching their white bellies, and the woodpecker's beak will scatter snow as he pecks at the peanut butter and suet cake.

There's another visitor this morning. A gray mourning dove has joined the other birds as the snowflakes cascade down.

~Jean Thompson Kinsey

But Now I See

To one who has faith, no explanation is necessary.
To one without faith, no explanation is possible.
~Thomas Aquinas

I bartered with myself, creaking back in forth in the rocking chair. *I'll check one more time.* Nestling my baby in the crook of my elbow, I scanned the penlight across his eyes. No response. Nothing.

A hot, angry tear rolled down my cheek, as the specialist's list of possible diagnoses echoed in my head. Vision problems. Blind. Retardation. "It's too soon to tell for sure," he'd said.

I took a deep breath and resumed rocking. Each night in the wee hours, Josh fussed. When the rest of the family slumbered, cozy in their beds, we rocked. His eyes searched continuously, but never seemed to find my own.

During the nights, I began to reconcile the baby I'd imagined with the baby I now held in my arms. I forgot about my previous post-pregnancy gripes like exhaustion and those extra pounds. I fretted less about Josh's flaky skin or his inability to sleep through the night. The future suddenly seemed far more uncertain and challenging than whether or not to sign up for an Aqua Baby class.

In the same rocking chair where my mother-in-law had rocked my husband, I prayed. At first, my prayers were selfish, asking God to spare our family from hardship. Soon, they evolved: "Please allow Josh to see the wonders of Your creation."

The night before Josh's baptism, my husband and I privately gave our son to God. We prayed for healing, but accepted whatever God planned for us. The next day, as our minister poured holy water over Josh's forehead, I felt only joy.

When Josh's eyes seemed to focus slightly the very next day, I decided I was just seeing what I wished to see. But each day brought new achievements to celebrate. He followed the penlight for a brief instant. He turned his head towards a bright light. He met my eyes and smiled. Finally, one night, we rocked in the dim evening light, gazing into each other's eyes.

When I brought Josh to the doctor for a follow-up assessment four weeks later, she met my enthusiasm with guarded hesitation. I didn't blame her; miracles don't make sense to the rational mind. Even I, the person who prayed for a miracle, found it difficult to accept.

Mid-examination, the doctor rolled her chair back to her desk to consult Josh's chart. She shrugged and asked, exasperated, "Is this even the same baby?"

I nodded, laughing. I'm not the same mother, though. I've been changed by a miracle.

~Jenny Sokol

Chapter 4

Miracles Happen

Dreams and Premonitions

A Heavenly Dream

We cannot banish dangers, but we can banish fears. We must not demean life by standing in awe of death.
~David Sarnoff

In 1994, I lost my brother Ron. In 2008, I lost my sister Micki. In 2011, I lost both my parents within two weeks of each other.

Losing someone you love is devastating. Mere words can't describe the pain and anguish of loss. My heart hurt so much, some days I couldn't do much more than breathe. Even that was an effort.

And where did they go after they died? That question bothered me most of all. I needed to know that my family was all right, no matter where they were. Not knowing their final destination just added to my pain. I begged God to let me know my family was okay.

Then I had a dream.

I saw myself lying in bed. The woman in bed didn't look like me but I instinctively knew it was me. The woman closed her eyes, and the next instant I was in her body. I was in pain. I hurt all over, a general achiness. I was extremely tired—even breathing was too much of a chore. I knew I was dying. I could feel my body slowly shutting down, but surprisingly I wasn't frightened. I had lived a good long life and this felt like the next phase—a natural progression. I didn't fight it. I found myself relaxing. I was ready to go.

Then I left my body with force—the only thing I can liken it to is being shot out of a cannon. It was quick and painless.

I felt weightless. My first thought was: I'm free! The body was so heavy and so cold; I was relieved to finally be rid of it. It felt like being immersed in a pool of heavy, cold clay, then someone pulls you out and you're free to move your arms and legs; you can twist and turn without any effort.

Then the euphoria hit.

Those who have died and came back usually can't find the words to describe how wonderful they felt after leaving their bodies. I am struggling to find the words, as words are so limiting. Euphoria comes closest to describing what I felt at the time.

As I shot into the air, my arms fully extended on both sides and transformed into butterfly wings. The colors of my wings were such an array of colors, all blended perfectly together. I knew those colors were as unique as my personality. Each design on my wings represented some part of my life. My wings were my pride and joy, my personal signature of having faced a crisis and risen above it. I knew others would see my wings and know instantly the intimate details of the life I had lived. Like an intricate tapestry, each color and each design meant something and blended together, telling the whole story.

I flew to the left and flew to my right and did somersaults in the air. And laughed the whole time.

As I neared what I perceived to be heaven, I saw a crowd of people. The crowd was so vast that I couldn't make out individual faces. I could tell they were waiting for me. All of them. I felt they were all family and friends who were gathered together to joyously welcome me "home."

After I "landed," I recognized the faces. I knew each and every one of them. Just like a football player who made an outstanding pass or a baseball player who hit the winning home run, and fellow players slap them congratulations on the arm and back, that's what I felt. Hands reached for me, touching me lovingly, as if in congratulations of a job well done.

I remember feeling "I'm home." Like I had been on a long, painful, tiring journey and now I could put those heavy suitcases down and relax. The struggle was over. Finally.

I stood, looking at the crowd and felt more love coming from them then I've ever felt in my life. I felt complete and whole. My mind and my soul and my body were in perfect harmony. Every good feeling I've ever had magnified a million times over.

The crowd slowly parted. I saw a figure standing in the back. As the last few individuals moved out of the way, I saw her.

She was smiling. And breathtakingly beautiful.

There was a soft golden light all around her.

"Mom!" I yelled as loud as I could, ecstatic to see her again.

When I had last seen her, she was on oxygen. Her hair had been streaked with gray, her eyes dulled from pain, and so thin and frail. The woman before me now was in the prime of her life. Her hair was soft, silky and brunette, her eyes bright, and her body healthy. I stood looking at her in awe and amazement, unable to speak.

"Death is not a punishment but a reward," she told me telepathically. "The world has it all wrong. They're afraid of death and worry about it all their lives. There's nothing to be afraid of. Death is wonderful; to be free of that body; to be free of all the cares and concerns we had on earth. You can see, I didn't die. We never die. Our soul is eternal. It cannot die. So don't be afraid of it. Death is a door through which we enter into joy."

When I woke up, it took me a while to realize it was just a dream. It all seemed so real. The colors looked so vivid, and the feelings so strong—how could it all have been a dream? Is it possible I actually visited heaven?

Most importantly, what did it all mean?

After spending hours reflecting, pondering and questioning, I finally came to a conclusion: It is what it is. My mother was specific. She meant what she said. And I am to take it at face value. Whether the dream was real or imaginary isn't the point. I'll never know the answer in this lifetime, so no point in questioning it further.

The real point is: the "dream" changed me.

Up until then I had always thought of death as a punishment. Awful, terrible, agonizing. Now I saw it for what it really is, a beautiful, joyous, liberating experience.

I don't know why God in all His wisdom predestined the body to die. But like a caterpillar that changes into a butterfly, the transformation is necessary.

Thanks to that dream, I'm no longer afraid of death.

When it's my time to go, I'll have a place in heaven among my friends and family. Much as I want to see them again now, I'm in no hurry to get there. I still have my life to live. I'll eventually get there. When it's my time.

Thank you, God, for letting me see my mom again. And more importantly, for letting me know death is not the end but the beginning of a wonderful new life. Death is merely a door through which we enter into joy.

~Pam Phree

30

Stairway to Heaven

A dream which is not interpreted is like a letter which is not read.
~The Talmud

Disturbing images of a burning staircase invaded my restful sleep that morning, waking me abruptly. Sitting up, I reached for the book of dream predictions I kept on my nightstand.

I flipped to the word "flames." The explanation made sense. I was to expect something hot and intense before the day was done. Well, I reasoned, it has been pretty warm lately. Continuing my search, I found "stairway" and gasped when I read the ominous words: "painful, horrible death."

It's just a silly book, I told myself. But before I even completed that thought, it felt like the pages were burning my fingers. I dropped the heavy paperback with a muffled yelp as a terrible premonition of doom came over me.

Seconds later, I remembered it was my friend Mira's birthday and we'd planned a girls' night out with three of our friends. Following dinner at her favorite restaurant, we were going to check out the Bluebird Cafe, a popular downtown Montreal nightspot.

I grabbed my phone and punched in Mira's number. She answered with a groggy hello.

"We can't go out tonight," I insisted. "Something terrible is going to happen!"

"What—no happy birthday?" she teased in her usual relaxed manner. "And what in the world are you talking about?"

I quickly told her about my dream, the book's prediction, and the awful sensation of combined heat and dread that tore through me.

Mira was a skeptic about the spiritual or paranormal, but also a loyal friend who tolerated my idiosyncrasies and superstitions with resigned humor. "We'll just go somewhere else instead of the Bluebird," she coaxed.

The moment she said that, I could swear I felt a hand on mine. A warm tranquility seeped through me.

"Yes," I heard a voice say close to my ear. "Yes, somewhere else."

"It's settled, then," Mira said with a laugh, and I went numb.

"I didn't say anything," I claimed.

"I just heard you say 'Yes, somewhere else,'" she insisted. "Anyway, I'll see you later. I have to go. Mom's making me waffles for my birthday breakfast. I'll pick you up at seven."

I hung up. I knew those words didn't come out of my mouth. I glanced at the book again. I was almost afraid to pick it up, but when I did, nothing happened. I carried it into the kitchen where my husband was already pouring coffee.

"Did you sleep well?" he asked, sliding a full cup toward me. "What's wrong?" he probed, seeing my pale face. Spotting the dream book, he grinned. "What drama are we in store for today?" he teased.

I thumbed through the pages to show him both words and what they foretold. As he read, his expression grew serious.

"You know I don't believe this stuff," he began, "but better safe than sorry. Maybe you should stay home tonight, or at least change the original plan."

"That's what we agreed on," I assured him. "Mira doesn't really care where we go. She just wants to celebrate. When she suggested a different place, it felt right—well more than right," I corrected, describing both the calmness that swept over me, and the touch and voice I heard. "Mira heard it too."

"Promise me you'll be careful." He frowned.

"I will," I assured him with a hug.

Mira showed up promptly at seven, following me to my bedroom while I finished getting ready.

"Everyone's okay with changing the club?" I asked, putting on mascara while she sat on my bed watching me.

"Yeah, but they all think you're nuts," she laughed. "Now, where's this doom and gloom book of yours?"

I pointed to the night table and she picked it up, leafing through until she found what she was looking for.

"Yep, that's what it says, all right—hot, intense, horrible, painful death," she concurred, returning the paperback to where she found it.

"You think I'm crazy too, don't you?" I accused mildly as I applied lipgloss.

"Not really," she confessed. "Normally I take stuff like this with a grain of salt, but when you repeated the words 'somewhere else' this morning, something about your voice got to me. It didn't even sound like you, but I just felt—I don't know—like it was a really good idea."

Before I could say anything, she glanced at her watch and urged me to hurry. "The others are waiting, slowpoke. Let's get going!"

After supper, we had to drive right by the Bluebird to reach our changed destination. As we approached, the girls started teasing me about my superstitious nature and I laughed along with them. Yet, as we neared the club, a strange silence fell over all of us. I felt that invisible hand grasp my fingers again as we passed and I shivered.

We had a great time that night—especially Mira. We all suspected she would soon discover that drinking to excess wasn't all that great an idea. Madeline, our designated driver kept begging her to hold off being sick, especially when we were forced to take a convoluted detour to get back home.

"Must be an accident somewhere," Jenna murmured from the back, and my mouth went dry.

Madeline dropped me off last, waiting until I got safely inside my building. I was surprised to find my husband wide awake, sitting on the couch waiting for me. He rarely stayed up past midnight.

"It's three-thirty in the morning," I pointed out unnecessarily as I bent over to kiss him hello. "Are you okay?" I asked worriedly when I saw his ashen face.

"Mack dropped in earlier to watch the game," he whispered. "I mentioned your dream because it was on my mind and I was worried about you. He just called and told me there was a fire at the Bluebird tonight. No one knows what happened yet, but a lot of people died."

He managed to catch me just as my knees buckled. As tears coursed down our cheeks, we prayed for the lives lost, giving thanks that our group of five was not among them.

That week, details of what happened were pieced together. It was reported that three young men, angry about being barred entry to the club, threw a firebomb into the staircase. The Bluebird Café was quickly engulfed in flames. Thirty-seven people died, including, I learned, one of my classmates from high school.

A month later, something compelled me to again look up those two words that saved us all from a horrible death. "Flames" remained the same. However, to my stunned amazement, the prediction for staircase said "lofty ambitions will come true" instead. When I showed the altered text to my husband, and later to Mira, both gasped in reverent disbelief.

Last year, on the fortieth anniversary of that tragic fire, a memorial was erected to the victims who perished in the flames. As I watched the ceremony on the evening news, I bowed my head and whispered yet another prayer to God, thanking Him again for the divine intervention that spared my life and the lives of my friends that horrible night.

~Marya Morin

31

The Hand of Fate

Everything comes gradually at its appointed hour.
~Ovid

My mother had been in a deep sleep for three days, taking in no food at all and a minimum of forced liquid. A "Do Not Resuscitate" sign hung over her bed. Every time I looked at the sign, I shuddered. The finality of the words chilled me, even though the heat in her bedroom was way too high.

She was eighty-eight years old and had reached the end of a long illness. She still lived in her own apartment, but I had arranged for round-the-clock nursing care; I did not leave her side during those three days.

On the fourth morning, a Sunday, I called my husband and asked him to pick me up and drive me home (some forty minutes from my mother's apartment) so I could get clean clothes. I had been wearing the same jeans and top for four days, having had no idea when I arrived that the end was so near.

As we drove home that Sunday, my husband and I decided that before we went back to my mother's apartment, we would stop at the funeral home to make arrangements. The doctor had said she would not last more than a few days at most, and the previous evening, the visiting nurse agreed with his prognosis. We felt it would be better to make the funeral arrangements while we were still relatively calm rather than after the emotional trauma of her death had set in.

I also wanted to stop at the grocery store so I could have some food in the refrigerator for the nurses and myself.

Once at my house, I quickly showered and dressed, then threw a few clothes into a shopping bag. We got back into the car. Suddenly, I told my husband that I had changed my mind about stopping at the funeral home. And I did not want to take time to buy groceries, either. Something inside me told me that we had to get back to my mother in a hurry—before it was too late.

I rang the bell in the lobby and the daytime nurse, Callie, buzzed me in. After the elevator ride up to the twenty-second floor, I saw Callie at the end of the hall, a look of amazement on her face. "It's some kind of miracle!" she exclaimed. "Your mother's eyes are open!"

Hurrying into my mother's bedroom, I was shocked to see that her eyes were open. Propped up in the rented hospital bed, she stared straight ahead. At first, I thought she was dead, and my heart started racing. But then she shifted her gaze and looked straight at me. She had a puzzled, questioning look on her face, as if to ask, "Where am I?" Or, perhaps, "Where am I going?"

Then a grimace passed over her face—a grimace that I have replayed in my mind over and over again. Was it a grimace of physical pain? Of fear? Of sadness? I think by then, she felt no more pain, so it must have been a combination of fear and sadness—deep sadness at leaving, and fear of the unknown. She needed the comfort of being in my arms when she began her journey.

I held her frail body gently, and spoke to her softly, telling her how much I loved her. And then I could feel, and see, that she was gone.

I asked Callie how long my mother's eyes had been open before I arrived.

"Only a few minutes," she said. "When I heard you ring the bell downstairs, I said to your mother, 'There's your daughter. Now you just hold on there. Don't you die before she gets here.' And she did hold on. She waited for you."

Thinking about the fact that something told me not to stop for anything on the way back to my mother's apartment, but to hurry as fast as I could; thinking about the fact that my mother opened her eyes when I rang the bell, and kept them open until I got there so I could say goodbye to her, I suspected Callie was right. It was some kind of miracle. It was the Hand of Fate.

~Arlene Uslander

32

Nightmare Ride

For safety is not a gadget but a state of mind.
~Eleanor Everet

I gasped when I woke. My chest heaved, and beads of sweat dripped down my face. The television flickered in front of me. As the living room came into focus, I lay on an unfamiliar couch, staring at photos of faces I did not remember. Where was I?

Then I remembered. After putting the kids I was babysitting to bed, I had curled up on the couch to relax. Their parents were due home around 11 p.m. that Tuesday night, and I had two hours to kill. I must have dozed off.

It had only been a dream, but it seemed so real. I had been driving down the familiar backcountry roads in Concord, North Carolina, when my eyes went heavy and I fell asleep behind the wheel. As my car hit the embankment, I screamed and suddenly jolted awake. But the fear of those last moments continued to grip me.

Besides a little fender bender, I had never experienced a real car accident. I opened my eyes wide, knowing I would have to make the drive home soon. I needed to be awake.

By the time I left the house that night, I was on high alert. The road was dark as I drove, but I wasn't taking any chances. I watched every movement around me, trying to stay awake.

I wasn't even supposed to be there that night. Babysitting was my sister's job, but she had a date, and I was on fall break from college. I needed the money so I took her place. Now, I wasn't so sure.

"It was only a dream," I muttered to myself as I rounded the bend and turned onto the next country road. "It was only a dream." But as soon as the sentence left my thoughts, my real nightmare began.

As I approached the ninety-degree curve ahead, I cautiously pressed the brakes. A friend had shown me the short-cut route to my home just two days earlier. It was very tight, and in the darkness, I slowed to feel my way around the curve. After the turn, the road would be straight, leading me home to my nice, warm bed.

Suddenly, the headlights of an oncoming pickup truck blinded me. I closed my eyes and braced the steering wheel. My car was barely moving, but I heard the squeal of brakes skidding across the asphalt. Something slammed into my door, cracking glass and throwing it across my seat. I felt my body spin with the car.

When everything stopped moving, my fingers tightened around the wheel. My shoulders shook as an eerie silence filled the car. I shook my head but time passed slowly as if in a fog. This time, it wasn't a dream. The sound of running footsteps approached the car.

"Are you okay?" A strange man looked at me through the window. A second man stumbled near the back of the pickup.

I nodded, unable to speak. I tried to open the door, but the driver's side was crushed inward, stopping just inches—about the width of a large hand—from my side. Behind my seat, the remains of my back door stretched into the center of the car. I unbuckled my seatbelt and crawled out the passenger door, still not completely comprehending what had just occurred.

Neighbors began to pour out of the surrounding homes, asking how they could help. After calling my mom, I turned around to look my car—the new car I had bought just three months earlier. It sat crumpled in a dirt lot off the side of the road. The windows had shattered. My punctured gas tank sprayed fuel like a water fountain.

My knees began to buckle as the reality settled in. I could have been killed or at the very least, seriously injured. Instead, I stood in shock. No broken bones. Glass covered my hair and jacket, yet I didn't have a scratch on my entire body.

The police soon arrived and arrested the two strange men from the white truck, who had been driving drunk after a company party.

In the days that followed, I experienced a lot of pain. I had muscle spasms in my neck and shoulders. The muscle relaxers my doctor prescribed upset my stomach. Every night I woke screaming from new nightmares—recurring ones that would plague me for the next year.

Later that week, my mom showed me the photos taken of my now junkyard-bound car. "The appraiser said it was a miracle that you made it out alive." She gave me a hug that could only come from a grateful mother. "Someone was looking out for you that night."

Yes, God was looking out for me. The dream I had earlier in the evening could not have been a coincidence. It made me more cautious than normal on the road. A split second slower and the impact of the crash would have cut my body in two. Two seconds later, I would have been hit head on. Either way, the end result would have been disastrous.

Eventually, the muscle spasms ceased and the panic attacks abated, allowing me to reflect on that fateful night. What if I had not agreed to babysit? What if I had chosen to take another way home? What if… the questions were endless, and I had no answers.

The Nissan dealer had told my parents that the manufacturer had installed steel reinforcements in the driver's side door. Why did I suddenly remember that? The smell of gas and alcohol made my stomach lurch for months. My dreams were full of swirling blue and red lights in the middle of the night. The fear that gripped me as I cried in my mother's arms the entire way home stayed with me for weeks until my dad convinced me to get behind the wheel of another car.

Most of the pain and fear from that night eventually dissolved. But one thing will never leave my memory—the width of a hand that held back the side of the car that crumpled around me. Yes, God was looking out for me that day and every day since. Only now, I recognize his presence more and trust him to take care of me in all circumstances.

~Carolyn Bennett Fraiser

Message at Midnight

Never drive faster than your guardian angel can fly.
~Author Unknown

L ate in the evening, driving rain pounded against the outside walls of our bedroom. By lamplight my husband focused on the book he was reading as I sat cross-legged, studying my Bible. Suddenly, an ominous feeling swept over me, but I couldn't figure out its origin. I could think of nothing in particular that was bothering me.

As my heart raced, I bowed my head and prayed, "What is it, God? Please tell me what is happening." Over and over, I prayed those few words until the confusion began to subside and a clear thought came into focus: Your child is in danger.

My child is in danger? Which child? I tried to think. My daughter and younger son were in bed asleep, so it couldn't be one of them. It had to be my older son, Mike.

I fervently began to pray. God, please, please! I don't know what is going on, but Mike needs you. Please be with him. Please take care of him. Please protect him. God, be with him. God, hear my prayer. Please don't let anything happen to him! Over and over and over I pleaded with God to be with my teenage son. He was in danger, and all I could do was desperately cry out to God in my prayer to save my son.

Tears poured down my face. By this time, my husband, who was capable of mentally shutting out everything around him when he read, was staring at me.

"What is wrong with you?" he asked. I had never before had a meltdown in a bedtime Bible study, and my husband seemed very puzzled that I had chosen this time and place to fall apart.

"Something bad is going to happen to Mike! Something is really, really wrong!" I told him.

"What do you mean? And how do you know?" he asked.

"I don't know how I know," I confessed. "I just feel in my spirit… somehow God is telling me that something bad is going to happen to Mike, and I've been praying frantically for him." I was sobbing and trembling as I shared this troubling information. Instead of discounting my revelation, my husband looked truly concerned.

Immediately, I returned to God with my plea. I really don't know how long I prayed, only that I prayed until the urgency slowly subsided and a peace filled me with the assurance that God had indeed heard my prayer.

"Honey, you've done all you can do. Just lie down and rest," my husband finally said. He turned off the light, and we both lay awake in the dark, listening to the wind and the rain.

This was the summer between high school and college for my son. His girlfriend had recently moved to a town some distance away, and he had driven this evening to see her as he often did over the course of the summer. During the day, it would have been a picturesque drive on winding country roads in the mountains of North Carolina, but not late on a rainy night.

From out of the darkness, a possum had darted in front of Mike on his drive home. He jerked the wheel to avoid the possum but then the vehicle spun off the wet road, hit an embankment and flipped onto its roof. A barbed wire fence entangled the front end of the car and held it in place; the rear hatch window shattered, and most of the car's roof crushed from the impact with the ground. Had passengers been sitting in the back seats, they would have been seriously injured or killed, for that part of the roof was flattened. Yet the portion of the roof over Mike's head was protected because it lay on top of a small drainage ditch and, therefore, was not crushed.

Suspended upside down by his seat belt, he released the latch and flipped himself over onto the glass scattered across the roof below. Carefully, he squeezed through the only escape route possible: a glassless window. A kind stranger, who happened to be out late on that rainy night, immediately stopped to help him. A highway patrolman arrived quickly at the scene and expressed difficulty believing that the young man standing before him had indeed survived the crash without a scratch.

When the phone finally rang in our bedroom, Mike's trembling voice broke as he spoke. "Mom, I've had a bad wreck, but no one was hurt." While my son may have felt confused by my joyous reaction, I believe his guardian angel, remaining close to my son's side, shared my indescribable happiness and smiled.

~Joan McClure Beck

The Unexpected Guest

Bricks and mortar make a house, but the laughter of children makes a home.
~Irish Proverb

The Spirit of Life will always find a way of supporting us when we have a deep desire in our heart. Sometimes the way the guidance flows to us can be challenging to accept. All that is required of us to receive the guidance is learning to be open. I can assure you from my own personal experience, the more I learnt to listen and trust the guidance, however it flowed to me, the easier my life became.

Our financial advisor, Mark, had been waiting patiently in our lounge in Jakarta, enjoying a cold drink, when my husband Graham telephoned with another update on the traffic situation. "I'm now only two miles from home and expect to be there within the next twenty minutes."

When Graham arrived he apologised for being late for the meeting. Mark laughed and said, "I live in Jakarta too, I know the traffic is very unpredictable."

I left them alone to talk while I went to the kitchen to check on dinner. Our cook Ngatmi had a very concerned look on her face as she said, "The roast dinner is ready for serving, madam." Then she looked at me with anxious eyes as to say, "What do I do?" I patted her on the shoulder and said, "I'll be back in a minute." As I walked into the lounge, I stopped abruptly as I could clearly see a third person in the room. I was startled.

Mark and Graham were standing, chatting and enjoying a glass of wine. Next to Mark I saw a cheeky-looking little blond boy hanging onto his right trouser leg. He stood wobbly on his feet and clung on tightly with both hands attempting to steady himself. Mark is a little over six feet tall and this small child stood no higher than Mark's knee. I sensed the boy to be around ten to twelve months old. As we do not have children, it was difficult for me to accurately estimate this child's age. This gorgeous little boy gave me a beautiful smile, glanced up at Mark and then he disappeared! Both Mark and Graham were oblivious to the child's presence.

It was such a clear and vivid vision. If I hadn't known better, I could have sworn the child had a physical presence in the room.

I retreated, walking back toward the kitchen door and out of sight. My mind searched for answers. Had Mark and his wife lost a child? Was this child simply missing his dad? Or even worse, could something horrible have just happened to the child? I slowed my breathing, opened up my energy and sensed the scene again. No answer came to me.

I was still baffled when the kitchen door flew open and my maid walked straight into me. "Oops," I said with a start. Ngatmi stood looking at me with her eyebrows raised slightly in anticipation of my telling her to serve dinner. I gave her a questioning look and she politely said, "Madam, what time are we eating?"

"Oh," I stammered, "I'll be right back." I rushed back into the lounge.

"Excuse me, Mark, is your wife in town?" I asked.

"No, she isn't," he replied.

"Well would you like to join us for dinner?" Before he could respond, I raised my voice and boisterously added, "We're having… Australian roast lamb!"

"Roast lamb!" he said excitedly. "Thank you, I would love to stay for dinner." I gave Ngatmi the thumbs up and she beamed with relief at being able to serve dinner.

During dinner, I casually asked Mark if he had any children. "No, we don't unfortunately, but we would love a child; we have been trying for many years. We have both had tests and nothing is wrong, so maybe it's not meant to be."

Graham gave me one of his looks, which said, "Where are you heading with this?" I smiled at him, then told Mark about what I had seen and explained that was why I had retreated so quickly from the room earlier.

"He is a strong little boy and so determined to be noticed. I could have reached out and touched him," I added. "I believe he is trying to tell you two to hurry up. He wants you to know he is ready and waiting. He gave you a glimpse of himself to encourage you not to give up."

Graham then explained my unusual gifts to Mark, who fortunately was very open-minded. "I don't do readings," I said to Mark. "If an incident like this happens it's for a very good reason." He was so impressed he rang his wife to tell her.

A few weeks later she returned to Jakarta and came to see me. We talked and I described the child to her. I explained slowly what I was sensing around her. "I am to tell you to give your husband a desert spoon of honey every day and you are to eat watermelon." I then went on to say, "I believe a door of opportunity is open to you both right now, otherwise I would not have seen this eager little boy. It's up to you two to decide what you do with this information, I'm just the messenger."

They heeded my words and commenced having honey and watermelon every day. Six months later, Mark contacted me to let me know his wife was pregnant. They were both very excited.

Eighteen months after first meeting Mark's wife, I met with her again and was introduced to their little blond-haired boy. I affectionately leaned over to the pram and said, "Hello again little one, remember me? You are definitely going to be tall, just like your dad."

I believe it's quite possible that the honey and watermelon may have only been a support mechanism, or a distraction. This baby was meant to come to them. The Spirit of Life blessed them by giving them a glimpse of their future child.

~Yvonne Fogarty

35

A Child's Faith

Young people need something stable to hang on to—a culture connection, a
sense of their own past, a hope for their own future. Most of all, they need
what grandparents can give them.
~Jay Kesler

I felt I wasn't in God's good graces during my college years, so I hung my head when Granny asked me to pray. She began, "Thank You, Lord, for blessing us with this food. We shore don't take it for granted, 'cause we been hungry before and know how that feels… " Then Granny starting humming ever so softly, "All my trials, Lord, soon be over… "

"Don't do that," I said.

"Oh, sweetheart, don't be silly." Granny put her hand on my cheek. "You know the Lord's gotta take me home before long. Besides, I done lived and loved enough for two lifetimes already."

The Bible talks about being content in whatever state we're in, but Granny walked the walk. This sweet woman, who'd picked cotton from age five and wore dresses made from flour sacks, created quilts for all her descendants with soft, colorful scraps she'd saved for years. My sixty-year-old quilt is thin and tattered now, but it took me from crib to college, then tenderly blanketed my children with the kind of warmth that only comes from multigenerational love.

As a child, I got to sleep in Granny's bed when we all slept over. I felt like "the chosen one." When I asked why I received the honor, she said, "The littlest grandchild ought to, so it can keep warm." I wanted her to say, "Because you're my favorite." But I knew that honor belonged to my brother George. And I couldn't blame her. It didn't matter that George was her favorite—what mattered was that she had always been mine.

When I was fourteen years old, doctors diagnosed Granny with terminal cancer and gave her six months to live. Exploratory surgery exposed malignancy "from hell to breakfast," the term I overheard in 1967. They sewed her up and sent her home to die, but no one ever told Granny she had The Big C.

I recall, like it was only moments ago, falling across my bed and crying all afternoon and into the night. Not even my mother could console me. I remember dropping to my knees and asking God to spare Granny and give me her pain.

The six months passed—and everyone expected Granny to die. Everyone except me. I'd been blessed with the unwavering faith of a child. What's more, Granny never even needed an aspirin for pain. There's not a doubt in my mind that God answered my prayer with an enthusiastic, "Okay, kiddo! You got it!" Eight years later Granny was still my living, loving, laughing heroine, enjoying life to the fullest.

In a hotel room in Spartanburg, South Carolina, with my arms folded beneath my head, I stared into the darkness. Alone, sober, and planning the route I must travel the next day, I saw an arm reach into the shadows and pull a white sheet over Granny's head. I lunged toward the vision, but it vanished as quickly as it had appeared. Nothing else.

My heart pounded. I felt like a bowling ball had hit my chest and knocked the breath out of me. I tossed and turned all night as I contemplated the vision's meaning. Common sense told me I'd imagined the whole thing—but this event was not common, nor did it make sense.

To this day, I don't know if God gave me a sign of Granny's imminent death, or if Granny's spirit somehow connected with mine in her moment of crisis. Whatever miraculous event happened that night in the hotel room, though, occurred at the exact time Granny was rushed to the hospital in Savannah.

The inexplicable premonition allowed me time to make the 250-mile trek to say goodbye. The answer to my prayer and the vision changed my life forever. My child's faith grew strong enough to withstand a lifetime of trials, not the least of which was my own battle with cancer thirteen years ago when God answered the second part of my prayer—giving me Granny's pain.

~Janet Sheppard Kelleher

36

Devil Winds and Moonbeams

God's promises are like the stars; the darker the night the brighter they shine.
~David Nicholas

They call them Devil Winds—the Santa Ana winds that scream across the hot desert, funneling through the California mountains before gaining force and tearing across the southland with tree-felling, fire-breathing ferocity. Each year they topple trees and down power lines. Each year they spark devastating wild fires that scorch acres and claim lives. And we were experiencing a big one.

We had just moved to our new home in the mountains above Palm Springs, and I was unprepared for the howl and force of that wind through 100-foot-tall cedar trees. As I got the kids ready for bed, my skin crawled.

"You've never liked the wind," my husband, Steven, said in an effort to calm me. "It will be fine. We're all here. We're safe."

I was known, back then, as the family worrier. Steven and I were "old" when we married. He was thirty-seven, I was thirty-four. We'd searched forever to find true love and had both believed we'd never marry when we'd suddenly found each other. I'd been diagnosed with infertility issues and we'd begun the adoption process when I got pregnant with Matthew. Two years later we beat the odds again and were blessed with a round cherub of a daughter whom we named Mary.

But, I was always afraid. I kept waiting to blink and have it all disappear.

"Mama, be by me." Blond and beautiful, Matthew knelt by the sofa and waited to say his prayers, breathing hard against his folded hands, still ruddy from his nightly wrestling match with his dad.

"Now I lay me down to sleep…"

And the wave of fear enveloped me again.

I nursed Mary as Matthew cuddled against my side. But the usual comfort of this nighttime ritual did nothing to ease my unrest. The moan of the wind through the trees shook my confidence just as it shook the windows of our cabin.

Steven had long since taken Matthew upstairs and tucked him into bed, but I could not let go of Mary. Upstairs, I stood paralyzed in front of her crib and rocked my sleeping child. I could not lay her down.

"Please God," I prayed, "I do not know what's wrong. But I'm scared. Protect my family. Protect these children. And give me faith in that protection."

I can't say I felt peace. What I felt was instruction. "Put her down. Let go. It will be all right."

So I did. Against every fiber of my being, I released my hands and laid my precious child in her crib. Then I kissed my sleeping son and went downstairs. Later, I checked on my babies and went to bed myself.

The next thing I knew the world ended. The roar was louder than anything I'd ever heard. My screams were lost in the explosion of sound. Bombs? Nuclear blasts? No matter how wide I opened my eyes, everything was black. The world went into slow motion. I jumped up on the bed, running circles trying to locate the direction of the noise, but it completely enveloped my black, black world. The walls of the house were clearly being ripped apart, but from where? How? I couldn't find Steven. I couldn't find sense.

Then, in an instant, it hit. The crash threw me off the bed, but my screams and Steven's frantic yells were intensely audible through the sudden silence. We groped for a light switch, but the power was gone. Like drunken madmen, we ran for the kids. No sound came from upstairs. In pitch-black darkness we stumbled up the stairs.

And there they were.

As we passed the doorway, the light appeared. The full moon acted like a spotlight on our precious daughter. Peaceful. Asleep. On her stomach with her legs tucked under her and her thumb in her mouth. Next to her in her crib, our beautiful boy cuddled up on his side, arm over his sister, his face peaceful and serene.

And just in case we didn't understand the blessing, the only light came from angelic moonbeams circling our sleeping—living—children's faces.

We fell into each other's arms and sobbed.

Seconds later, we heard a knock on our door. Neighbors with flashlights had arrived to check on us. With them, we grabbed our sleeping babies and ventured out.

A 150-foot cedar had once stood beside the deck off our bedroom. The deck was gone. So was the cedar. It had ripped out of the ground in the wind, taking the deck with it. A gaping crater replaced the deck and the tree's roots stood twelve feet in the air. The tree had smashed fences, buckled the road and taken out all the power in town. "I saw it!" proclaimed one man. "I stepped outside 'cause I heard a noise. I'd run back in to call you—the tree was wobbling like a spinning top. But it fell before I could call."

In unison, each neighbor shined his flashlight down the length of the tree and across the path of destruction as the howling wind whipped our hair and tugged at our nightclothes. It reached from our yard, through our next-door neighbor's yard and into the yard of a neighbor two doors down and across the street with its full, wispy branches beating against the steps of the preschool in the wind. Chain-link fences were crumpled like aluminum foil. Split rails were kindling. The tree had imbedded into the asphalt a good eight inches.

But, no one was hurt.

In fact, the tree crashed at the only angle it could land and not kill someone — a lot of someones. It had fallen in the only direction that would not hurt someone. We were spared and neighbors in three adjacent houses were spared.

A shiver ran up my spine as the enormity of our "near miss" hit me. Mary was asleep on my shoulder, her sweet baby breath warm against my neck. Steven's eyes locked mine by the reflection of the flashlights and, knowingly, I watched as he pulled Matt tighter against his chest as the relentless wind suddenly calmed. As it did, treetops settled into their statuesque positions and the full moon beamed down between the branches and onto our small band like those theatrical spotlights that descend with the word of God.

"My, my, my, " whistled our neighbor. "Can you believe that nobody was killed? That's got to be a freak of nature."

"Or a miracle," offered Steven as we all stood assessing the damage.

That night taught me about God's miracles, about faith, and about listening, for yes, there may be devil winds out there — but there are also moonbeams.

~Susan Traugh

Miracles Happen

Divine Appointment

Let Me In

… I was a stranger and you invited Me in.
~Matthew 25:35

"What's taking so long? Move out of the way! Other people have places to be too!" The construction in front of the Emergency Room entrance was more than I could handle, and the cars trying to find parking places for the physicians' offices were beyond frustrating. The hospital complex parking lot was congested with construction workers, cranes, and people all coming and going. On top of that, it was July, and I know Hell was probably cooler that day!

As usual, I was running late. So late that I was actually running dressed in my suit, my hose, and my heels! I was exhausted and just needed to park and run some equipment into the respiratory department. It would only take a couple of seconds, and then I could pick up my baby girl. At that time in my life, it felt like she was always the first one dropped off at daycare and the last one picked up. I had promised her that morning she would not be the last one today, and I could not bear the thought of being late again.

I found a parking place, whipped in, grabbed what I needed, and headed for the building. As I passed through the first set of sliding doors, I saw a woman standing there. She looked lost or like she was waiting for someone. It wasn't that I didn't care, but she was a stranger, and I was in a hurry. I shuffled past her, dropped off the equipment, and headed back to my car.

I noticed her again on my way out. When I was almost to my car, I could hear Him saying, "Go back."

"Not today God," I thought. "I really have places I need to be, and it's going to take me forever to get out of this parking mess and even longer to get to the daycare! Then I have to run by the grocery store, because I realized at breakfast that we were out of milk! Please God, not today."

He did not let up though, and I felt the lump in my throat getting bigger and bigger. I knew I didn't really have a choice. "Fine! Fine!" I said out loud, throwing my hands up in the air. At which point, I noticed a couple watching me from the sidewalk. Clearly, they could not hear God speaking to me, but they could see me talking to myself. "Great!" I thought. "Maybe I'll be admitted and can have a nice long vacation!"

I headed back to the hospital. My heart pounded nervously, and I knew God had a reason to turn me around. Most people don't take kindly to strangers butting in because God said they should, but I could sense this was different. The automatic sliding doors opened, and I stepped inside. I glanced at the woman for a second. She was probably in her seventies and very beautiful, but she seemed so fragile. Then, for the first time, I really saw her. I could see the emptiness, the loss.

At that moment, her face glowed, and my heart softened. I heard God's voice gently saying, "Let me in," and I let her in. I put my arms around the woman and began to pray. She was shaking and held on to me so tightly. Then she began sobbing and I felt the release of all her emotions as I stood, holding us both up. Time passed, people passed, and I began to cry with her. So many things went through my mind. I kept thinking about her standing there alone, keeping her composure, and just desperately waiting for someone, anyone, to notice her pain. I felt ashamed of almost missing that divine appointment.

Then she began to speak softly, telling me that she and her husband of many wonderful years had been to lunch earlier that afternoon. As they waited for their food, he complained of chest pain, and then immediately he went into cardiac arrest and died. The paramedics tried to revive him but he was truly gone. She explained that he had not been sick and had never had any heart problems. She talked about the plans they had and the things they had yet to do. She had lost track of time. She didn't know how long she had been there, waiting for family to arrive from out of town, and I stayed with her.

She held my face in her hands, and she brushed my hair back the way my mom always did. She called me her angel and thanked God for sending me. I had no idea what to say, but God gave me the words she needed to hear. I reminded her how much God loved her and that He was with her and with her husband. We stood together a bit longer.

Then she saw her family pulling into the parking lot. She pointed them out, hugged me, and thanked me again for waiting with her. As I walked way, I thought about all the strangers I had passed who were hurting, needing a smile, a kind word, or a shoulder to lean on. Surprisingly, I made it out of the parking lot with no traffic problems, and I made every green light on the way to get my daughter. I stopped to get milk and found an extra $20 dollar bill folded up in the side pocket of my purse, so we had ice cream too! I made it home earlier than I had in weeks, and my little princess was happy and healthy.

I've thought back to that day several times over the years. I never knew her name, I never saw her again, but she changed my life. I knew the divine appointment was as much for me as it was for her.

~Chrissy Conner

The Voice

No one is a firmer believer in the power of prayer than the devil;
not that he practices it, but he suffers from it.
~Guy H. King

Applause thundered across the dinner theater as we *Godspell* thespians bowed to the standing ovation. When the clapping subsided, we bee-lined to the dressing room and smeared on cold cream to remove our heavy make-up.

"You sure wowed them with your solo, 'All Good Gifts,' tonight," Claire said.

"Thanks. Your 'Day-by-Day' was beautiful, too." I glanced around the room for the girl who gave me a ride home each night, but I didn't see her. "Has anybody seen Deb?" I hollered over the fray.

"Deb? She left with Robert to go grab a bite," a fellow cast member said.

My shoulders sagged. How was I supposed to get home? I lived four miles from the theater, and no buses ran at this time of night. I couldn't afford a taxi, and since none of the other cast members lived near me I hesitated to beg for a ride.

I changed into jeans and a T-shirt and mulled over my dilemma. Maybe a long walk home would tire me out and I'd get a good night's sleep.

I plodded toward home, trying to avoid the streets with seedy bars and a bad reputation. I picked up my pace when I heard footsteps following behind me. But the ominous stranger gained ground until I could almost feel his breath on my neck. Hadn't he ever heard of personal space?

My heart pounded and I tried not to panic. Cars whipped by and music blared from a fraternity house nearby. Surely he wouldn't attack me on a busy street. Finally, I stepped aside and gestured for him to take the lead. "Why don't you go ahead of me?" I said in a shaky voice. "I seem to be slowing you down."

He grunted, barely acknowledging my offer, and strolled ahead of me. I dawdled until he was a healthy distance ahead, then crossed the street and headed down the secluded street on which I lived. After a four-mile trek, my feet ached and I was ready to flop into bed. Just six houses away now.

I scolded myself for my paranoia. The guy was probably wrapped up in his own worries and was clueless about the panic he'd caused by tailgating me.

Suddenly, my mouth was clamped shut in a vice-grip. Arms like those of a giant octopus snatched me from behind and dragged me off the sidewalk. I immediately recognized my assailant as the creep who had stalked me earlier. He must have doubled back and followed me down the dead-end street.

I kicked and fought and bit and clawed in a futile attempt to escape, but I was no match for this madman. He shoved me to the ground behind a stone fence. I suddenly recalled, just one month ago in Barre, Vermont, a girl my age had been raped, strangled, and dumped behind a stone fence on a quiet street, just like this one. The horrifying reality stabbed me like a sword. I was about to be raped and murdered, just like the Barre girl.

In desperation, I jerked my head away from his hand and let out a blood-curdling scream. I opened my mouth to let out another roof-raiser, but he slammed my jaw shut. "Shut up! Shut up, or I'll kill you." His eyes, wild and crazed, glared at me with contempt. With one tug, he ripped off my T-shirt and jammed it into my mouth as a gag. His hand tugged at the zipper of my jeans, while his knees pummeled my thighs into the ground.

My heart pounded at a dizzying rate. "Help me, Lord," I pleaded. "Send somebody to rescue me. I'm about to be raped."

But no one came. In a last-ditch effort to escape, I jerked my chest up, but he smashed me down again and tightened his grip on my arms. "You're not going anywhere," he spewed, a diabolical gleam in his eyes. "I've just started in on you."

He pried my jeans from my uncooperative legs.

I couldn't overpower this psychopath—every time I tried, he slammed me back to the ground, and with a gag in my mouth, I couldn't scream.

"But you can pray," a voice whispered in my head.

"Somebody help me! I'm about to be raped," I pleaded silently to my only source of hope. Over and over I petitioned God with this same prayer, knowing I was powerless, but He was not.

My attacker loosened his trousers.

Suddenly, I heard footsteps pounding down the sidewalk and a man hollering, "Leave her alone! Leave her alone!"

My assailant bolted.

A man clad only in pajama bottoms helped me to my feet. "Are you okay?" he asked, concerned eyes peering into mine.

I burst into tears. "Thank you so much for coming. You saved my life." I clutched his arm, never so grateful to meet a stranger in my life.

He escorted me to his house where his wife fetched a new T-shirt for me and a mug of chamomile tea to calm my frazzled nerves.

While we waited for the police, we rehashed the events of my attack. But then my hero dropped a bombshell. "When I heard you holler, 'Somebody help me, I'm about to be raped,' I knew I had to come."

My heart lurched. "There's no way you could have heard me say that. I was gagged."

He scratched his head. "Well, I don't understand it, but I clearly heard a voice say, 'Somebody help me, I'm about to be raped.'"

His wife piped in. "The weird thing is, I never heard it, and I was lying in bed right next to him. But Ron insisted he'd heard it, so he threw on his pajamas and dashed out."

My heart stopped. "Those were the exact words I had prayed. In my head."

We stared at one another, stunned. How was that possible? Had he read my mind?

With sudden clarity, I knew God had intervened and transferred my desperate prayer into this man's brain, just as though he had heard the words audibly.

A police siren blared and I spent the next several hours providing a police report.

My life had nearly been snuffed out, but God miraculously allowed me to live. And live I have, to His glory. I married my long-time sweetie, Nathan. I've sung in a touring Christian group, finished medical school and practiced primary care medicine for twenty-five years. Thanks to my second chance at life, I've published stories, nurtured two wonderful children, tended a cottage garden, and bicycled around Glacier and Banff National Parks.

How apropos that the words in my *Godspell* solo were "All Good Gifts Around Us, Are Sent from Heaven Above." Even today, I marveled at the truth of those lyrics. He does send His children good gifts!

~Sally Willard Burbank

Butterscotch

Everything that occurs in your life is part of God's plan to wake you up.
~Leonard Jacobson

R onnie is disabled and lives in an efficiency apartment on the other side of town. I used to take care of him when I was a nursing assistant, and we remained good friends even after I left the field.

One evening last week, I visited Ronnie. As I got ready to leave, we noticed his precious tabby cat Butterscotch, always the center of attention, was nowhere to be found. We called and searched for him to no avail. Ronnie asked me to check the back screen door to see if perhaps Butterscotch had slipped out unnoticed. As I looked out the door, the yellow-and-white striped Butterscotch ran across the yard and through the alley. I hollered back at Ronnie that Butterscotch did get out and I was going after him.

I did the fastest walk I could manage on two bad knees in pursuit of Butterscotch. Each time I called him he would stop, turn and look at me as if to make sure I was following him. And just as I got close enough to nab him, he would take off running a few more yards ahead of me. By the time I got across the large parking lot, I was praying, "Dear God, I know you are so busy, but if you could just please stop Butterscotch I would really appreciate it! Besides, my knees are killing me!" As we both neared the end of the parking lot, I saw the fence separating me from the dark brush and busy roadway. This would mean the end of my pursuit.

"Butterscotch, please, just stop!" I hollered one more time. He turned around, looked me right in the eye, and then vanished over the fence. I was out of breath and knew that Ronnie would be devastated! He had raised Butterscotch from a kitten. I couldn't delay letting him know. I called Ronnie. "Ronnie," I breathed into my cell phone, "has Butterscotch ever run away like this before?" I was mustering up the courage to tell him his beloved Butterscotch was gone.

"You know, as soon as you left, I called one more time for Butterscotch and he came right up behind me. He never left the apartment," Ronnie replied. "I have been looking for my eye glasses so I could see to dial the phone to let you know."

"Oh, thank God!" I exhaled and took a huge sigh of relief. "Okay, I'll be back at your place in a couple of minutes." I stopped for a second to wipe my tearing eyes and offer a brief but sincere prayer of thanks to God for sparing Butterscotch.

One thing I have always tried to do when things like this happen is determine what God's purpose might be. You know, you run late for work in the morning because you can't find your keys only to discover that you missed being in an accident by a few cars. That's how I try to deal with the negatives in life. All I knew was that I was hurting all over from semi-running to catch a cat that wasn't even the right cat. And, I had a long walk ahead of me back to Ronnie's apartment.

Halfway back, a voice called out from the darkness. "Miss! Miss! Can you help me Miss! Miss! Please, help!" From the shadows, a figure of a huddled man appeared seemingly out of nowhere. As I got closer, he continued his plea. "Miss! Miss! Please help!" I made my way quickly over to the man and put my arm on his shoulder. He immediately turned his head away and vomited.

"Sir," I said, "what's the problem?"

He turned back to me, sweating and his breathing labored. "I think I'm having a heart attack. I got some bad chest pains, I can't stop throwing up. I can't get anyone to answer their door. I don't have a phone. Can you help me?"

I immediately called 911, gave our location, and relayed his symptoms, pulse and respirations to the operator. I stayed with the man until help arrived, trying to keep him alert, calm and breathing. The man, whose name I later learned was Gerard, was having a heart attack right in front of me! The ambulance arrived in a few minutes and rushed Gerard to the hospital. According to the first responder who thanked me for assisting, I probably helped save Gerard's life.

I have always firmly believed that things happen for a reason. I may not always know immediately what God's plan is, but if I pay attention and let Him take the lead, He will show me. So the next time you lose your keys when you are running late, pause for a second before letting the frustration consume you. It could be God's way of slowing you down or delaying you so you avoid an accident. Or, like me, what seems like an inconvenience actually puts you somewhere you are needed to make a difference in someone else's life. When you allow God to take the lead and trust that He has a plan, that's when true miracles can happen.

As I made my way back to Ronnie's apartment, the reality began to set in. I actually helped save a man's life! It was surreal. I paused for a moment at the screen door. Lo and behold, the "real" Butterscotch was there to greet me, his outstretched paws gently plucking at the weave of the screen in eager anticipation.

"Ronnie," I said, overwhelmed by the chain of events, and scooping up Butterscotch for a warm hug, "you are not going to believe what just happened."

~Michele Dellapenta

Wrong Turn or Right?

Chance is perhaps the pseudonym of God when he did not want to sign.
~Anatole France

I had just finished my grocery shopping, and it was already dark outside. The parking lot was lit, but everyone walked quickly, watching for anyone in the shadows who'd grab a purse or grocery bag. The proximity of other shoppers made me feel safe and I hoped my presence did the same for them. Speedily I tossed milk and ice cream in the trunk, checked the inside of the car for intruders, then got in and locked the door. The front seat of the car was still cozy warm from the Arizona sun, cozy enough to make me drowsy. I turned on the A/C and struggled to stay alert for pedestrians.

Once on the wide street home, I could relax, enjoy the evening and think of the food my family would soon eat. The traffic light at a busy intersection turned red. I stopped without thinking of much more than the ice cream in the trunk. It would be softened and easy to scoop! Yum! As if on automatic pilot, I turned right. Oh no! I'd meant to wait for the green light and go straight ahead toward home. Now I was heading in a totally different direction and would need to make a U-turn. No problem; there'd be a break in the traffic to get into the left lane.

Absentmindedly I kept skimming along the far right curb. As the next traffic light turned red I realized it was too late to make a U-turn. I had three lanes of traffic between me and where I wanted to go. Paused at the stoplight, I blasted the A/C and took a deep breath. Wake up! Look where you're going! Just across the intersection, I saw a pharmacy with a large parking lot—a good place to turn around.

That's when I spotted a familiar person, standing at the shadowy edge of the parking lot. It was my friend, Amy, her leg in a brace and her hands full of shopping bags. She was surrounded by three young men in black muscle shirts, their heads shaved and arms covered in tattoos. It didn't look safe for Amy. She did not have a car and was trying to get past the group to a bus stop.

Quickly I turned into the parking lot, honked the horn and shouted, "Hi, Amy, do you need a ride?"

She looked relieved to recognize my old clunker of a car. Quietly and politely, she nodded goodbye to the men and said, "God bless you." Before she even finished speaking, the three guys slipped through the shadows and disappeared. Amy jumped in the car and locked the door. She said the men wanted money to ride the bus, the same bus she would have ridden home, alone. She had stalled in finding her purse, saying kind things to disarm them, wondering what to do next. And then I arrived with a car and a loud voice. As we left the parking lot, we spotted the three men getting onto the bus. They had bus money after all.

I drove Amy to her house, waited until she got safely inside with her shopping bags, and then drove home. By then I'd forgotten all about the ice cream and didn't care if it had melted. My husband was glad to see me home. "We worry when you're out after dark."

"Oh, don't worry about me," I said, blowing it off and unpacked the groceries. The next day we saw on TV a mug shot of a man who looked just like one in the group that had stopped Amy. He was one of a team of robbers arrested for armed theft near the pharmacy where I'd accidentally driven.

Talking with another friend Lydia, I told her how I'd made a wrong turn, overshot my neighborhood and ended up by the pharmacy. It had been dark and yet I spotted our friend Amy and recognized her need for help. Lydia gasped as she realized how close the danger had been and how unusual it was for me to get turned around driving. "Someone was looking out for Amy." And I knew Who the "Someone" was.

~Genie Eide Stoker

My Breast Cancer Angel

Angels have no philosophy but love.
~Terri Guillemets

I sat at my desk twitching and fearfully glancing out the window. It was raining like I never saw it rain before. But it wasn't the rain I was afraid of, it was the thunder and lightning. With tears in my eyes, I turned the page and continued pretending to read my book. However, when an almost blinding bolt of lightning shot across the sky followed by an earsplitting boom of thunder, I almost knocked over several students sitting in their desks as I ran to hide behind the nun's long black habit. She laughed as she lovingly put her arms around me and quoted her favorite scripture, "For He shall give his angels charge over thee," before calming my fears. I was in the third grade then, and from that day to the present, I no longer fear anything. Sister Maria's logic always included an angel or angelic activity for everything, and before that school year ended, so did mine.

No matter where I went or what I was doing, I believed I had an angel watching over me. But as I grew older, my childlike faith and belief in their existence began to fade until I seldom thought about them.

On my fortieth birthday, someone gave me a beautiful figurine of an angel, and that began my collection. Although I no longer believed in angels, I liked to collect them.

One day while in a store browsing, I noticed an angel figurine with a light pink breast cancer ribbon on her chest and the words faith, hope and believe written around the hem of her light and dark pink robe. She was absolutely beautiful, perfect for my collection. I wanted to buy her, but I wasn't out shopping for angels, and I didn't know anyone with breast cancer. As I reluctantly placed her back on the shelf, I thought I heard a soft, but firm, voice whisper, "Buy her." I quickly turned around to see who said it, but nobody was there. For weeks after, thoughts of the angel and the voice consumed me. However, I assumed it was all part of a foolish childhood belief, and I was no longer a child.

A few months later, a routine mammogram, followed by a sonogram and biopsy, revealed Stage II breast cancer. After the shock of it wore off, thoughts of the breast cancer angel came to mind. I returned to the store to buy her but she was gone. I wondered what was going to happen to me since I hadn't obeyed the voice. I shuddered at the thought. I searched every store that sold angels but I never found her.

After my surgery, I opened my eyes for a moment in the recovery room and saw my mother, my fiancé and a nurse standing behind them dressed in pink-ribbon scrubs. The next day, although I slept most of the time, I vaguely remember a nurse taking my vital signs and giving me a shot. But I clearly remember the nurse in the pink scrubs was there too. She stood by the side of my bed, smiled and told me I was going to be fine.

When I finally became more alert, I asked my mother if she knew the name of the beautiful nurse in pink-ribbon scrubs. She said no one fitting that description was ever in my room. "Yes, there was a nurse in the room," I said, "she was standing behind you and Wilson." My mother said she didn't know who I was talking about. When I asked my fiancé and the other nurses the same question and described the woman, they all said the same thing: they didn't see or know of anyone in the unit fitting that description.

The night before my release, I saw the nurse dressed in pink hurrying by. Excited, I called out, "Nurse! Nurse!" Too groggy, weak and hooked up to too many contraptions to quickly get out of bed, I hit the call button to the nurses' station.

"Can I help you?" came the question.

"Yes, can you please ask the nurse dressed in pink if she'd stop by my room?"

"The nurse dressed in pink? Hold please." A second later, she said, "I'm sorry but there's no one on staff dressed in pink tonight. Is there a particular nurse you'd like to see?"

"Yes! The one in pink, she just passed by my room."

"I'll be right there." A few minutes later, a nurse knocked and entered. "Are you in pain?" she asked.

"No, I just want to talk to the nurse in the pink scrubs," I answered.

"As I stated before, there's no one on staff or on this floor dressed in pink tonight. If you're okay, I need to get back to the desk. Ring if you need anything." She turned and left the room. Disappointed and confused, but knowing what I saw, I slowly drifted off to sleep.

For months, I was in and out of the hospital, but I never saw that nurse nor did I ever ask for her again. However, I often thought about her—her beautiful smile, consoling voice and reassuring words. Not only did they uplift me, they seemed to sustain me. I felt like a third grader again. I no longer feared or worried as battle after battle raged. I now had a sense of peace and assurance in the mist of my storms.

Years after my surgery, I walked into a store and saw an angel figurine dressed in pink ribbon scrubs with features just like the nurse in the hospital. She had long, flowing light brown hair, the same bright eyes, perfectly arched eyebrows, stunning smile, high cheekbones and that unforgettable heavenly look. Without any doubt, I knew it was her—it was my breast cancer nurse. Better yet, my messenger—my breast cancer angel. I held her close to my heart and whispered, "Thank you." I bought her, but not for myself. Since I'm now considered cancer-free, I bought her for someone who needed her much more than I did. And like Sister Maria, now I too will always believe that there are angels in our midst.

~Francine L. Baldwin-Billingslea

Angels Among Us

Knowledge is knowing that we cannot know.
~Ralph Waldo Emerson

Piles of dirty, crusted snow lingered in the shade of the hospital as my daughter Nicole labored to deliver her twins. She had been in labor for eighteen hours but those stubborn babies refused to come out. The two nurses assigned for her double-birth had tried everything to get the babies to drop into the birth canal but nothing worked.

Nicole anxiously watched the heart monitor. The babies were getting tired and their heartbeats were slowing. She pleaded with the nurses and the OB/GYN to do something.

The doctor was used to a birth turning sour. He quietly told the nurses to prepare Nicole for an emergency caesarean.

But the operating room was busy with another woman and her baby; Nicole would have to wait. Nicole's husband, Ian, took her hand. The large twenty-four-hour clock ticked silently as they stared at the green iridescent blips of the laboring hearts.

Nicole was just about to be transferred to surgery when a nurse in blue flowered scrubs entered the room. She was a stranger, unknown to the doctor and his team, but she offered to help. The nurse explained she had just finished a practicum in London, England. The British were using a new method that was successful in helping mothers in this situation. Everyone moved back, making room near the bed. The nurse told Nicole to grab hold of the iron rail above her head and twist her body until her belly was on its side; then she was to push. Nicole grabbed the rail, twisted and bore down. With the first push, Keira slipped into position in the birth canal. A few more hard pushes and she slid out and was whisked away.

Sometimes with twins, the mother labors for the first child and the second flows through the opened door. That didn't happen in this case. The second baby, Brynn, still didn't move. Nicole kept staring at the heart monitor by the bed. The blips were further apart and fainter. Frantic, she yelled to the doctor, "Get the baby out! Now!"

The doctor found the head, grabbed on with forceps and pulled Brynn out.

The ordeal was over. It was quiet in the room and the babies lay cocooned in flannelette and pink knitted tuques. Ian remembered the mystery nurse and said, "I should go find her and thank her."

He went to the maternity wing's nursing station. "Do you know of a nurse who's just returned from a practicum in England? She helped my wife deliver our twins."

The nurses in pink, yellow and red flowered scrubs looked up from their files and shook their heads. He searched the halls, enquiring of all the doctors and staff if they knew of a nurse who had just returned from England. No one had seen or heard of such a person.

In 1993, the American country music band Alabama recorded their hit, "Angels Among Us." The refrain says: I believe there are angels among us, sent down to us from somewhere up above.

It seems that an angel in a nurse's blue scrubs helped Nicole birth her twins that day in early spring.

~Jeannette Richter

Night

Everyone entrusted with a mission is an angel.
~Moses Maimonides

The last bus pulls away. What now? I've missed my connection. I yank the threadbare coat around my thin nurse's aide uniform. It barely reaches my hips. The white nylon pants contain no warmth against the bitter night's wind. Shuddering, I swallow. I'll walk, no choice, no money for a cab. It's about four miles.

"Stay by the street lights," the voice inside me instructs. Who cares if it's through the worst section of town? That's where I live now. It's all I can afford since leaving home three weeks ago. A room with a mattress. Food tightly sealed in cardboard boxes, providing inadequate protection against mice. Maybe in a few months I'll be able to afford a room with a bed in a nicer section.

It starts to drizzle. I jerk my hood in place. Squaring my shoulders, walking briskly, hoping to slip into the night unnoticed. My rain-soaked pants cling to my calves. The weak light from the street lamps elongates my shadow, throwing it into darkened alleyways. Safety is behind the four walls of my room, snuggling under my grandmother's comforter.

The houses now are worn, steps crumbling, some windows boarded, some dimly lit behind torn shades. I wonder about the people inside. Hopefully they're warm. My shadow no longer keeps me company as the streetlights disappear. It's a struggle to keep my imagination in check every time I pass an alleyway. I refuse to play the victim. My mother blaming me for my father's nightly visits. I've carried the burden of night for years.

My breath catches. Footsteps sound behind me. The night is gathering its powers. A man's voice yells to someone. My numb hands pump at my sides picking up my pace. The footsteps behind me mirror my speed and expand. My fear is palpable. I hear voices murmuring to each other. They sound closer. My tears fall, mixing with raindrops hitting my face. I pray in earnest.

Out of nowhere a car pulls up besides me. I freeze. Glorious rays stream out the car's roof light contrasting with the dark letters TAXI. My breath catches again. The passenger door opens. The golden glow from the interior light accentuates the driver. His shoulder-length white hair and flowing white beard are beacons against the dreaded night. Familiar soulful eyes grace my heart.

"Get in," he says.

"I have no money," I reply.

"Get in now. You're not safe."

I obey. Strangely I don't feel cold in my wet clothes sitting silently besides him. He drives to the building that houses my sparse room, never asking for directions. He turns to me.

"Remember you're never truly alone."

I nod in agreement. I open the car door and walk to the porch steps as if it's a dream, turn to wave goodbye. I glance up and down the street. No evidence he was there.

Smiling, I touch my hand to my heart. I now cradle my own dawn pulsing deep inside me. The knowledge of a loving cosmic presence sustains me.

~Anne Merrigan

My Worry Stone Miracle

Some things have to be believed to be seen.
~Ralph Hodgson

A few months after my husband Bill died, his hospice nurse, Pam, moved to Florida. But before she left, she gave me a worry stone with the word L-O-V-E on it. I carried it in a pocket inside my purse, and had it with me when I attended a ceremony in honor of the donation I gave hospice after Bill's death. Many families who had made similar donations in honor of their loved ones also attended. One by one we were called up front to accept a plaque with our loved one's name on it. While waiting my turn, I held the worry stone in my hand.

A few weeks after the ceremony, I reached into my purse to get the worry stone and it wasn't there. I searched everywhere but couldn't find it. In the meantime, my ongoing distress with the cemetery over my husband's gravestone, as well as their mistake with placing the vase, prompted me to write a letter expressing my frustration. More than four months had passed since my husband's death, and his grave still did not have a permanent grave marker.

A new general manager at the cemetery called in response to my letter and asked to meet about the matter. He was not with the cemetery at the time of my husband's death, but had talked with everyone involved and had reviewed my file. He had even been to the gravesite to inspect the temporary grave marker. He said he understood how I felt and immediately offered to reimburse me for the cost of the marker.

As I was leaving, he happened to mention that he had noticed a small stone on the grave marker when he visited the gravesite, and didn't know if I had put it there. I asked if the stone had L-O-V-E written on it. He didn't know, but said we could go to the gravesite to check.

To my amazement and disbelief, I saw my worry stone sitting on the lower right edge of the grave marker! I told him how I searched everywhere for it and it was a miracle he even mentioned it to me. He suggested that it possibly had fallen out of my pocket during one of my visits. As I drove away from the cemetery, totally stunned, I asked myself, "What just happened?"

My last memory of the worry stone was at the hospice ceremony. It must've fallen out of my lap when I stood to accept Bill's plaque. I did not carry the stone in any of my pockets and have never carried my purse to my husband's gravesite—there was no reason to. I always left it in the car and locked the door.

I would never have purposely put the stone on Bill's temporary grave marker, because the permanent one could replace it at any time. I also would not have placed it near the edge of the marker. It would've fallen off and been lost when the marker was replaced.

I have heard stories like this that have no plausible explanation, but never thought some greater power actually moved an item from one location to another. However, I have no other explanation for what happened to my worry stone. I only know that I did not put it on my husband's grave marker and that miracles do happen.

~Margaret Chandler

Chapter
6

Miracles Happen

Guardian Angels

45

An Underwater Revelation

I believe in prayer. It's the best way we have to draw strength from heaven.
~Josephine Baker

One of our favorite summer getaways was the lake an hour away from our home. Though my dad had to work and only came on the weekends, the rest of us made the most of our time. Our rented cabin wasn't luxurious, but for kids it had the best amenity of all—a short walk to the lake. Several times a day we would head out for a swim. If Mom wasn't with us, my oldest brother was in charge.

"Come on, all the other kids are already there!" my brother, Bob, shouted as he paced the cabin's front porch waiting for me.

"You mean Susie is there already. She's the only one you notice," I said as I skipped out the front door. My other brother, Gary, was already sitting on the front steps. He covered his mouth to hide his giggles over my teasing our big brother.

Bob's cheeks flushed a slight red. "You don't know what you're talking about. Do you have your towels and suntan lotion so we don't have to come back?"

Gary and I lifted up our stuff to show we were ready to go. Once we arrived at the lake, we dropped our towels and other possessions on the ground. Dutifully, we put on the suntan lotion though it was hit or miss. Before we split up, Bob sternly stood over us and said, "You kids stay out of trouble. Stick around where I can see you."

I was six years old and the youngest in my family. I loved swimming whether here at the lake or our wading pool at home. Only I didn't really swim. My idea of swimming was more of splashing about in the water at waist level with other kids my age. We would bob up and down in the water, throwing our arms about in a pseudo-style of swim strokes. I thought that was all I needed to know about swimming. It looked like what the big kids were doing.

That particular summer day, I watched my older brother inflate his brand new rubber raft. It was as tall as he was and its sparkly blue color glistened in the sun. It looked like so much fun as he paddled out to the deeper water with the others who had similar rafts. Right then and there I decided to follow him, so I could get on the raft as well.

Gleefully, I ran out in the water after him, not really paying attention as the water around me got deeper and deeper. I just kept bobbing up and down bouncing off the lake's floor. All of a sudden the lake bottom dropped from under me. I sank about ten feet, though to me it seemed like the deepest abyss.

In a panic, I began to flail about. But that didn't bring me to the water's surface; instead it kept me under. In despair I saw others swimming above me, but I couldn't reach them. The worst part was seeing my brother's raft float past me overhead like it was taunting me. I thought without a doubt, I would drown. Closing my eyes and feeling a dire sense of helplessness, I prayed, "God, please help me!"

Almost immediately I heard a calming voice in my head. I remembered our pastor telling us at church, "God can talk to each of us individually, just like in the Old Testament. We only need to listen. This relationship isn't just for super-holy people, but for anyone who is willing to put their trust in Him." This wonderful voice had to be God because there was an overwhelming sense of peace and calmness in it. With my eyes closed, I let that tranquility fill me. If I died now, I thought, I'd be forever wrapped in his love.

Yet God had other plans for me. My life wasn't going to come to an end in this lake. This amazingly serene voice told me to let myself sink down to the bottom. It made no sense to me, but I took a chance and trusted God's lead. Soon my feet hit bottom. From there I was gently instructed to softly tiptoe forward and everything would be okay. Without hesitation, I followed these directions with the water slowly getting shallower and shallower, until at last, my head was out of the water.

Gasping for air, I began sputtering and crying. Soon my big brother was next to me and scooping me out of the water. Hurriedly he brought me to the dry land and wrapped me in a towel. I felt safe and secure as he held me, but it was nothing like the comfort I knew from the voice in the water.

Gary ran back to the cabin to get our mom. Rushing over, she knelt down beside me and asked, "Are you okay, honey? I know you've had a big scare. Your brother should have been watching you."

Seeing how upset she was, I wanted to make her feel better. After a short cough, I said, "Don't be mad at him. It was my fault. I didn't stay by the water's edge like you've always told me to do."

"But honey, it was his job to keep an eye on you."

"It was okay; someone else helped me."

Scanning the faces of the other people in the beach area she asked, "Who was it? I'd like to thank him."

I smiled. "It was God. He was there to help me. God told me what to do."

Mom looked at me skeptically at first, but then smiled. "I do ask him to watch over each one of you daily, so I guess it shouldn't surprise me when he does."

With one arm wrapped around me and the other one held up in the air she said, "Thank you, Lord, for watching over this dear little child of mine."

The scare stopped me from going back in the lake that afternoon, but I did return to the water a couple of days later. Only now, it was at our community pool where I was enrolled in swimming lessons. Mom wanted to make sure there wasn't another opportunity to put

God to the test. However, she still kept praying for his protection against any other mishaps we might find ourselves in.

Before that event I had always said my prayers before I went to sleep at night. Now they took on an even greater meaning and reality. When I ended with "Thanks, God, for watching over me," I knew he really did!

~Christine Henderson

46

Angel on a Dusty Road

The guardian angels of life fly so high as to be beyond our sight,
but they are always looking down upon us.
~Jean Paul Richter

My husband Dave and I were traveling to a mission station. We had enjoyed a breathtaking sunset over the Mexican landscape, appreciating the various forms of cactus and their black silhouettes against the setting sun. It was nearly dark. As we approached five young children standing along the left side of the road, my husband slowed the car—not knowing what one of the little ones might do. The littlest one started across the road, then returned to the other children. We noticed the older ones scolding her for running into the road, but we continued to drive slowly, still being uncertain of the little one's behavior. Being teachers, we knew the unpredictable behavior of children. We were in a foreign country and took every possible precaution.

When we reached where the children stood, the littlest one again darted across the road. A split second later, we saw her head disappear beneath the center of our car's hood. In that same split second, we heard that heart-stopping, terrifying thud. It happened so suddenly we didn't have time to think. She disappeared beneath the hood of our car as we heard the awful thud. The car jerked to the right, dropping into a rock-lined ditch.

As the car came to a screeching halt, our brains could not comprehend what had just happened. We had killed a little girl on the way to minister to others. Although I am ashamed to admit it, my first thought was to run... run from the reality of what had just occurred to the safety of my own country, to the farthest possible place from this stretch of road. I had never killed even an animal on the road. Now I was facing this nightmare.

There was a crowd of women and men with their machetes standing around. That frightened us even more, for there had been only the children just moments before. From where had those people come, and what did those men plan to do with those machetes? The women were speaking to the children in Spanish. The men said nothing—they stood there, their faces grim, hands on their machetes. We were terrified.

My husband had stepped to the side of the group in an attempt to watch the men, so that he would not be taken by surprise if they decided to use those awful-looking things. He would do what he could to protect me, but what were his chances against several men, obviously upset, carrying machetes?

Then we saw the little girl—not lying under our car or on the side of the road. She was standing with the children with whom she had been waiting to cross the road! She had a few scratches on her face and one on her arm, but other than that she seemed fine.

I had taken Spanish in high school and college, but I forgot nearly all of it in the terrifying fear of the moment. We stayed a few minutes longer, then slowly made our way back to the car. We were concerned about sudden movements because we did not want to frighten any of the adults standing nearby—especially the men with those machetes! My husband looked under the car, certain that we had ruptured the oil pan or damaged another part of the undercarriage.

Convinced that everything seemed in order, Dave slid behind the wheel and slowly drove away. He commented as we left that it was miraculous the car had suffered no damage, considering that the drop off was cluttered with jagged-looking rocks.

We had not even taken time to do a final check of the front of the car. That was not on our list of priorities at the moment. The little girl was safe, and that was all that mattered. With our hearts in our throats and prayers of thanksgiving in our hearts, we drove the remainder of the way that night in silence. Perhaps we simply were not able to put into words the terrible experience we had encountered, but I know both of us were offering up our own words of disbelief at what we had seen and been spared.

Later at the hotel I was in our room unpacking, and my husband was outside near the car. He needed time alone to process what had happened, and I let him have his privacy. If he wanted to talk, he would come to me.

A few minutes later, the hotel room door opened and I heard, "Carol, come out here. I want you to see something." My heart stopped. Was I going to see pieces of that little girl's skin hanging from a part of the car? Was I going to see her blood smeared on the paint?

"Come and look at this car." Dave took me to the front of the car and, in utter shock, I saw no dent in any part of the car's hood or grill. How could that be? We had seen her head disappear there. We had heard the thud.

"Now come and look at the driver's side of the car." I thought he had saved the worst for last. The car had accumulated a lot of dust on that dirty road, but in the glare of the hotel's parking lot lights I could see it.

There, running the full length of the car, was the evidence. The image of a little hand had made its path in the dust. Five little fingers had coursed their way the full length of the car. We stood in absolute silence, staring at each other, as the reality of what had occurred made its way into our minds and spirits.

We had had an encounter with an angel on that dusty Mexican road. A little girl's life had been spared and, perhaps, ours as well. Dave and I knew an angel had pushed that little girl out of the path of our oncoming car. That priceless child had her angel come to her in her time of need—when it was literally a matter of life and death.

~Carol Goodman Heizer

Protection in a Dangerous World

It comes down to whether you believe in seven miraculous escapes a week or one guardian angel.
~Robert Brault

I believe angels are present and active in our world. I like to imagine a vigorous, yet harried, protector tasked with keeping me out of harm's way. This job is made more challenging because I also believe that life is a daring adventure or it is nothing at all. I am driven to climb it, swim it, ride it or paddle it whenever it's possible to do so.

I like to think my angel enjoys a good adventure, too. I can almost hear him howl with joy as he rides the rapids on the front of my kayak. But I also believe he's by my side when I'm driving in rush hour traffic or walking through a dark parking lot. Help has been sent to me in many ways over the years, and I have learned to pay close attention so I recognize these sacred moments when they arrive.

Sometimes my "life preserver" comes in the form of a loud, decisive voice that seems to originate from within me and leaves no room for misinterpretation. One time, this happened during a pre-dawn jog on a humid, tropical morning. I came upon the gates to a local park. As I approached the entrance, as I'd done hundreds of times before, I heard a resounding "NO!" At the same moment I felt as if I'd hit an invisible wall and, despite the forward momentum of my run, actually bounced backward. Needless to say, I crossed the park off my itinerary for the day.

I believe I was saved from something sinister that morning, but the irony of divine intervention is that I don't always know what danger I would have faced. Sometimes it's a leap of faith, the childlike trust that I was indeed spared. Other times, it's all much clearer.

"Turn now!" A voice boomed in my head as I came home from work one evening. I usually turn left into my neighborhood from the south, but it's also possible to come straight into the entrance from the east. These roads meet at a four-way stop sign. I did as I was told, and a few navigational adjustments later came to a stop directly in front of my neighborhood. Cold chills raced down my spine when I noticed the car that had been in front of me and the car that had been behind me on the road from the south had collided in a very serious accident.

I have also felt the undeniable touch of an angel. In the middle of a triathlon several years ago, a woman careened into me during the bike leg of the race while traveling around thirty miles per hour. We were both thrown from our bikes, but I had the clear, specific sensation of being caught and placed gently on the ground. The woman who hit me broke her clavicle and wrist and split her elbow open to the bone. I walked away without a single bruise, abrasion or the jarring feeling that comes from taking a bad fall.

On one occasion, I was climbing a ladder anchored into a steep mountain as I trekked around Mont Blanc in France. As I neared the top of the long climb, hundreds of feet in the air, my foot slipped from one of the rungs. My fatigue and heavy backpack made me less agile and I had the fleeting realization that I was going to fall. A hand clamped firmly around my wrist and held fast until I had regained my balance. The feeling of that hand was so real that I assumed it belonged to my husband. I looked up to thank him, but saw nothing above me but empty space and blue sky.

One intervention required a bit more "visibility" from my Heavenly helper. My sister and I hiked along the Appalachian Trail one summer day and came to our last junction. It was a clearing from which the trail leading to our car would veer right and down. Despite the fact that we were only a few miles from the road, we were still deep in the isolated woods. As we approached that intersection, the all-too familiar voice rang out in my mind: "Don't stop!" It was then that I noticed three men sitting against a tree in the clearing and clearly heard one of them say: "Here they come."

The sense of danger was palpable. I firmly grabbed my sister's arm and casually said hello to the men without slowing. They remained seated as we crossed within a few feet of them.

"Hey ladies, what's your hurry?"

"Sorry, we're meeting some friends for dinner and we don't want to be late," I lied. "Have a good one."

"Hey, wait, we just want to ask you a question."

I met my sister's eyes and knew she was feeling the same sense of trepidation. I glanced back and saw the men, now a few yards away, climbing to their feet and understood they were not going to let us simply walk away.

As they approached, a large black bear stepped out from behind some thick brush and, amazingly, positioned itself between us. He stood calmly at the head of the trail without exhibiting any of the normal alarm you'd expect to see when a bear encounters a group of people. The expression on the men's faces turned from malevolence to terror and I knew their fear of that bear was stronger than their desire to harm us.

I took advantage of the opportunity, pushed my sister and yelled: "Run!" We ran as fast as we could over the rock-covered trail and didn't stop until we reached our car. I glanced back frequently but never saw any sign of the men gaining on us. We memorized the license plate number of the car parked in front of us at the trailhead and sped straight to a Park Ranger's office to report the incident.

A week later the ranger called to update us on the situation. It seems that the men had been wanted in connection with several brutal attacks on women. The police now had them in custody. The men admitted they had seen my sister and me exit our car and head out for a hike with daypacks and, terrifyingly, were waiting for us in that clearing. The ranger confirmed our fear that they did in fact intend to harm us. "You were lucky those old boys were out of their element that day." He chuckled. "They actually believe a bear purposely blocked the trail! Isn't that the craziest thing you ever heard?"

I knew it wasn't luck that saved us that day and I know that bear's appearance was no accident. I am terrified to think how close we came to real harm and silently thanked God, yet again, for His protection.

To the ranger, I simply said: "Yes sir, that's crazy, all right!"

~Vicki Kitchner

A Miracle for Mellanie

Miracles, in the sense of phenomena we cannot explain, surround us on every hand: life itself is the miracle of miracles.
~George Bernard Shaw

"The worse accidents always happen close to home." I grew up hearing that expression in our small Georgia town, with its winding roads and heavy deer population. Those country roads taught my older sister Mellanie and me many lessons. Living in the boondocks, we learned how to navigate around animals, oncoming cars, and sharp curves. We made it to our early twenties accident-free.

Newly married, my husband and I lived in Perry, Georgia. We were expecting our first child in January. I was excited to head home for the weekend to help plan my sister's upcoming wedding. It was early October; the leaves would be beautiful on the 100-mile drive and I welcomed the cool, crisp air.

On Thursday morning, something was bothering me. I felt restless, so I decided to start packing a little early.

By mid-afternoon, I felt exhausted and sat down for a nap. Then the phone rang.

"Amy?" the voice asked.

"Mr. James?" I replied. He was the local warden at the county prison back home, and also a close family friend.

"There has been a car accident, sweetie." His voice was soft.

"Who?" I could barely breathe.

"It's Mellanie; she has been taken to Newnan Hospital," he offered.

"I am on my way." I quickly hung up the phone.

I called my husband, grabbed a bag, and we jumped in the car. I prayed as each mile passed.

My mom met us in the emergency room along with my sister's fiancé, Jeff.

"What on earth are you doing here?" she asked.

"Mr. James called me," I told her.

"Well, we didn't want to worry you, but I am glad you came." Mom hugged me.

"What happened?" I finally caught my breath.

"She was pulling out of the driveway, headed to work. She says she didn't see it," Mom began. "It happened right in our driveway."

The worst accidents happen close to home....

"She didn't see what?" I asked.

"The eighteen-wheeler." Mom's face was ashen.

"Mellanie was hit by an eighteen-wheeler?" I couldn't believe it.

"She hit him head on," Mom said, a tear rolled down her cheek.

Mellanie was in her small, two-door Chrysler.

"She just didn't see it," Mom repeated.

As we impatiently waited for the doctors, Mom filled me in on the details. She told me that she and Grandma saw the mangled car in the driveway as soon as they returned from shopping. The truck driver had no injuries and the truck had already been towed.

"We didn't know what had happened until Jeff called," Mom said.

"I'm glad she was able to call Jeff. That is a good sign, right?" I asked.

"She didn't call me... James Williams did," Jeff said. He clutched his Styrofoam coffee cup with both hands, his brow creased with worry.

"I am so glad Mellanie was able to get in touch with a neighbor." Mom nervously paced the floor.

"Where is he?" I looked around the emergency room full of strange faces.

"I haven't seen him; he left before I arrived. Mellanie was sitting on the grass with the truck driver when I got there; I drove straight here," Jeff said.

We attempted to fill the hours with small talk.

"How are you feeling?" Mom glanced at my stomach.

"Okay." I hadn't thought about the baby in hours. I rubbed my swollen abdomen.

The baby wiggled a time or two, reassuring me that all was well.

The Restricted Area doors swung open.

"McCoy Family?" a little, plump nurse asked.

"Here." My mom jumped to her feet.

"Come with me," she instructed.

We followed the nurse down a maze of hallways. She gently pushed open a door to her right.

"Come on in," she said.

Mellanie was quiet, lying in the bed with her eyes closed. Her nose and mouth were crusted over with blood. She had black eyes. Both her knees were propped high on pillows while two nurses carefully tended them. They were covered in bruises, blood and glass.

"She was lucky she had excellent first aid. She could have bled to death without it," the doctor said as he walked in behind us. "She has a concussion. There is broken glass embedded in her nose, forehead and both knees. As soon as we get her cleaned up and bandaged, we will let her go home, provided she remains perfectly still for the next few days."

Mellanie opened her eyes and tried to smile, but could not hold back her tears.

"I didn't even see it, the sun was so bright," she whispered. "I remembered seeing the prison detail cutting grass to my right. Mr. James was supervising and he waved to me. I waved back and then everything went black for a second." Mellanie sobbed. "He was so sweet. I don't remember anything, except for the dirty faces of the prisoners that took me out of the car. They were covered in dirt and grass, but were very gentle with me as they lifted me out of the car."

"I am so glad they were working on our road that day," I told her. "You could have sat in that car for an hour waiting for someone to come by."

Over the weekend, we all took turns caring for Mellanie. She would moan and cry as we pulled out pieces of glass, but she was grateful to be alive.

Our mom was the local baker, so she decided to bake a cake for James and the prisoners who had helped Mellanie.

"I will be right back. I am going to run this cake down to the prison camp," Mom announced.

"I want to go; Mellanie is in good hands with Jeff." I gently patted my sister's head and waddled to the door.

Mom and I signed in at the front desk of the prison. She placed the large, decorated sheet cake on the desk. Its vanilla aroma filled the dark, gray room.

"I want to thank Mr. James and his men for helping my daughter," Mom proudly said.

"We will go and get him." The clerk smiled.

Mr. James looked surprised to see us. "Donna, Amy," his friendly voice boomed.

"I baked you a cake to thank you for all your help with Mellanie the other day." Mom offered him the cake.

"I appreciated the phone call," I added.

Mr. James looked puzzled. He just shook his head. "I was sure sorry to hear about her accident, but I wasn't there."

"No seriously, we appreciate it." Mom assumed he was being modest.

We both explained Mellanie's recollection of the accident.

Mr. James stepped behind the desk and grabbed a large book.

He pointed to the entry. "Donna, according to our log, our last grass cutting on Rocky Mt. Road was August 26th."

"Well, what... on... earth?" Mom's southern drawl lingered in the air.

We are not quite sure who helped my sister that day. She insists that it was the familiar face of Mr. James along with the prisoners from the local work camp. Our family is positive that we were granted a miracle that day… a miracle for Mellanie.

~Amy McCoy Dees

Over the Edge

Hope keeps you alive. Faith gives your life meaning, blessings,
and a good end.
~Rex Rouis

As my car spun wildly out of control toward a 250-foot drop into the ocean, all I could do was pray. This wasn't the Thanksgiving vacation I had looked forward to when my fiancé and I had planned it several months ago! My mind raced through the recent events that brought me to what appeared to be the end of my twenty-four-year-old life.

We had planned to visit luxurious bed and breakfast inns, take long leisurely drives in the country and perhaps enjoy a wine tasting or two as a way to reconnect and take a break from our sixty-hour workweeks. But the discovery of his infidelity and my subsequent angry departure had put an end to the dream.

Instead, I substituted a solitary drive up Highway 1 — the coastal route from Los Angeles to the wine country north of San Francisco. In November you can see spectacular vistas, stunning sunsets and few people — all the beauty with none of the crowds. The weather is cool, but not yet rainy. A week away would give me ample time to think and plan.

And it had. I enjoyed the fresh, cool air as well as the spectacular and scary drive up the ridiculously-narrow and curvy highway. Several parts of the road are carved out of cliffs that drop straight down to rocky shorelines, and negotiating these areas was stomach-churning at best.

I made it as far as Mendocino, and had enjoyed the charming hippie atmosphere after the somewhat over-the-top wineries in Napa and Sonoma. The time away had allowed me to face the fact that my life would change in major ways, and I had come to terms with starting over, as painful as it might be. In fact, I had decided to cut my vacation short and return home. Worn out by driving difficult winding roads, I planned to drive home the less scenic route, via a major four-lane highway.

However as I left the B&B that morning, the owner spoke of the spectacular forests that Weyerhaeuser maintained—the incredible natural scenery and opportunities to see abundant wildlife. The only drawback: viewing this lushness called for one last curvy drive down Highway 1 through Bodega Bay. When I questioned him about the unfamiliar route, the inn owner assured me it was an easy thirty-two-mile drive after which I could head to the interstate.

The drive toward the coast was stunning—through old growth forests and carefully managed meadows full of wildlife. Heavy fog shrouded the area in mystery that morning, and the views seemed a perfect end to a difficult week. As I turned south onto Highway 1, I felt full of peace and the determination to begin again.

Unfortunately, when this occurred in the early 1970s, only locals used the road to Bodega Bay, and it was pitted, potholed and without guardrails. There were sinuous S-curves still wet with fog that had my tires squealing, even when I slowed to a crawl. About halfway through, a large pickup truck and trailer began impatiently following me.

On a stretch of straight road, the pickup raced around me. Apparently in front loomed a hard left S-curve. But the driver had slammed on his brakes, swerving and throwing the trailer so closely in front of my fender that it blocked my view until I almost drove off the curve.

I pulled with all my might to try to get around before it was too late. But with the wet road and my lightweight vehicle, I went into an all-out spin. As the truck sped away, I felt myself helplessly spinning closer and closer to the cliff.

How would it be to die at twenty-four? Had I done all I was "meant" to do? Could I really answer positively for my life? I found a deep sense of regret rising over wasted, overworked and angry hours. This feeling replaced even my fear of the absolute certainty of the crash to come. I felt the tires hit the edge of the gravel and larger rocks, and the car tipping downward. Will I feel the crash? I don't want to feel the crash, Lord. Or maybe I'll just drown in the sea below... Oh, God, help me!

I noticed the sun glinting on the ocean below and saw the tires go off into space. Then my seatbelt broke. I was thrown over to the passenger side and mercifully blacked out.

Sometime later I woke up to the sound of fists hammering on my passenger side window. When I opened my eyes, I saw a crowd of people surrounding the car, which sat in a ditch forty feet away from the cliff I had gone over.

I fell out of the car into the mud and felt strong arms pick me up. I had broken ribs, had massive bruises to the right side of my body and a concussion, but I was alive! How could that be?

After confirming I would survive, everyone, including me, stood in stunned silence at the side of the cliff, amazed by the story a car of sightseers told about driving toward me and seeing everything as it happened.

They had watched in horror as my car spun into the air and tilted down toward the sea. Then, amazingly, it had come back upright, and flown away from the edge.

When I limped to where it had happened, I clearly saw where all four tires had spun off the edge and where the bottom of the car had scraped on the boulders jutting out the cliff below the road. I also saw where the entire car had come back onto the road some ten feet away from the cliff then slid sideways, with no tire marks before where the slide began. It looked as if my car had been picked up and tossed like a toddler's plaything.

I sat in wonder on the edge of that cliff for a long time, crying in gratitude for another chance. That day I learned the profound truth that miracles are real, and that we each can pray for one in our lives.

~Kamia Taylor

Mayday

The soul can split the sky in two and let the face of God shine through.
~Edna St. Vincent Millay

"Stop it. Stop spoiling my fun." Mom's words of warning invaded my thoughts. I imagined her wagging finger pointed at me, reminding me how dangerous flying in small private planes could be.

Should I listen to her and forego the invitation? Nah. Mom always viewed life through a critical lens. So, I pushed her voice out of my head and determined to have an enjoyable afternoon. After all, the day was cloudless, bright and filled with promise for the first time since I had moved into my new apartment 250 miles north of where I attended college. My date—a handsome amateur pilot—wanted to log some flight time and invited me along.

I was twenty-three years old, freshly graduated with a Masters in Know-It-All, newly employed, and recently unattached from a twelve-month relationship that went sour. Like someone consuming alcohol on an empty stomach, the mixed drink of companionship and adventure dulled the loneliness and left me intoxicated with hope.

Grabbing my jacket, purse and the lunch goodies I prepared, I took one last admiring look in the mirror and headed out the door.

The young man completed his safety check, logged our flight plan, and welcomed me into the two-seater. Its single propeller roared to life, and we accelerated down the runway. Squeezing my eyes shut,

I let the power of the thrust pin me to the seat. When I opened them, cars and buildings shrank into a toy town, and people became small dots on the terrain below. I left my troubles behind.

This pilot was trained only to fly visually. Instead of navigating with instruments, he charted our course by visible landmarks and markers on towers. He pushed a map into my hand, pronounced me co-pilot/navigator, and showed me how to match landmarks below with those on the map. Because of his newness to the area, coupled with my inexperience at navigating from aloft, we occasionally strayed off course. No worries. Putting our heads together we eventually found our path again and safely landed at our destination an hour later.

Sprawled on the blanket, we nibbled at the picnic lunch while trading bits and pieces of our lives. When the sun sank toward the horizon, we prepared to leave while we could still see land markers before nightfall.

With one leg of the trip behind me, I confidently assumed my navigator seat. Map in hand, I located every landmark. Not one course correction was necessary. How silly Mom's fears were.

The weather shifted fifteen minutes outside of home base. Clouds moved in, visually blocking landmarks. Thick haze hid the downtown skyline that rose only moments before in the distance. No amount of straining to see penetrated it. We searched below for any hint of our location, while the clouds thickened.

Not knowing how we might land, my breathing turned into short gasps of panic. My companion's brow furrowed, and his lips pressed into a thin line, telegraphing his growing concern too. "Don't worry. We'll be fine," he said.

I didn't buy it. Mom's words haunted me. Between blinding clouds and all those course corrections that ate up precious fuel on the way out of town, I worried today I would die.

The gas gauge moved toward Empty.

My friend admitted the obvious. "We're well past our airport." With the city nowhere in view and night rapidly overtaking the sky, he offered a terse suggestion. "Let's look for a landing strip."

I managed a strangled "okay," and we both fell into silence. Only the propeller's steady hum filled the cockpit. Seconds passed like hours.

Please, please, God, let me live through this. Please let us find a place to land. I prayed. I pleaded. I bargained.

As the gas gauge rested on E, I thought God might not be listening.

Five more minutes passed when, as suddenly as they formed, the clouds parted long enough for a hangar and airstrip to appear. It looked like a tiny island in the ocean, sitting in the middle of a large, deserted field.

Saved. Thank you, God.

My pilot circled for the approach. Salvation was moments away.

The engine sputtered.

Please, God! I screamed silently as the young man pumped the gas knob to ensure every ounce of reserve fuel reached the engine.

He began the descent.

The propeller hesitated again.

Then, stopped. Completely still.

Silence filled the cockpit. My friend grabbed my hand. "Don't panic," he said. "If I keep the nose up, the plane will glide."

"You gotta be kidding."

"It will glide," he repeated. "Trust me."

I closed my eyes and prayed while we floated toward the farmland bordering the narrow strip of cement below.

"We're dropping too fast," the pilot said. My eyes flew open. "I have to put the plane down in the field. The wheels within those plowed furrows. Or we'll flip. Hold on tight."

Please God, please God, hear me. God, where are You?

Below us, pilots poured out of the nearby hangar and watched our free fall.

As I held my breath, the wheels touched the ground. Exactly within two plowed furrows.

My pilot's grip tightened on the steering wheel while the plane rolled within the trenches and halted… 100 feet short of the runway.

Our audience of pilots broke into applause. Once we jumped from the plane, they slapped my companion on the back, congratulating him for doing the almost impossible—landing a plane in a furrowed field without flipping it, and without a working engine.

Only that evening when safe at home with both feet on the ground did I realize God had answered my mayday call. Not just my physical one in the plane but also my spiritual mayday. I was back on course.

~Gloria Ashby

Night Bull

One thing you can say for guardian angels: they guard.
They give warning when danger approaches.
~Emily Hahn

Across the parking lot, I watched a gantry crane load containers onto a ship while I returned phone calls. My office overlooked the turning basin of Houston's ship channel. And my fascination for the sea and all that rode on it teased at my attention as I chatted with reporters as my company's media spokesperson. Today's project meeting had been lengthy, meaning a lengthy list of calls to return. At the beginning of these, the hull's rust-colored waterline rose high above the water. Now, with the sun in the western sky, the ship had ebbed into the bayou, the waterline barely visible, a full load for the Swedish flag vessel.

My secretary buzzed. "Your mom's on line two."

My stomach clutched and I promised a callback on the line one conversation and then took some deep breaths for what awaited. Until recent months, a manager herself, Mom never called during working hours. But since the holidays, she had, several times, the message similar to today's: "I took your dad to the hospital... can you come?"

Of course. Who wouldn't? Not old by today's standards, Dad's body seemed to be wearing out—heart, lungs, and intestines—and I was their only child.

Home lay north from Houston about 300 miles, an easy drive after clearing Houston's tangled sprawl. But creeping through those first hundred miles could take two to three extra hours. I checked on flights into Dallas/Fort Worth. All full.

"I've got to go home," I said to my boss on the way out the door. "I think I've covered everything. Can I switch the calls to you for the next couple of days?"

He nodded. "Want someone to drive you?" His hand rested on the intercom button, ready to summon our intern, I was sure. Our secretary must have told him it was Mom. Also the adult child of a declining parent, he understood my fear.

"No. I'll be fine. The drive will help... wish it were shorter though." Did I ever. In truth, driving at night, watching the flicker of lights in houses along the way did produce a calming effect. I just didn't know if I could get there in time.

I stopped by my house, thirty minutes in the wrong direction, to pick up some clothes, give Mom a call back, and let them know about when I'd be in.

"Honey, be careful," she said. "Do you want to speak to Daddy?"

Of course, she'd say that and I knew I'd hear the same from him. I did, and loved them for their care. He added, as usual, "Remember, you and your mom are all I've got. That car's carrying a precious package."

"I'll be fine, Daddy. I'll stop by the hospital when I get in town. It'll be after hours but I know my way around." I said the same to Mom along with, "Gotta go. Want to beat the worst of Friday afternoon rush hour." I wouldn't, though. It had already begun.

While talking with them, the phone cradled against my shoulder, I slapped together a sandwich of meatloaf leftovers and filled a thermos of vanilla bean coffee rather than stop along the way. After all, this might be the last time I could see or speak to him.

Mom was tired. Daddy had been ill for years, the last three months so much more so. I could hear the flatness in her voice, usually chipper no matter the hour or event. All of that added to my haste.

One route from my house took me on back roads, a good ninety-five miles parallel to the clogged I-45N. Usually I didn't take this road at night. It was lonely. Today, clouds quickened the darkening day. But it would be faster. Besides, I had a good car, nearly new. It's a pretty route, up through the tall pine trees and gently rolling pastures. I put the windows down after leaving the city to take in the scents of fresh pine mingled with wood smoke from houses buried in the surrounding forest. Besides, it helped to clear my head after the sandwich. I pulled over to pour a cup of coffee to beat sluggishness before it arrived.

This worked, carrying me to the turnoff onto a smaller, narrower, two-lane, curving, hilly road that would take me to the highway for the rest of the trip. I'd driven it many times, just not this late. I turned up the music to keep me company and shush the thoughts of what waited at home. Jimmy Buffet could get me singing along anytime.

All of a sudden, out of nowhere, a huge bull, black like an Angus, straddled the road's faded yellow midline. I stomped on the brakes. My God. Where had that come from? I'd seen large bulls before, but none like that. In the eeriness that only pitch-black night can produce, he loomed as big as a house. Having stopped in the middle of the road, I eased off to the grass strip to recover what was left of my composure. Now where was the beast? Just moments ago, he'd scared the life out of me. My car's headlights pierced the black. No bull. I walked around, ready to dive back in if I saw him. No bull. Sirens sounded in the distance, the highway not far off.

My hands shook. I gulped deep breaths and poured another tumbler of coffee. I'd not been sleepy or dazed. I'd seen the bull and now it wasn't there. My mind playing tricks? Settling down, I re-started the car and crept onto the roadway at a sedate fifteen miles an hour, not the eighty-plus I'd been doing before the Black Angus appeared.

Cresting a hill, my car's high beams shone on a rolled-over car and a broken pickup. The screech and whine of sirens yanked to a stop where I would have landed moments ago but for the sudden appearance of my friend I call the Night Bull. I parked and waited while they moved people, at least one in a body bag, and tended to others before loading them into the ambulance. A wrecker arrived and opened one lane. I looked around for the bull one more time before passing by the wrecks. I never saw my friend, Night Bull, again.

When I got to the hospital in Fort Worth, my folks asked about the trip. "Long, but okay," I said. "I had some help from a friend."

~Carmen Goldthwaite

Ricky's Angel

God blesses him who helps his brother.
~Abu Bakr

The victim of a rare genetic disorder causing his muscles to deteriorate, my son, Rick, required frequent visits to the doctor. This was a major undertaking, and on the best of days we would return home exhausted.

Even with a hydraulic lift, Rick's scooter was a beast to load and unload. It took some time to get both him and the scooter in or out of the van. People were neither patient nor polite about delays in the patient loading zone, so we skipped that convenience, instead parking at the far perimeter of the lot where we had plenty of space and, if we were lucky, a little shade.

The doctor was running an hour behind that day and by the time we left, Rick was fatigued from sitting on the scooter without the neck and back support he so badly needed. It was a hot day, really hot, even for Phoenix in July. But Rick didn't mind the heat, courtesy of blood thinners, and I was grateful that at my age I could make the walk.

"It's kind of creepy out here," I commented as we walked to the van, the heat visibly rising off the blacktop. "Not a sign of life anywhere."

"You've now entered *The Twilight Zone*," he snickered, knowing that show gave me the heebie jeebies.

As we made the transfer from the scooter to the van something went horribly wrong, and before I knew it Rick lay flat on his back on the ground, completely helpless. As he was wearing only a lightweight cotton shirt, the blacktop immediately started burning his skin. He was too close to the van for me to push him into a sitting position, and at 6'2" and over 200 pounds I had no chance of moving him.

I didn't have a cell phone. It was a long way back to the building and I would have to leave Rick alone.

"Can I help?"

I turned and found a strange man standing there.

"He fell," I said weakly. "He's getting burned."

The stranger nodded and stepping past me, he leaned over, scooped Rick up as if he were a small child and sat him in the van. As he stepped away I swooped in and fastened the seatbelt. It felt as if a cool breeze was blowing over me, the relief was so great.

As I tried to swallow the lump in my throat I turned to thank the man who had saved us from certain disaster.

"Where did he go?" I yelped.

I looked around but he was nowhere to be seen. No cars were moving, and given the distance involved I didn't see how he could have gone out of sight in the few seconds that had passed. For that matter, in retrospect, I couldn't imagine where he had come from in the first place.

"He's gone. He just vanished!" I said as I got behind the wheel and jammed the key into the ignition.

We didn't speak on the drive home. Falling was Rick's greatest fear and we still had to get him out of the van, onto the scooter, into the house, back off the scooter and into his chair. He was very tired and would be able to offer even less help than usual. Each transfer was another chance for mishap.

Home and safely in his chair, Rick dozed off almost immediately. I collapsed at the breakfast bar sipping a tall glass of cold water with a lemonade chaser and thought about what had happened. Surely there was some logical explanation. We did not speak of it that evening and I put it out of my mind.

That night as I lay in bed, I found that I had not put it out of my mind at all. I thought and thought but could not come up with an explanation. Early morning light crept in my window before I fell asleep.

When I got up I was still puzzled. Usually I would spend the morning puttering in my kitchen, but that day I found all I could do was sit and think about the previous day's events. I believed in angels, I supposed, in theory, but I was not prepared to tell anyone I had just had a chat with one.

I was still sitting there when Rick came around the corner on his scooter. Usually he went straight to his chair. We would not speak until he finished his struggle to get settled, at which time I would bring his morning pills and orange juice and we would exchange our first words of the day. But that day he stopped right in front of me.

"It must have been an angel," he said simply.

"What?" I asked a bit stupefied.

"Yesterday. It must have been an angel," he repeated and went to his chair. Speechless, I went to get the orange juice.

As I collected his morning pills, one of Rick's sisters arrived to watch TV with him, as that was all he could do anymore. Sometimes she would convince him to go for a ride around the block as she walked alongside his scooter. I was always glad for him to have somebody to spend time with.

"What's new?" she asked.

"We saw an angel yesterday," he replied.

"Oh? What happened?"

"Tell her, Mom," Ricky said as I handed him his pills.

Of all my children, my youngest daughter was the most likely to believe in something that could not be proven, yet on some level I wished that he had not brought it up. But it was out of the bag now and I knew she wouldn't let it go, so I told her about what happened, finding myself feeling a little defensive as I did.

"How could that man have just disappeared like that? And how could he have picked Ricky up so easily?" I demanded, the tone of my voice almost daring her to disagree. "I've thought and thought and there's no other explanation."

"I think you're right," she replied simply.

"What?"

"I think you're right," she repeated. "It was probably a guardian angel." With that, the two of them turned to conversation about what to watch on TV, as if an angel popping in was just the most natural thing in the world. I went to the kitchen.

My son is gone now. My daughter never had any trouble believing an angel had rescued us. While I always knew that was the case, I had some trouble actually accepting it. I suppose I was worried some "logical" explanation would come to light and I would be left feeling old and foolish. But now it's a comfort to know that Rick has somebody to watch over him until we arrive to take over… as we've been known to do.

~W. Jones

Chapter 7

Miracles Happen

Divine Intervention

53

David's Story

Luck is where opportunity meets preparation.
~Denzel Washington

Each year in the early spring there is an Annual Open Call at Wilhelmina Kids & Teens, a leading modeling and talent management company of which I am president. It is a widely publicized event and a chance to get discovered. It is always well attended, with a line around the block at the company's offices. Everyone on line is waiting to become a star. It is a huge event and my staff and I have a great time meeting the candidates on this high-energy day.

I spend a lot of time walking the line so I have a chance to talk to the aspiring youngsters in a low-key atmosphere when they are comfy and casual and not under the spotlight. This way I can get a better sense of who they are and make sure not to miss anyone.

One year, I spotted a very exotic young teen three-quarters of the way around the block. He was small for his age and quiet, and I just knew the camera was going to love him. He and his family had recently moved from Morocco. He spoke perfect English and a remote French/North African dialect, which I knew would come in handy for a movie part someday. His parents had taken their life savings and opened a coffee shop downtown. It would be perfect—the mother's job allowed flexibility and they lived in Manhattan, so auditions and Go Sees (auditions for print work) would be easy to coordinate. His name was David.

Over the course of the next few months David went on some Go Sees and auditions. He booked a few jobs but nothing significant.

Then came the breakthrough I still remember. It was a snowy Friday afternoon in the dead of winter. I received a phone call from the London production office to which I had submitted David for a role several months earlier. I thought the role was perfect for him, plus the role required knowledge of the French/North African dialect that David already knew. Shortly after I had submitted him for the project I followed up with a call to the casting director and was told the project was on hold. They said when they got the "green light" they would be in touch. That's what they always say, but it rarely happens.

Well, they were in touch. The director wanted to meet David and he was flying in from London for one day, Saturday, to do so because shooting started in London on Monday. Wow, the director flying in on the weekend just to meet David. Perfect. They must have been really interested in David.

We worked on all the details for the director to meet David and his mother, Solange. To make things easier for the director, I suggested they book a suite at one of the airport hotels. They could spend a few hours working together and get to know each other, because this young man would have the title role in the movie.

The snow that started Friday continued heavily through the night, and the director's flight to New York was cancelled because flights were not landing. The snowplows could not keep up with the snow to clear the runways.

All the airports up and down the Eastern Seaboard were closed. I had been up all night watching and listening to the weather reports. It was not looking good. All I could think was: Oh no, would they book their second choice, who lived in London, and be done with it? Would David miss the opportunity of a lifetime? Would the stupid weather prevent the director from making it to New York?

Early Saturday morning I got a call from my friend Lori. Lori is an early riser and always thinks everyone is up as early as she is, so it is typical for her to call me at 6 a.m. I was already awake from being up all night watching the weather, so it was okay. She told me she would not be able to meet me for lunch. She'd had a last-minute business trip to London and her return flight could not land at JFK because of the weather, so it was diverted to Boston. Wow—sorry about the lunch but what great news. The Boston airport was open—have the director fly to Boston and have David take the train up to Boston and meet him. What luck that I had a date with Lori and she called to cancel. Now all I had to do was get the director on the flight, and how was that going to happen?

Next thing, my boyfriend Robert, who was in Costa Rica, called to ask how I was weathering the storm. I told him how crazed I was with the David-and-the-director situation. He took down all the information. He told me he would call his friend on the Board of Directors of British Airways who owed him a favor and would get the director on a flight. Oh my god, was it going to happen? Was I that lucky? Was David actually going to meet the director?

As all this was happening, Solange kept calling me for updates. Every time she called she told me she had lit a candle in David's room so the director could find his way to David.

The next twelve hours were a haze. Robert ended up getting the director on a flight that landed at JFK that morning. It was the only flight that landed until the afternoon. It was as if the angels cleared the runway for the director to find his way to David. The director and David spent three hours together. When the director walked out of the room, he was like a proud father. He announced that he and David would be spending a lot of time in London and so would Solange. She was going to play the role of his mother. Who knew she was an actress?

A warm fuzzy show biz story but wait—the part I didn't tell you was that the family's coffee shop was downtown, a block away from the World Trade Center, and it was destroyed earlier that year by the 9-11 attack. The family was broke, living hand to mouth, and the money David and his mother would earn from the movie was enough to pay for all the restaurant renovations and part of David's college tuition. David is very lucky his mother lit that candle.

~Marlene Wallach

54

The 115-Pound Miracle

Nothing has more strength than dire necessity.
~Euripides

"Hand me that wrench, Tammy."

I did what my Pappaw Luther said. I was about ten years old, and hunkered down near a car he had jacked up and was working on. A light gray one with a black top.

I didn't give his mechanic work a second thought. He'd lain under cars before, fixing them, and I'd seen him do it a dozen times. He lay on his back underneath in the gravel, only his head and shoulders visible. The rest of him, from chest down, was under the car.

It was a pretty summer day. Life on my grandparents' farm was quiet that day, with almost everyone having attended the funeral of a relative. My mother didn't want to attend, so she volunteered to babysit all the kids—my siblings and cousins. Usually the yard would be full of running, playing, laughing kids.

It was a one-hundred-acre farm, and my pappaw worked on the car in front of his house.

I liked hanging out with my pappaw once in a while. He was a man of few words, but when he talked, he liked to explain how things worked and what he was doing. He was a diesel mechanic and farmer, and could build or fix anything with his hands. I looked up to him and thought he could do anything—invincible.

That's why my brain was so frozen and stunned when the jack slipped and the car fell straight down onto his chest with a sickening thump.

He couldn't move, and the only sound was a slight gasp of "Get Dana," so I ran as fast as I could toward the trailer my mother, sister, and brother lived in.

My mouth opened to scream to my mother as I ran, but no sound would come out. My voice had frozen in my throat.

Finally I reached the door, and I screamed, "The car fell on Pappaw! The car fell on Pappaw!"

My mother and I ran back to the car, and he still lay as he had when I left—trapped under the car on his back.

My mother gripped the bumper of the car and lifted it, urging, "Scoot out! Scoot out!"

Pappaw scooted in the gravel, and my mother scooted the car over and set it back down.

My mother couldn't have weighed more than 115 pounds.

I couldn't believe my eyes. At ten, I knew something extraordinary had happened, but, on the other hand, it seemed like a perfectly normal thing for a person to do when a car crushes someone's chest.

My mother ran to the farmhouse to call an ambulance.

"I don't want to go to the hospital," my pappaw said. "With this hole in my sock."

Well, he did go to the hospital, and the doctors were amazed that he only had some bruises.

"It should have killed him," the doctor said.

At the time I thought of the incident as amazing, but now as an adult, I believe it was a miracle. Two miracles really. One, that my mom lifted the car and scooted it over. And, two, that Pappaw had only some bruises.

People claim adrenaline, and I don't doubt that. But the truth of the matter is, not everyone in a state of panic can lift a car, and not every person who has a car fall on his chest survives with just a few bruises.

All I know is that I witnessed firsthand the power of miracles that summer day so long ago.

~Tammy Ruggles

55

A Time for Miracles

If God brings you to it, He will bring you through it.
~Author Unknown

Every once in a great while, I have the dream. I'm eight again. I'm watching blood from my mother's head drip onto the blades of spring grass. Her hair is wet. The blood is thick and won't stop falling. I'm screaming. I'm crying. Life is vanishing from Mom's body.

Only moments before I'd been a worry-free second grader. Dad was tinkering outside in his workshop. Mom and my four-year-old brother were mowing the lawn. I remained inside while my baby sister slept in her crib. My black-haired baby sister who nearly died of congenital heart defects, and now, finally was at home with us. We considered her a miracle from God.

But God wasn't finished performing miracles. That quiet spring evening, God had many more miracles in store for my family.

Although charged with checking on my sister, something propelled me outdoors. Looking back, I consider this a miracle in and of itself. It put me in the right place at the right time. And for the events about to transpire, every second mattered.

Upon stepping outside, I found my little brother hysterical. "What's wrong?" I asked.

"Mommy's hurt!" he choked.

I looked up to see Mom bent over the tractor at the back of our property.

"No, she's not," I assured him. "She's fixing the tractor."

To mow the lawn, my parents used a set of blades hooked to the back of a small garden tractor. The tractor's tires had been wrapped with chains, which allowed for better traction in the garden.

"No!" he wailed. "She's hurt! She's hurt!"

"C'mon," I said. "I'll show you."

My brother wouldn't budge. I skipped across the yard. As I approached Mom, it still looked as if she were bending over performing repairs. I leaned down, getting close to her face, to ask what she was repairing. Then, my agonizing screams filled the air too. No one can prepare for such a tragic sight, especially a child. Mom's face and hair were drenched in blood, her head wedged beneath the seat of the tractor. But somehow, someway, in that horrifying condition, with oxygen cut from her airway, another miracle happened.

Mom spoke.

"Get… your dad," she instructed, in a raspy, gasping voice.

Immediately, I dashed across the lawn to Dad's workshop. Cutting and sawing, he hadn't heard anything. We rushed to Mom. Petrified, Dad tried frantically to free her. The efforts proved futile.

"Mom! Mom!" I screamed, terrified.

And then, Mom spoke again.

"Get… the kids… in… the house," she said. "Call… the… ambulance."

Mom's words came out slow and slurred, but deliberate.

We raced for the house. I grabbed my brother. Dad called for an ambulance and rushed back outside. At that moment, though knowing Mom teetered on the precipice of life and death, a sudden calm came over me. My fear subsided. My tears ceased. Everything became clear to me and I understood that my brother—who'd been guided safely off that tractor—shouldn't witness the events outdoors. I closed the curtains, turned on the television, asked him to watch, and directed him not to look outside.

Later I discovered what transpired beyond the walls as we waited. The ambulance crew struggled to release Mom from her pinned position. Then, another member of the crew arrived—a former state-wrestling champion, who, amazingly had gone to school with Mom. But at that moment, he didn't recognize her. Gifted with great strength, adrenaline soaring through his body, the man seized that tractor seat and ripped it from its foundation. The air flowed again to her weak body. But she still remained trapped. Mom's sweater had wrapped around an axle. Her classmate removed the tire and cut Mom free.

On the way to the hospital, Mom nearly succumbed to shock. With her blood pressure dangerously low, the crew feared coma or death. To prevent this, Mom needed to stay awake. Besides a crushed head and oxygen deprivation, her left arm hung nearly detached from her body. She was bleeding to death. The friend, who saved her life, finally recognized Mom. He spoke her name.

"Who is it?" Mom asked.

"It's Jack," he said.

Barely able to see, Mom looked upon his face. And she remembered. When Jack talked, she responded. Had Jack not been there, I wonder if perhaps Mom might have surrendered to sleep.

Throughout most of the night, Mom remained in critical condition. Mom's sister stayed with us kids. My aunt's presence brought comfort. She would take care of things that night. I lay in bed awake, aching for Mom, when finally my aunt delivered wonderful news. Mom would live.

When Mom regained consciousness, she explained what happened. As she mowed the lawn with my brother on her lap, suddenly the unthinkable occurred. The bottom button of her cardigan sweater caught on the tire's chains. Mom tugged to break free, but quick as lightning the mighty force yanked her beneath the tractor tire, which repeatedly ran over her face before pinning her head under the seat.

Over the next few months, Mom underwent orthodontic repairs and plastic surgery on her face. Though extensive, it could have been much worse. Before mowing the lawn, miraculously, Mom had removed her glasses. This act was out of character. Mom always wore her glasses. With them on, she would have likely been blinded.

Surgeons also performed reconstructive surgery on Mom's arm. But though attached, the limb remained immobile. Experts warned of lifetime paralysis. Once again, the Lord intervened. A doctor suggested electroshock therapy might reignite the damaged nerves. Mom went diligently, working to regain mobility and strength. She pushed past excruciating pain and fatigue. For months we watched. For months we waited, willing that arm to stir. Then, one autumn day, a joyous event occurred—her little finger moved. And one by one each finger slowly awakened from hibernation, followed by the hand, and then the entire arm.

Many don't believe God performs miracles in the current age. But my eyes and heart have personally known them. I didn't witness the parting of the Red Sea, observe hills filled with horses and chariots of fire, as did Elisha and his servant, or see Jesus raise Lazarus from the dead. However, my eight-year-old eyes witnessed God's loving intercession and precious deliverance. I can't say why God intervenes in some instances and not others. But I do know, in my heart, that our creator actively participates in our lives, and his reassuring love propels me onward with continued hope.

~Lisa Mackinder

Would You Give It Up for Me?

The value of consistent prayer is not that He will hear us, but that we will hear Him.

~William McGill

I am a first-generation Canadian. My parents came to Canada from Denmark in the 1950s and I was born in Calgary six years after they arrived. I think as soon as I was weaned from a bottle, I was introduced to coffee. When I was about two years old I would get about a quarter cup of coffee, the rest of the cup filled with cream and sugar. As I got a little older the mixture got blacker and blacker. Coffee was an important part of my life.

Then, one cold Sunday morning early in January 2000, I was putting on make-up and fixing my hair, trying to finish quickly so that my husband Charles and I could have some time to enjoy our second cup of coffee before heading to church. This had been our custom for twenty-one years. As I combed my hair and looked into the bathroom mirror, I heard a distinct voice say: "Would you give it up for Me?" I thought Charles had spoken so I turned around, but saw no one. Then I heard the voice again very distinctly say, "Would you give it up for Me?"

I stopped brushing my hair. "What? Give what up?"

The voice again said, "Would you give it up for Me?"

I felt, more than understood, that I had just had an audible encounter with God. And for some reason God was asking me to give up coffee.

I went downstairs to my husband and told Charles what I had just experienced, and that I needed to stop drinking coffee immediately. Charles did not question my sanity, as I thought he might. Instead, he said, "If you think God is telling you to stop drinking coffee, you must stop and I'll stop too, to support you."

Over the course of that year, many times I wondered why God had asked me to stop drinking coffee, but I would not question His wisdom. We had the youth group come to our home for a New Year's party to usher in 2001. As we prayed together, our youth pastor's wife, Cathey, said something that remained in my thoughts for a very long time.

"We welcome in the New Year," she said, "but even as we do that, we think about how we need to stay focused on God throughout this year. This might be a year of challenges, of good times and of bad times. We might be called upon to offer help and support to each other. We might have to say goodbye to friends. Someone right here in this room might not be here with us next year."

I thought about those words, even though I knew she was thinking more along the line of kids moving away than anything more ominous. A month later I suspected God used her to prophesize what the future year held for me.

In January 2001, I had a full physical and went for a routine mammogram. The technician normally does not reveal findings to patients, but she let on that she thought she saw something unusual and sent me immediately for an ultrasound. Three weeks later a biopsy confirmed I had breast cancer. In early March 2001, I underwent a mastectomy followed by four rounds of chemotherapy.

I could relate countless stories during that two-year battle with cancer, where God spoke to me through prayer, scripture, and God's people. As Cathey had prophesied, the youth group was instrumental in lifting me before the Lord in prayer that year. Many of those young people remembered her words and banded together to surround my family with unconditional support as I battled cancer. My entire church family ministered to me through random acts of kindness and service. The worship team even came to my home and led a mini-worship for me when I was too sick to venture to church. I received countless e-mails from friends around the world. Truly, God used them all to encourage me through the entire experience. I could, and probably will, write a book about my journey with God through that cancer experience, but I know the first chapter would focus on why God told me to give up coffee in the first place.

Doctors, nurses and technicians later told me that the lumps discovered in my right breast were so small that the technician almost missed seeing them in my mammogram. She had asked me before the test if I was a coffee drinker and I had told her I gave up coffee the previous year. I didn't know it at the time, but later learned that in some women heavy coffee drinking can cause little fatty cysts to develop in breast tissue because of the caffeine. This can sometimes throw off a mammogram reading. If I had not given up coffee, the technician might have thought that those tiny lumps were nothing more than cysts caused by my caffeine intake. However, since I was not a coffee drinker at the time of the test and had been off it for over a year, she decided to investigate those lumps. As a result, that early detection of cancer saved my life. My surgeon told me that my particular form of breast cancer was extremely aggressive, and had the lumps not been detected when they were, I probably would not have survived the year.

I have thought often about God telling me to stop drinking coffee. It sounded like a strange thing at the time, but I obeyed without hesitation. God asked, "Would you give it up for Me?" The more I have thought about it over the years, the more I am sure those words didn't have as much to do with giving up coffee as it was my giving up everything to God.

I have come to realize that the moment God speaks to you is the time He wants you to respond to Him. I had no idea what was happening within my body, but God did. His timing was perfect. Had I disobeyed, I would not have lived out that year. It was a life-or-death decision for me and I didn't even know it at the time. I pray that in the large things and small things, whenever He asks me to "give it up for Him," no matter what He asks of me, I will respond immediately, "Yes, Lord!"

~Lynn Dove

I Won't Let You

God understands our prayers even when we can't find the words to say them.
~Author Unknown

The sun was shining bright on a warm but windy afternoon in early November. It was a perfect day to be out and about in Tampa, the downtown oasis where I was entering my third month of college. So far my first semester was nothing like I had planned, and I was frustrated that my depression had returned with a vengeance. The stress of being around constant parties was eating away at me, so I turned to a professional for help. At the time, I was on my second antidepressant and my body wasn't adapting well. The little white pill that I took once a day impacted my life in so many negative ways. I had terrible stomachaches and stayed awake all night. I hadn't eaten or slept in days when I decided to go for a stroll—to the bridge right outside of campus.

It was nothing fancy, just a small white drawbridge that connected the university with the skyscrapers of downtown. Judging by all of the familiar faces I saw, it was a well-traveled path by students. I held my hair back as I walked. The wind was so fierce I thought I would be blown right into the path of the cars speeding by next to me.

When I approached the highest point of the bridge, I leaned my elbows on the white stone railing and looked out over the water. The river next to the school was a dazzling forest green and sparkled from the sunlight. On some days I would see dolphins jump and swish their tails at the students tanning in the park a few feet away. I took a deep breath and exhaled, lifting my feet onto the bottom rung of the stone railing. My head hung low as I stared into the green abyss below me. Fear started to build. Many times I had thought about suicide, but I had never gone that far. I leaned forward. The water looked shallow, and I cringed at the thought of landing on one of the pointy rocks protruding from the slow current.

In my list of plans for my final farewell, I only had two steps left to complete: stand on the top of the railing, and jump. Before making my next move, I gazed over the horizon and whispered what I thought would be my last words: "Goodbye world. I'm sure I won't miss you."

As soon as I picked up my right foot to climb to the railing's edge, a powerful gust of wind hit me, almost making me lose my grip. For a moment, I thought I was going to fall backwards. I continued to try and lift my right foot, but the wind didn't let up. It even started to howl. But what I heard didn't sound like the ordinary whistle — it was almost like the wind was speaking to me, shrieking the word "no" over and over again. It gave me chills but I was stubborn, determined to hit the water. No matter how much I tried to lean forward or climb on top of that white stone, it was useless. The wind was just too strong to fight against. After about a minute or so of struggling, I put my feet back onto the walkway and let go of the railing, frustrated. Seconds later, the air stood still.

At that moment, I knew exactly what had just happened to me. God saw what I was trying to do and wouldn't allow me to commit suicide. It was His way of telling me that I needed to stay here on earth and continue living. I looked up at the sky and whispered "thank you," then walked back towards the campus. After that day, I never returned to the bridge. When I was so close to ending my life, God helped me to see what I didn't realize on my own: life is precious. It shouldn't be cut short.

~Jess Forte

My Last Whisper

Certain thoughts are prayers. There are moments when, whatever be the attitude of the body, the soul is on its knees.
~Victor Hugo

"What the heck!" I screamed, trying to fathom what was wrong with my car. I didn't have much time as my car raced toward the twenty or so cars lined up at the stop sign, waiting for their turn to get on the main road. The traffic was always horrendous this time of day when the daycare center—on the main road—dismissed the morning classes and took in the afternoon kids.

I had put my foot on my brake as I approached the stopped cars, but instead of slowing down I raced faster than ever. When I tried the brake again, it sent the car speeding as if I had floored the gas pedal. I tried to reach down to feel what was wrong, but it was impossible. My car was going too fast and I started swerving into oncoming traffic, causing a few horns to honk. There was bumper-to-bumper traffic on the main road ahead, and the oncoming traffic was heavy too. I couldn't veer off the road because there was a fence and a ditch next to it. Therefore, not only was I going to crash, I was going to take other cars with me—maybe even kill someone.

My children's faces flashed in front of me. "Please don't let me kill any kids, please," I mumbled to myself. I knew the preschool was the reason for the traffic jam, and many of the cars would be carrying children. As I watched the cars in front of me grow closer, I pictured my sixty-mile-an-hour car smashing them accordion style. There was no way out and no way not to hit someone.

I was seconds away from impact when I whispered, "I need a miracle," and then turned the wheel hard to the right. The car flew into the air, bounced, and was about to hit those bumper-to-bumper cars on the main road.

Then, suddenly, my car came to a complete stop. I was shaking so violently it took me a minute to realize that not only had I not hit anyone on the main road, I'd come to rest far from the traffic jam. In fact, there wasn't one car around me. I was far up the road and couldn't even see the intersection I'd just been at. How I got so far away from the cars on the main road made no sense at all. I don't know why or how, but I was okay and so were the other cars.

Trying to pull myself together, I reached down to find that someone had tossed some empty pop cans under the driver's seat, which had wedged under my brake. When I stepped on the brake the cans molded to the edge and hit the gas pedal, sticking in place. Each time I stepped on the brake the cans pressed the gas pedal down more. It took me a few minutes before I could get the twisted cans off the pedals.

Taking a deep breath, I started the car and turned around to head home. As I passed by the children playing outside at the daycare facility my tears flowed freely. The sight before me was a miracle. No smashed cars, no ambulances waiting; business carried on as usual. The last words I had uttered flashed in my mind, and I knew that when I said I needed a miracle I truly got one. I will never ever forget the terror of that day or how it miraculously ended safely. But I am forever grateful that my last whisper was heard and answered.

~Jill Burns

A Gentle Warning

We have two ears and one mouth so that we can listen
twice as much as we speak.
~Epictetus

"Go home," something inside me seemed to say. "You need to leave now." I had no idea where this warning was coming from, but it wouldn't stop. I tried to brush it aside as I stood watching a line of children waiting their turn to sit on Santa's lap at the Sun Valley Mall, a shopping center thirty miles east of San Francisco.

Just two days before Christmas 1985, my husband and I had left our two young children with his parents while we did last minute shopping. First, we'd had dinner at a restaurant adjacent to the mall and then walked over to join the holiday shoppers. A heavy fog settled over the mall but this didn't dampen the spirits of last-minute shoppers. Lighted Christmas trees, carolers, and a Santa's Village set in the center of the mall created the perfect environment to forget one's cares and abandon oneself to the holiday season.

"Let's meet at the Santa village," I told my husband, as we each headed in different directions for shopping.

With people rushing to and fro and carrying overflowing shopping bags, a special magic filled the air. Usually, I savored the hustle and bustle that only Christmas can create, but a nagging sense of danger cast a shadow over my joy.

The thought kept going through my head: "You need to leave

now!" I stopped shopping and headed back to the designated spot where my husband and I were to meet. If he didn't come soon, I'd go look for him.

Trying to brush aside the urgent feeling to leave, I watched a line of children patiently waiting to see Santa. Protective parents hovered and clasped tiny hands. Cameras clicked and bulbs flashed. Younger children cried when parents placed them on Santa's lap. Older children smiled and shyly recited their wish lists in the jolly man's ear. I smiled to myself: Treasured memories to keep for a lifetime.

I should have brought our children, I thought. They'd love to see these Sesame Street figures in the display.

But this was our "date night," a tradition that started after our children were born. Each year, we'd arrive at my husband's parents for Christmas, and they'd insist we leave the children and enjoy an evening together. Usually, this meant an early dinner, some shopping, and a movie.

This year would be no different, if only that sense of impending danger would leave me alone.

When my husband arrived, I said, "We need to leave. I'm not sure why, but I have an uneasy feeling. I can't explain it, but something inside me keeps telling me to leave."

"I thought we were going to a movie," he said.

"No, we need to go home," I said. "I just have a strange feeling."

Fortunately, he didn't argue. As we walked across the packed parking lot, the fog was denser than I'd ever seen. The mall looked like an eerie ghost shrouded in a heavy veil, and lights from the stores almost faded away.

"Are you sure you want to go home?" my husband asked again, as we climbed into the car.

"I feel uneasy being out," I said. "Let's go back to your parents'."

Once we arrived at my in-laws' house, the warning inside my head stopped. A great sense of relief swept over me, yet I didn't know why.

The next morning, my father-in-law greeted us at the breakfast table by holding up the morning newspaper. "Read this," he said.

Splashed across the front page were the words: "Plane Hits Mall; 3 Die, 50 Injured: Bay Area Shoppers Panic as Wreckage Spills Flaming Fuel."

"This could have been you," he said.

Not only had the plane crashed into the Sun Valley shopping center just moments after we left, but it crashed in the exact spot where I'd been standing—Santa's Village! My heart sank. What about those poor children? What about the parents? "Oh, God," I prayed, "please take care of everyone who was injured. Please comfort those who lost loved ones." How could this have happened just two days before Christmas? How could it have happened at all?

Only then did I tell my husband and his parents about the sense that kept warning me to leave the mall. "I believe it was the Lord," I said.

"If you had ignored it," my father-in-law said, shaking his head, "you'd probably be dead or seriously injured."

Why I got the warning, I'll never know. But I had no doubt this was divine protection. Five more minutes could have been the difference between life and death.

To this day, I grieve for those who lost loved ones that terrible night. If only they had heard that same gentle warning.

~Jeanne Getz Pallos

60

Miracle at Dawn

Greater love hath no man than this,
that a man lay down his life for his friends.
~John 15:13

s my daughter and I said our goodnight prayers on February 20, 1997, we ended it with "God, please keep your hand on Daddy tonight." It was not an uncommon prayer for us. With my husband a captain in the Houston Fire Department, this simple prayer was always part of our bedtime ritual whenever Stan was on duty. We crawled into bed and fell asleep.

About half past five the next morning, I woke to the ringing of the telephone. *Who is calling me at such an early hour?* I hurried to silence it.

"Mrs. Shockley?" The voice was a man's.

"Yes."

"This is Chief Holleman, safety officer with the Houston Fire Department."

"Yes, sir," I said, my voice uncertain.

"I need to talk to you about your husband."

Suddenly, my heart raced.

"Stan's been involved in an accident. We've got him at Hermann Hospital right now... "

I could hardly breathe. "What kind of accident?" I managed to ask.

"Well," the chief said, "Stan and his crew were just arriving on the scene of a church fire, when part of the church's structure collapsed onto the cab of the pumper."

"Collapsed? Were they in the pumper?"

"Yes, ma'am, I'm afraid they were. Nobody but Stan was hurt. We believe he's going to be okay," Chief Holleman said, "but I didn't want you to hear it on the news. They've got him in the trauma unit at Hermann right now, checking him out."

"Is he conscious?" It was my voice, but, oddly, I felt like an observer eavesdropping on someone else's bad news.

"He blacked out earlier, but he's conscious. What I'd like you to do right now is just hang tight. They're running some tests on him and I'll call you back as soon as I know more."

"I want to be there," I said, a sob catching in my throat.

"Let me get these test results, and I'll call you back. Okay? Just try not to panic. I'll be in touch soon."

"Thanks for calling." I was practically hanging from the telephone. I fell into a chair in the darkened kitchen, numb. Dear God, I pleaded, please let my husband be okay.

Most of Stan's years in the department have been spent in the heart of Houston's downtown. He's witnessed a multitude of hair-raising sights, and received a number of awards for heroic lifesaving efforts. He's even had some close calls, but never had he required hospitalization. The phone call from Chief Holleman was the call all families of firefighters fear.

As I stumbled from the kitchen, the phone rang again. An official from Hermann Hospital was making the customary call, informing me my husband was in the trauma center. Upon inquiry, I was told Stan had lost a lot of blood and had been knocked unconscious for a "significant" amount of time, but the fact that he was able to recite his name and address was a "good" sign.

In minutes, Chief Holleman called again. He was sending a car to take Anna and me to the hospital.

The dreaded moment had arrived. I had to tell my daughter,

then ten, that her father—her buddy—had been injured. She lay sleeping peacefully on my bed.

"Anna, Mother needs you to wake up, baby," I said. "I need to tell you something."

She cracked one eye.

"Daddy's been hurt at work and we have to go to the hospital and see him."

Her eyes flew open. "What happened, Mom?"

Choking back sobs, I told her all I knew. We held each other and prayed together. "No matter what we have to face today, Anna," I told her, "God is going to help us get through it." Suddenly, I was filled with a sweet peace as I realized the truth in my words to my daughter.

She squeezed my hand, her eyes shut tight, a thin stream of tears trickling down her cheeks.

A few minutes after six, Chief Kelley arrived at the house. We climbed into his vehicle and headed toward the medical center, making small talk along the way.

Arriving at the emergency entrance, Houston's fire chief and Chief Holleman were there to meet us. We hurried inside toward the trauma center. "I need to warn you," the chief said. "Stan looks pretty bad."

The trauma center buzzed with hospital staff and a host of men and women from the fire department. When I entered the room, I was surrounded by HFD personnel, all offering their sympathies and wanting to help in any way. Never have I felt more among friends than I did that morning. A brother had been injured, and the feeling of camaraderie was powerful.

In the middle of the activity, I saw my husband propped up on a gurney, a pallid, bloody mess. A surgeon stood behind him, stitching up a large gash in the top of his head. It was not a sight for the weak. Be strong, I told myself, as I inched forward.

When my eyes met Stan's, volumes of unspoken words passed between us. It was a moment frozen in time. A moment full of the deepest emotions imaginable. I clutched his bloody hand and whispered, "I love you so much."

The two-alarm fire and my husband's injuries were the morning's top news stories. Stan's crew was the first to arrive on the scene of the pre-dawn fire at the abandoned Good Hope Baptist Church. As the driver pulled around the corner to catch a plug, Stan reached for the microphone to make his initial report. That's when part of the church's front structure came crashing down onto the roof of the cab, directly above the passenger seat, where my husband sat. The last thing Stan recalled was leaning forward to steady the microphone.

The collective weight and force of the falling structure was later estimated at about 3,000 pounds. So great was the weight it blew out all of the tires on the pumper, and made a horrific V-shaped dent just above the passenger seat. Had Stan been sitting upright, the blow would probably have killed him instantly, or left him with severe spinal injuries.

Stan was knocked unconscious and quickly began losing blood. His dedicated crew and fellow firefighters worked feverishly to free him from the wreckage. Chief Raney, one of the district chiefs who helped pull Stan out of the truck, later told me that when he saw Stan's face, he felt sure he was not going to survive. In Raney's words, "I've seen death, Mrs. Shockley, and Stan had the look of death on his face."

But, thank God, he did survive. Outside of twenty-five stitches in the top of his head, and the expected aches and pains from such a severe blow, Stan was okay.

Shortly after his release from the hospital, we drove to the shop where the pumper had been towed. As we crawled up and surveyed the tangled wreckage on the passenger's side where Stan had sat, he and I just looked at each other in a wide-eyed stare. No question about it, a real miracle had occurred.

~Dayle Allen Shockley

61

Disappearing Act

All that I have seen teaches me to trust God for all I have not seen.
~Author Unknown

I sighed as I concentrated on the slick road ahead of me. The windshield wipers made easy work, clearing away the fine mist settling over my car as I drove.

"What's wrong, Mommy?"

"Nothing, honey, I'm just frustrated." I smiled at my daughter, Kyley, sitting next to me in the passenger seat and quickly checked the rearview mirror to make sure my little guy was doing okay. Josh sat nestled in the back seat of my two-door sports car, seemingly content.

I turned my attention back to the source of my frustration, the truck in front of me driving entirely too slowly. I only had a little farther to go until I could turn off of this narrow country road. I wasn't at all concerned with the fact that the farm-to-market road I would take next was even lonelier and narrower than the one I currently traveled. At least I wouldn't be behind this truck. I did feel a momentary twinge of sympathy for the truck following behind me, knowing he would soon be stuck behind this Sunday driver all on his own.

As I approached the intersection where I would turn, I flipped on my turn signal and that's when it happened—the truck in front of me turned onto my exit! I followed behind him and was surprised when I noticed the truck behind me in hot pursuit. What was going on here? This old rural route hadn't seen this much traffic in ages.

I drove a short way, cursing my luck when I became alarmed. The slow-moving truck pulled a rickety flatbed trailer. The trailer had begun whipping back and forth. I imagined it coming unhitched and flying towards us. I had to get past this truck!

We were on a flat stretch of road and I saw no oncoming traffic. I pulled out and began to accelerate when the trailer drifted into my lane, nearly hitting my car. I slammed on my brakes and jerked the wheel hard. I no longer had control of my car. With my foot planted firmly on the brake, we careened into a nearby field. I held the steering wheel tightly and became terrifyingly aware that we were headed straight for a tree. I jerked the wheel again, sending us into a spin. The car spun and spun, still headed for the tree.

I'd always heard of people who talked about their lives flashing before their eyes during life-threatening events but I had never fully grasped what that meant. I now knew. I processed what seemed like hundreds of simultaneous, coherent thoughts in what had to have been a matter of seconds. I thought about my daughter on the passenger side and my son seated behind me on the driver's side, meaning this would end badly no matter how my small car landed on that tree. I thought about a man in our community who had recently lost his wife and how my husband, Joey, was going to be like him, a widower. I thought about how completely helpless I was and how there wasn't a single thing I could do in that moment to help me or my children. I suppose it was that desperation that prompted me to do what so many before me had done when they too realized they had no other hope; I called out to God... literally. I screamed the same words over and over, "Save us God! Save us God! Save us God!" And in one anti-climatic moment, it was over.

We sat in stunned silence.

"Are y'all okay? Kyley! Joshua!" I turned to my daughter and then twisted in my seat so I could see my son. They nodded, a mixture of shock and fear etched into their little faces.

The truck pulling the trailer never stopped but I watched as the truck that had been following behind me pulled onto the side of the road. A man in his late fifties emerged wearing an unmistakable look of concern.

"I'll be right back. Y'all stay here."

I got out of my car and did a quick survey of my vehicle. It didn't seem to have any major damage, just a lot of grass and dirt everywhere.

I headed towards the stranger. I assured the kind man that my children and I were fine. I turned back towards the final resting place of my car and stood silently as my eyes darted back and forth.

"What are you looking for?" the man asked.

I felt a little confused and a bit sheepish when I answered. "I know this is going to sound crazy, but I could swear I was headed straight for a tree." I looked over the empty, grassy, field, not a tree in sight.

He shook his head in disbelief and responded with a shocking revelation. I wanted to hear more. I wanted him to elaborate but a distinctly familiar sound coming from the direction of my car interrupted our exchange. The shock had worn off and my children's terrified cries had found their way to me.

"Don't leave. I need to go check on my children. I'll be right back." I reluctantly left the stranger standing by his truck.

I hurried over to my car and did my best to reassure my babies. They seemed to settle down and I looked up just in time to see the stranger pulling back onto the road and drive away.

In the days following our accident, I shared the story of the disappearing tree with a few close relatives. I was aware of how strange and improbable it sounded, that I had been headed straight for a tree that had somehow vanished. I decided pretty quickly that it was a story best kept to myself. People would either think it was the adrenaline and I had imagined it in my panic or they would think I was crazy. I'd have thought the exact same thing. As a matter of fact, through the years I had tried to dismiss it as just that, a manifestation brought on by the stress of the situation. Only there's one thing I couldn't get past, one truth from that day that wouldn't allow me to simply "dismiss" the awesomeness of what I had experienced—the words of the kind stranger.

He had asked me what I was looking for and when I told him, he spoke the words that will be forever embedded in my soul.

"I know. I saw it, too."

I've had people ask me if I think the stranger was an angel and I feel very strongly that he was not. I believe he was simply placed there that day to do one thing: to bear witness, to affirm what I already knew in my heart but had been all too willing to second guess and deny for the sake of worldly acceptance. I experienced a real life miracle. I called out to God and He delivered me.

~Melissa Wootan

Chapter 8

Miracles Happen

Messages from Heaven

Life After Life

God has not taken them from us. He has hidden them in his heart,
that they may be closer to ours.
~Author Unknown

"G ranny?" Johanna's breathless voice greeted me from the phone. My heart skipped a beat. Had she lost the baby?

She continued. "I wasn't going to tell anybody about this. They'd think I was crazy. But now, I just have to tell you the good news."

Ah. So the baby must be all right. I knew that Johanna was enduring a peculiar pregnancy. The doctor had warned her not to get pregnant because she had a clotting disorder that would endanger both her and the baby. But, as sometimes happens, she got pregnant anyway.

Now, she was in the seventh month of pregnancy, and the fetus was not growing. The doctors called it "intrauterine growth retardation." They had a name for it, but they didn't have a solution. Every two weeks, they did tests: sonogram, blood pressure, urinalysis. They could detect a heartbeat, but the fetus was only about three inches long. It hadn't grown for several months.

When she told her doctor that their church was faithfully praying, he simply raised his eyebrows as if to say, "Lot of good that's doing!"

"What's the news?" I asked, hardly daring to breathe.

"The night Granddad died, he visited me."

My dead husband visited her? I understood now why people might think she was crazy.

"That night, I was in bed, sleeping beside Tom. I woke up, smelling cigarette smoke. It was the same way Granddad used to smell."

I recalled that Don did have a distinctive smell when he was still a smoker. I could tell without looking whenever he was in the room with me.

"Wow! Then what happened?"

"I opened my eyes, and he was standing there, across the room from me. He walked over to the bed, smiled, and sat on the bed. I could feel the bed go down. It wasn't some ethereal ghost or anything, it was Granddad."

"I don't think you're crazy, Johanna. I think you really saw him—or something like him. What time was it?"

"About 2 o'clock in the morning."

I did a quick calculation. Don had died in Honolulu at 4 p.m, which was 10 p.m. on the East Coast. Adjusting for the time zones, he'd made it to Atlanta much faster than any jet plane could make the trip.

"That's wonderful," I said, thoughts racing through my mind. I'd often thought about life after death, heaven, all that. When I became a grieving widow two weeks previously, I wondered if what I'd been taught was true, or if it was a cultural fairy tale like Santa Claus. Did churches, society in general, conspire to create a myth about heaven to make us feel better? You know, patting us on the shoulder and telling us our loved one had "gone to a better place?"

If Johanna truly had seen Don a few hours after his death, then most assuredly, there was life after this life. "What happened next?"

"He smiled, leaned over, put his hand on my belly and began to talk to the fetus. I couldn't understand what he was saying, but he went on a long time; it seemed like a half hour or so.

"Then, he stood up, smiled, and gave me the best hug I've ever had. I could feel his warm body pressed lovingly against me. Then he walked out the door.

"I got up and wrote down everything I could remember about it, figuring nobody would ever read it, but I wanted to record every detail for my own benefit.

"That morning, while I was fixing pancakes for the family, I began to feel life for the first time. The fetus was moving around."

"Awesome," I breathed.

"Today I had my two-week checkup with the usual tests—and they did them all twice. They couldn't believe the results the first time around! The fetus is growing, growing faster than they could imagine."

Johanna's giggly excitement was matched by my own. Was it possible? Was there hope for this tiny smidgeon of a person?

Because of the clotting disorder, doctors discussed taking the baby by caesarian at eight months, but when the time came, everything seemed to be going well. The fetus was growing. Johanna seemed to be healthy. They decided to watch and wait.

I flew to Atlanta to care for the other children during the coming birth, and I got to read Johanna's journal from that strange, glorious night. It was just as she had told me, along with lots of reminiscences of her dear grandfather.

The baby, named Elena after me, was born on her due date and weighed over eight pounds! A week later at her checkup, the doctor said, "I've heard of other cases where the fetus did not grow. Intrauterine growth retardation. But I've never heard of a case where the fetus suddenly started growing and then was born healthy."

He added, "There's no medical explanation. This had to be a miracle."

Little Elena is now six years old, an energetic, healthy, normal girl with a lively imagination. As for me, I no longer doubt there's life after death. It's no fairy tale.

~Elaine Olelo Masters

My Midnight Miracle

We acquire the strength we have overcome.
~Ralph Waldo Emerson

Living was no longer an option! I was taught that God would not put more on us than we could bear. But that was surely not true, considering that in less than three years, I had faced the death of my only child—murdered in a carjacking attempt—and the death of both my mother and father.

A person should not have to live with such pain. Grief and anger filled my life. My sister lived far away and was busy with her family and two sons. When we talked she kindly told me to call her any time. But those nights when I lay awake crying my heart out, I did not call her. I just cried, cried, and cried.

Always very responsible, I made my preparations carefully. Not only did I own my own business, but I served as president of an international professional organization.

When my son, Paul, was murdered, I updated my will. As I planned to end my life, I felt comfortable that my home and belongings would be disbursed as I had requested. Instructions were left regarding the organization's files.

As I read a newspaper ad, a plan formed in my mind. A church singles' group would fly out of Dallas on Thursday evening to Jamaica and return the following Monday. How convenient! Yes, I would go and attend the functions, but I would not be on that plane back to Dallas Monday morning.

No one would miss me until enough time had passed for me to fulfill my plan. I am terrified of water and never learned to swim. It would be so easy. Just wade into the water until it was over my head. I wouldn't be able to swim and that would take care of the problem.

I called to make my reservation. I told the director of the singles' program that I would make my own travel arrangements and that I preferred a room alone.

Time passed quickly. I had little time to grieve as I busied myself making my final preparations. I wanted to leave everything perfect. Late hours that I usually spent crying were spent organizing things both at home and at the office.

When the day of the trip arrived, I contained my excitement as I gave my parting words: "All of you will be just fine. The Office Manager knows how to take care of things just as well as I do. I wish you all the best."

I planned even those words so no one would look for me for at least a week. By then, I would not be hurting anymore. Yes, death would give me peace.

Thursday was a blur, and at last I was on my way. I felt wonderful knowing my pain would soon end. We arrived in Jamaica and checked into the hotel. Everyone was celebrating the Labor Day weekend. I was just as happy as everyone else, but for a different reason.

On Friday, Saturday, and Sunday I counted the hours until the final Beach Party was over. I mingled just enough to be polite. I could not wait for the party to end. Everyone dreaded having to return home to go back to work on Tuesday. I joined the conversation but knew I would not go to work on Tuesday. I would not even have to face Monday.

Before going to the party I dressed in a white tank top, white skirt with a pair of white shorts underneath the skirt. Meticulously, I hid my passport, credit card, driver's license, and the key. Giving one last look around the tiny room, I breathed a sigh of relief. I would not need any of those things again.

No one noticed as I slipped away and walked toward the seashore.

Each day I had looked for a place to leave all my pain behind. And I found the perfect spot!

Some of the group mentioned an inlet where the water seemed shallow, but as they walked in the sand, it suddenly dropped off into very deep water. I had marked the place in my memory and went there every day to be sure I knew the way. Soon I found the location, removed my skirt and my strappy sandals and hid them in the brush. I did not want anything to interfere with my plans.

The moon was full and there was no wind, just the gentle lapping of the waves on the shore. As I began to walk, I allowed my thoughts to return to why I did not want to live. Paul. I would never see him alive, but tonight I would be with him.

Paul was always so responsible and never worried me. When he would go out with friends we would agree on a time for him to be home. He was never late. Even the years he was in college, many times he would call to tell me what he and his friends were doing and that they would be in by midnight, as they all had jobs as well as classes.

Finally I allowed the tears to flow and sobbed deeply. I was tortured not knowing where Paul was. Was he in Heaven? Was he in Hell? Exactly where was Heaven? No one has ever found Heaven. No one has ever found Hell. Nothing mattered. Tonight I would finally be with Paul again.

As I cried I said aloud, "Paul, if I just knew where you were I would be okay." From somewhere behind me, I heard the soul of my son distinctly say to me, "I am where I was before I was with you and I am okay."

I whirled completely around. I was alone on the beach.

The full moon shone almost as bright as day and I could see no one. Again I said, but louder this time, "Paul, if I just knew where you were I would be okay." Again I heard the same words. I did not imagine that I heard the words. I had not been partying with the group. I was fully awake. I knew I heard the words, twice.

As I fell to the sand with heartrending sobs, I allowed the pain in my soul to pour onto the sand. I still sat on the beach as the sun rose.

Somehow those words from above had brought the peace I needed to survive.

Making my way back to the hotel, I managed to get the clerk to unlock my room and I entered that room a new person. The events of that evening changed me forever.

The flight back to Dallas cost triple what I had paid for my one-way ticket there, but now I knew I could and would survive.

Though that trip was several years ago and I still grieve the death of my child, my life began to have meaning again.

Arriving home, I destroyed my notes and once again participated in life. Daily, I am grateful God gave me a special miracle that saved my life.

~Thomas Ann Hines

Always a Daughter

I love my father as the stars—he's a bright shining example
and a happy twinkling in my heart.
~Terri Guillemets

M y late night radio show had put a crimp in my dating years. Then I got a promotion to a morning show but that came with a 4 a.m. wake-up call so that didn't help my love life either!

Finally, I said yes to a blind date and met the man of my dreams. Mike is a great chef and a master carpenter. He could build a restaurant and cook in it too! He loves to laugh, he loves family and he loves the New York Yankees. I was never much of a sports fan, but I knew the New York Yankees because I talked about them with my dad.

It wasn't long before Mike called my father and asked for my hand in marriage. That was a blissful October. My engagement ring is a blue sapphire with twelve diamonds around it. Yankee colors and a diamond for every time Joe Torre took the team into the post season!

Things turned quickly in November when my father took ill. A rare virus went undetected by his doctors. He passed away in February. After he passed, as I stood outside the hospital, I looked up at a scraggly tree and said, "Dad, you're here now, you're part of all this. Everything I see and hear in nature, that's you." I saw no reason to stop our conversations.

People went back to their normal routines but I could not shake my sadness. I was so close to having my father walk me down the aisle. My conversations with him were constant. "Why did you leave me NOW? What about those Sunday dinners I planned eating egg-plant and watch the Yankees on TV?"

I wore the weight of his passing physically. An MRI revealed a herniated disc so large the technician came out of the booth to see me safely down the hall. "Jeez! You've got to be careful!" I walked with a cane. Walking down the aisle seemed like a cruel joke. Mike was growing impatient with my daily crying spells. I explained that I needed to hear from my father. Since I saw him in nature everywhere, I decided that he would send me a tree!

When I was a little girl, Dad would plant sapling trees. One day I had helped him plant trees in a neighbor's yard.

"He'll send me a tree," I repeated to Mike.

The next day, the nursery delivered a beautiful weeping cherry tree. Friends had ordered it weeks earlier. They had no way of know-ing what meaning it held for me.

The tree only increased my demands. "So you can send me a tree but you can't be here for my wedding!" I spoke to Dad non-stop in my head.

Shortly after that, Tom, a co-worker, was selling raffle tickets. He was to MC a charity concert at which someone would win ten thousand dollars. As I wrote out my check for a $100 raffle ticket, I was mentally throwing down the gauntlet to my father. "Okay Dad, this is it. I need a big sign and I need it now. If I am supposed to marry this summer I want you to pay for it." Tom handed me the ticket. It was number 159.

I took the ticket home and showed it to Mike and said, "Dad's going to pay for our wedding." I kissed the ticket and put it next to my father's Yankee cap that I kept on the mantle. The night of the drawing I put my cell phone on vibrate and went to sleep.

When I turned it on the next morning I saw that I had a missed call from Tom at 11:10 p.m.

I didn't have to listen to the message; I knew I had won the ten thousand dollars.

I jumped up and put that ball cap on my head. "Dad wants me to get married. Dad wants me to get married!" I was laughing and crying and calling every relative and friend to tell them the good news.

My father, Antonio Romelo Morabito, was born on July 8, 1929. He grew up in a two-story stucco on Highland Avenue in the Hudson River town of Verplanck, NY. The small yard is covered by grapevines. My cousin lives there now, and on July 8, 2008 that's where I married Mike. The number on the house? 159.

~Kacey Morabito-Grean

Voices of Angels

Music is well said to be the speech of angels.
~Thomas Carlyle

"Thanks," Dad said, as he took the chocolate milk-shake I bought for him on my way to the hospital. He smiled. "I'm really glad you're here."

I was visiting him at St. Mary's Hospital in Florida after his hip surgery. The operation was successful but he looked frail and his strength seemed to be waning.

"I have a complaint," he said. "Would you mind finding out where that music is coming from and ask the person to turn the radio down?"

"I don't hear any music, Dad."

"Well, I do. Someone in another room must be hard of hearing and has the volume up too high. Tell him to turn it down. It's too loud."

"Okay," I said. "I'll check it out."

I walked down the corridor and listened outside all the patients' rooms. There was no music coming from any of them and the hall-way was silent, too.

"No one has a radio on anywhere in this area," I reported, when I returned to his room.

I sat on his bed and put my head next to his to see if I could hear the music from his vantage point.

"I don't hear a thing, Dad."

Excited now, he said, "Listen! It's playing right now! Don't you hear it?" Pointing toward the window near his bed, he said, "It's coming from there."

I heard nothing. When he saw the blank look on my face, he became agitated. "I'm not making this up."

"What's the music like, Dad?"

"It's a chorus humming the same tunes over and over again. Peaceful, calm tunes. Only it's softer now than it was a few minutes ago."

Still, I heard nothing.

I called the nurse on duty and she checked every room on the floor.

"No one is playing a radio or a TV," she reported back to us. "I'd better call your father's doctor."

"Could he be hearing things as a result of the anesthesia?" I asked the doctor.

"That's unlikely," he answered.

"Well then, do you think the pin inserted in his hip is picking up a radio station?"

The doctor didn't think that was likely either. He said that in either case Dad would hear different songs, an assortment of melodies, not just the same music over and over again. If it weren't for the fact that my father was lucid and articulate in every other respect, the doctor said he'd think Dad was hallucinating. He told me Dad's body had undergone trauma and he seemed weaker than he should at this point in his recovery. However, if he was hallucinating, that wasn't good and they would keep a close eye on him.

"I told them the music stopped," Dad told me the next day, his voice weaker than before. "I don't want everyone hovering over me and thinking I'm out of my mind. I heard them talking and I don't need a psychiatrist or sedatives, which they'd give me if they thought I was still hearing the music. So, I assured them the music stopped."

"Has it really?"

Hesitating, he answered me. "No, but you won't tell, will you?"

I looked at my father, a normally energetic eighty-eight-year-old who loved life and only wanted to get better. It was obvious, though, he was losing strength daily.

I took his hand. "It'll be our secret. So, what exactly does the music sound like, Dad?"

He grinned. "Well, like I said, there's no variety. Just the same music repeating itself. I'll try to hum what it sounds like."

He set his face in concentration.

"Hmmm…. hmmm…" he hummed. "I can't seem to grasp the melodies. They're just beyond my reach. And I really enjoy listening to them."

"You do?"

"Oh, yes. They're very peaceful, like unformed words murmured by a chorus of angels—such beautiful chanting."

Each day when I came to visit, I asked, "Any new songs today, Dad?" And even though he seemed to get weaker, he'd laugh and we'd joke about what we'd come to call "our angel voices."

I knew that Dad heard them and he understood that I knew. It was our secret.

Several days later when I walked into Dad's room, I stared in disbelief. He was animated and sitting up in bed. He gave me a strong hug.

"The music is gone," he said. "It stopped, with no warning. It didn't gradually fade away. It just stopped."

"I'm sorry, Dad."

"That's okay. It wasn't so good hearing things that no one else could hear. But it was nice while it lasted."

The nurses told me everyone was surprised by my father's sudden improvement. They would watch him carefully for another day or two and then he could go to rehab.

Many weeks later, the surgery and subsequent rehab had drained Dad of his sudden spurt of energy. His health was failing and I brought him to my home in Massachusetts with round-the-clock nursing care.

One evening he motioned to me to sit near him on his bed.

"Open the window for me."

"Open it? You're always so cold and it's freezing out."

"That doesn't matter. I feel hot. And besides, I think I'll hear the music better with the window open."

My heart flipped. "Music? Is it what I think it is?"

"Uh huh. Remember those angel voices I heard in the hospital? I hear them again. You know, our secret."

My heart was heavy as I opened the window.

Dad's spirit and health deteriorated quickly and he died two days later, the cold air streaming into his room along with the soothing voices of angels sent to chant a melodic welcome to heaven.

~Linda J. Cooper

A Divine Goodbye

Blessed are those who mourn, for they shall be comforted.
~Matthew 5:4

One brisk, fall morning in 2001, I held my lifeless toddler in my arms, tears rolling down my cheeks. I would have given anything for a simple goodbye. I longed to hear her chuckle. I wanted to see her climb onto the ottoman and perform a silly dance again. I craved all the things I'd never do again. No more cleaning paint-stained overalls or muddy shoes soiled during playtime. No more pushing the tire swing or hearing her squeals of joy.

I needed closure. I put my healthy three-year-old daughter to bed one night and she was gone forever the next morning. I felt my options were to withdraw and become bitter or allow God's healing hand to work deep within me. Yet grief still took its toll. I avoided people. Isolation was comforting. In my solitude, I cried out to God. I gave only Him all my feelings: anger, pain, sorrow, confusion, and fear. My only request was to know my daughter was okay. As a mother, I wanted reassurance and my final goodbye.

Days ran together. I drifted in and out of sleep. I self-medicated to calm my nerves (or so I told myself). It was just more escape. The reality that my firstborn child was gone became more and more apparent as each day passed without her. Despite the pain, I continued to pray. Eating, praying, and sleeping were the three main elements of my daily routine. I couldn't proceed with my life until I knew she was okay.

According to my Christian beliefs, she should be playing in heaven and filled with joy. But my faith was shaken. I just needed to know, as her parent, she was happy. I prayed for a sign.

One night, soon after I made my petition, my prayer was answered. To this day, I'm not sure if it was a dream or a supernatural encounter. Madison visited me. I saw my precious daughter one last time. I smelled her sweet essence and even felt her warm embrace as she ran up and hugged me. I heard her precious voice. "Hey Mommy. I'm okay. It's nice here. I like it. It's really fun." I was overcome with delight! I fought back tears as I let her know I was glad she was happy in her new heavenly home. I held her in my arms until she said it was time to go.

She started walking away, but then quickly whipped around. She placed her hand on her little hip and, with her sassy voice, lectured, "Mommy, you didn't tell me." She flipped her hair and rolled her eyes. I looked at her with a question in my eyes.

"He's a guy, Mom," she declared.

"Who?" I asked.

"God, Mommy. God is a boy."

I couldn't hold back my amusement. I giggled. "Yes, dear, God is a boy. I thought you knew that."

She walked away into the white, puffy clouds.

"I love you my child," I called out as I watched her go. I heard her sweet voice call back, "I love you, Mommy." I woke and could still felt her presence around me. We had our last goodbye.

That one encounter allowed me to move on with my life. The hole in my heart will always be tender. But through God's love, I can move on and face my future with hope. Now, support groups, journaling, praying, and remembering are the main elements of my daily routine.

I think about Madison every day. I'm learning how to remember and celebrate her memory by cherishing our good times. I have gained the strength to share my healing journey with others. Hopefully, my story can help them let go of their pain while embracing sweet experiences shared with their loved one.

I believe losing a child is the biggest heartbreak anyone can experience. Watching someone you brought into this world leave is unnatural. Life never seems so precious until it is gone. Love is never sweeter than that of a child. In my pain I had an awakening of my senses. The promise of Matthew 5:4 came true; I was comforted in my mourning.

My final goodbye with Madison catapulted me into a new level of faith. I cherish life more. I love without limits. I take more risks. I try to take in every precious moment God gives me. Not even death can take away the memories we build over a lifetime. Madison may have only lived on this earth for three years and ten months, but she gave me a multitude of precious memories. I will never understand why God took her to be with Him at such a young age, but I accept His will. I know she is content. It was God's grace in these dark circumstances that drew me closer to Him.

~Delena Richeson

Standing Tall

When someone you love becomes a memory, the memory becomes a treasure.
~Author Unknown

My mother, at times, was a proud and stubborn woman. It wasn't always easy being her daughter. We certainly butted heads during my teen years. And she was constantly on me about my posture. At 5 foot 8 inches tall, she carried herself like a model. She had me practice standing against a wall for five minutes each day, then walk while balancing books on my head without dropping them. This was her method for attaining perfect posture.

I would ask, "Mom, who does this? I don't see the point; do I have to keep doing this?" We often argued over my posture.

Over the years, she continued to remind me about my posture and often at inappropriate times. To keep the peace, I never said too much. I knew she meant well, but one day I finally told her to stop. However, she continued to comment on my posture until the last days of her life. Like I said, she was stubborn.

At seventy-seven, Mom developed lung cancer. She took this diagnosis the way she had taken the breast cancer news fifteen years earlier. She survived then and she would again. Determined to beat it, she started chemo and radiation treatments. However, after two treatments, she had to stop. Her body couldn't take it. She needed full-time care, so she came to live with me.

Family and friends came to visit. Everyone knew her time was short. Between her frequent naps, we talked. She often spoke of her mother, who died of pneumonia when my mother was only seven. It was her biggest heartache and she cried during these talks. One afternoon, she recalled her mother instructing her to stand with books on her head. She wanted her to walk like a lady and be proud of herself. Her mother had explained, "Phyllis, you can tell a lady from across the street by the way she carries herself. You must practice this every day while your bones are growing—your back will grow straight. Then as a grown woman, you won't even think about it. It will be your natural walk."

Mom thoughtfully continued, "I remember her showing me how to stand and walk with books on her head. However, they fell to the floor and we laughed. Of course, the same thing happened when I tried it. We laughed again. Then mother would walk beside me to catch the falling books, until I got it. So, when I think of my mother, I remember walking and laughing together."

My mother's face looked beautiful as she talked. She found love and peace in this treasured memory. I understood then, and felt remorse. She had tried to pass this one thing from her mother to me. With tears, I told her how I felt. She tenderly said, "Never mind all of that now. Your walk is fine, just keep your shoulders back and your head up."

I wished I had known her mother—my grandmother. I was sorry my mom had to grow up without her mother. Then the reality of losing Mom hit me. I cried in her arms for the last time.

In the last week of her life, other visitors came to see Mom. One day, as I started to go into her room, I heard her talking. I looked and saw only her. "Mom, who are you talking to?" I asked, thinking she was talking to herself. She smiled and said a relative's name who had passed on. I didn't say anything, but thought her medication was making her see things. Two days later, I found her upset, waving her arms and yelling.

"Colleen, look at all these people. Why are they here? I don't have time to talk to them all!"

I looked around and said, "I don't see anyone Mom."

She replied frantically, "What do you mean you don't see any-one? They're all around the bed—right there, look!" She pointed in all directions. I needed to calm her down, so I quietly said, "Mom, they are here to see you. I'm not supposed to see them. After all, they came to see you, not me. If you're tired, tell them to come back later."

This worked. She agreed to talk to a few. I left the room, nodding to her guest. However, I did not believe anyone was there. Then one evening, right before her passing, I paused just outside her door. I saw my mom as I hadn't seen her in months. She was sitting straight up and reaching for something at the foot of her bed. She appeared engaged in a real conversation with someone. She would ask a question, wait for the response, then reply. I stood transfixed, listening. Her face looked relaxed. Gone were the lines of pain and stress. My mom smiled at someone at the foot of her bed, but I saw nothing. The exhilaration radiating from her surprised me; I could feel it. I stepped back, then heard these words in Mom's "little girl" voice: "There you are. You look just like you looked the last time I saw you." Pure joy covered Mom's face as she gazed at the foot of her bed.

Suddenly, I realized I was witnessing something phenomenal. Goosebumps rose on my arms and neck. I turned quietly to retreat, to let my mother have this incredible moment. I must have made a noise; Mom turned and motioned for me to come in.

Mom's face had color again. She looked better than she had in months and seemed so excited. Her beautiful green eyes glistened with delight. Before I could ask, she declared, "Look Colleen, my mother came to see me. She looks just like she did the last time I saw her when I was seven." She pointed to the foot of the bed and beamed with love and happiness. I felt so overwhelmed I could not say a word. Tears streamed down my face for my mom's joy.

I have always believed in God and life after death. However, up until then, I was unaware passed loved ones could come to help us cross over to the next life. This made losing my mom a little easier. For now I know when my time comes, she will be at the foot of my bed, arm in arm with my grandmother, two elegant ladies—standing tall.

~Colleen M. Leftheris

Two Hundred Miles

Life is a series of thousands of tiny miracles.
~Mike Greenberg

"He's gone." Those two small words came across the phone line loud and clear at 1:58 a.m. on May 15, 2013. Spoken by my sister Sandy's best friend Teresa, they had the power to wake me right up. She was calling to tell me that Sandy's husband of twenty-three years, Mark, had just passed away after a heartbreaking, six-month struggle. He was only fifty-one years old.

Tears gathered quickly in my eyes. "How's Sandy?" I asked.

"Not great."

Teresa tried putting Sandy on the phone, but Sandy was too upset to speak.

I hated the long distance. I wished I could pack up right then, drive the two hundred miles between our homes, and wrap my little sister in my arms. I had family and work commitments the next day, though. It would be afternoon before my husband Jeff and I could tie up loose ends and get on the road.

As I sat in my trusty rocking chair, trying to comfort myself with its steady to and fro, I knew that I wouldn't sleep for the rest of the night. I couldn't imagine what Sandy was going through. I'm a firm believer in the claim that "God's timing is always perfect," and I've repeated that mantra often in moments of crisis or lack of clarity, but

I couldn't see His purpose in this. Mark's fast decline and terrible suffering seemed nothing short of cruel.

A big bear of a man with a ready smile and gentle nature, Mark had been a carpenter by trade but was forced to look for other work due to the economic downturn. He still found time to do the things he loved however: playing his guitar, volunteering on a Search and Rescue team, cooking—and eating! I could still see him striding into my parents' house with his hearty "Hi, Mom," before heading outside to help Dad man the grill. But the one thing he loved more than life itself was Sandy—and she loved him. In all their time together, I never once saw them snip at each other. And while they had no children, the love they shared was almost child-like, pure in a way that's refreshing in this age of on-the-run texts and meet-you-there social events. Wherever you saw Mark, you saw Sandy; wherever you spotted Sandy, you encountered Mark. They were truly soul mates and best friends.

But now my sister's soul mate was gone.

It had all started innocently enough with back pain. Soon that pain had progressed to a point that made walking difficult for Mark, and a trip to the Emergency Room had him facing a battery of tests. Sandy called me from the hospital. "They think it's cancer, Sis," she whispered.

"Oh my God," I said, shocked. "Oh honey, I'm so sorry. I'm praying for you both."

The diagnosis was indeed cancer. Late-stage metastatic lung cancer, to be precise—particularly heart-wrenching since Mark hadn't been a smoker—and the disease was everywhere. He had multiple tumors along his spine, which accounted for his increasing inability to walk, and more tests confirmed tumors in his brain, bone, and liver as well.

The news couldn't have been more devastating. By the time Jeff and I saw him several short weeks later, Mark was confined to a wheelchair. I thought I had prepared myself, but his appearance left me stunned. The robust man I knew had seemingly transformed overnight. He was pale and had lost weight and most of his hair. As the months sped by, he deteriorated at an alarming rate. Each visit left me feeling helpless.

And then came Teresa's phone call.

I was so grateful to have her there with Sandy, but I knew Mark's death was hard on her too. She'd lost her own husband the year before, so she felt Sandy's plight deeply. They were both young widows now, a sad bond that strengthened their friendship more. As Teresa and I continued to talk, I decided not to call my mom and tell her about Mark's passing until morning, at our usual 6:30 time. There was nothing she could do at 2:00 a.m. anyway, and I wanted to let her rest.

But at 6:30, our phone call had barely begun when Mom left me speechless. "I already know about Mark," she said.

I paused. "You do?"

She went on to relate a strange happening that had occurred in the middle of the night. At 3:00 a.m., alone in her villa just five minutes away from me, she was awakened by a noise, a distinct tap-tap-tapping. She didn't know where the noise was coming from—it wasn't coming from the wall or the glass on her window; it wasn't someone knocking at her front door. The noise was quite persistent, yet she wasn't afraid.

Then all of a sudden, she sat straight up in bed and had this very strong sense of Mark's presence. She knew she wasn't dreaming, but she just couldn't shake the feeling that he was standing right there at the foot of her bed. And then she heard him say, clear as day: "Bye, Mom." It was the same hearty voice she'd always known, said in the same full-of-life way. After that, she saw in her mind a single red rose. She could almost smell its sweet scent, feel its soft petals and the prick of its thorns.

"And as we all know," she told me matter-of-factly, completing her story, "a single red rose means 'I love you.' I didn't have a chance to say goodbye to Mark, but he took care of that for me."

I sat enthralled. It truly was one of those goose bumps moments.

Days later, when we gathered for Mark's memorial service, we all brought something to show. Sandy displayed Mark's guitars. His siblings, Debbie and Mike, shared cherished family photos, while I added some jewelry boxes he'd made. Teresa and her daughter Morgan, intent on injecting humor, brought the Nerf balls they used to "pester" Mark with and the little Nerf basketball hoop my youngest sister Christie had contributed. And last but not least was Mom's red rose, standing tall amidst it all like a lovely splash of heaven.

On May 15, 2013, at 1:37 in the morning, Mark passed over to God. But before he did, he found his own unique way of saying goodbye to Mom, of traversing those two hundred miles in a blink. I believe fully that a miracle happened that night—that they happen all around us all the time. More often than not, they are everyday occurrences, tiny nuanced incidents that we label as "strange." They are far from strange, though. They are the ties that bind us, the arms that hold us, the love that connects us, each to the other and to the divine. We just have to be open enough to see them.

~Theresa Sanders

An Unexpected Journey

Earth has no sorrow that Heaven cannot heal.
~Author Unknown

She wasn't supposed to die that way. Nor was she to die so soon, so suddenly. We often talked of how she was my best friend. What would I do without her? But on December 9, 1995, her seventy-first birthday, she woke up "dizzy." In a half hour my mother was dead.

It was right before Christmas and so much was going on, including her birthday celebration. She was supposed to host another birthday party, for a friend's three-year-old, in eight days—she was that kind of woman. So I was not surprised when people poured into the house, doing what they could, saying what they thought would help, and being there for us. While I was able to stay calm for Dad's sake, I really only wanted one person there—my mother.

Mom had chosen the Christmas tree. It was out on the sun porch, and Dad said we needed to put it up. He also insisted after her funeral we have the party for little Brandon as she had promised him. He was too little to know why she wasn't there. So we went through the motions, and I cried surprisingly little; I just felt like I had to hold the guys together. My sister was also in deep sadness. But maybe she was right—I saw death at the hospital constantly and was numb to the sting of it.

One of my mother's closest friends was a pastor who had once preached at our church. He had lost his favorite aunt just eight weeks earlier, and so I leaned on him for two reasons: he knew how to help with grief counseling and he had experienced it himself. So we talked.

I asked him where she was. I needed to know. A lifelong Christian, I never thought about where we went immediately following death, until it took my mother. He said with a soft smile, "She's with Jesus. Remember the crosses—when He told the thief that repented 'Today you will be with Me in Paradise.'" I smiled, trying to accept his answer. But I just couldn't be satisfied, even though I knew I should be.

This is how I went through the holidays too, just wondering. People in my church said things like "Your mom is spending her first Christmas in Heaven" with a smile on their faces. I wanted to say, "How do you really know?" I just wanted to feel better. I said the same prayer every night: "God please let me know she's with You. Please." And then the next day would be the same. It went on for months.

One night, no different than the others, I lay in bed staring at the ceiling. Again I prayed and asked God to please take care of my mother, since I could no longer see her. Then something miraculous happened.

I was no longer looking at the ceiling. I was floating over a road, looking straight ahead, and saw a "Y" in the road. I noticed the sheen on the road, the thick bushes and the huge tree ahead. I didn't get a chance to look long, because I suddenly was somewhere else. I was looking at a house—close up—made of sand-colored stone bricks, with two windows in the front. I saw thick greenery in front of the windows and around the house, and they bloomed with the most colorful flowers. I had never seen that kind of flora before in my life! Amongst them were beautiful birds, some flying, some just walking beneath the bushes. Then I realized the windows had no glass in them! What kept the birds from going in?

And then I was inside.

I was in a living room and heard voices. Everything was muffled though, like I had cotton in my ears. I could hear, but not make out the sounds or words.

And then I realized who I was looking at—my maternal

grandfather! Even though he had passed away when I was three, I was very close to him. I remember so many things about him, and there he was, talking to… my mom! She sat across from him, and they appeared close in age now. I wanted to hear what they were saying. To my right came this slightly younger girl, with very long red hair. While I had never laid eyes on her before, I knew it was my sister Linda. She died one year before my birth. I just knew it was her. She came into the room with such grace and then… I was staring at my ceiling again. In my bedroom. Wide awake. I knew I hadn't fallen asleep. I knew I had been given a gift. The tension I felt was now replaced with the most peaceful feeling. It was a calm I've never felt before or since. With a "Thank you, God," I knew He had allowed me to see her. Knowing I'd join her someday, I fell peacefully asleep.

I have repeated this story to very few people. I did tell my current pastor, who said he had heard similar stories, and believed I was given a glimpse of Heaven. I know I did, and I also know that I didn't just see my mother, but also my future home. And that was even more than I had prayed for.

~Sharon Knopic

Miracles Happen

Angels Among Us

Elena's Angels

Insight is better than eyesight when it comes to seeing an angel.
~Eileen Elias Freeman, The Angels' Little Instruction Book

It was mid-afternoon and I had collapsed on my bed, wondering if I should take a nap, and feeling guilty for even considering it. Instead of resting I should have taken advantage of my nine-year-old daughter Elena's nap to pay overdue bills, open the scores of get-well cards stacked on the front table, and do the laundry that had piled up during Elena's three-month hospitalization after her aneurysm rupture. But I hadn't had a good night's sleep in weeks, and it felt so good to lie there, even if I still had on my shoes.

Closing my eyes, I reveled in the stillness. It was so quiet. Church quiet. No alarms signaling a high blood pressure, plummeting oxygen rate, or racing heartbeat. No doctors or nurses interrupting us for exams, vitals or meds. All I heard was the shuffle of our Golden Retriever, Buffy, as she checked on me before curling up in her usual place on the rug outside Elena's door. And the steady hum of the baby monitor, telling me Elena was finally settling down to sleep.

Sleep. Before I knew it I was dreaming of a day in our lives before our world turned upside down. It was a Sunday afternoon. We'd just returned from church. The day was warm, our moods bright. Instead of going in for lunch, Elena ran for the back yard. She mounted a wooden swing, pumped her legs, and flew so high.

"Watch me!" she shouted. "Mom? Mom!"

I jolted awake, my heart racing. A few seconds passed before I realized I was not outside watching Elena fly. And I was not camped out on the lumpy faux-leather recliner next to Elena's hospital bed either. I was home. In my own bed. In my own room. So why couldn't I shake the feeling that something wasn't right?

"Mom?" Elena called me through the baby monitor on the bedside table. "Mom!"

The hair prickled on the back of my neck. Not a dream. Real. I bounded out of bed, and clambered down the stairs.

The last time I had rushed to Elena's side was a hot, steamy day in July. The sky was so blue my eyes hurt to look at it. The cousins were over, playing dress up. All was well until Elena's oldest sister, Liz, came racing upstairs. "Something's wrong with Elena," she said breathlessly.

We found Elena curled in a ball on the basement floor. She was dressed like a Disney princess in a bright yellow gown, groaning and holding her head like it was about to explode. I'll never forget the sound. It was deep, guttural. Primal. Remembering it now as I hurried to Elena's room made my chest ache.

I rushed into the room and sat on her bed. "What is it, sweetie?" I asked, trying to hide my fear. "What's wrong?"

"It's too loud," she said as she clutched her blue blanket.

Elena liked to fall asleep with music playing. But her *Little Mermaid* tape had ended nearly an hour ago, leaving me unsure what to make of this. "What's too loud?" I asked.

"The angels," she said.

"Angels?"

For the record, we're not an angel family. We don't display them around the house, except during Christmastime. We don't talk about them, unless questions come up after church. But Elena hadn't attended worship in months. And since it was only October, we didn't have any angels displayed around the house or neighborhood. None that I could see anyway.

"Are they here now?" I asked.

Elena pointed at the upper right hand corner of the room. It was empty except for a few cobwebs and a handful of "Get Well" balloons.

It was possible she was talking about the balloons; but being balloons they were just floating around, seen not heard.

"How many are there?" I asked.

"Three," she said without hesitation.

"Three?" It was a small room, which made it difficult to imagine how there was room for one angel, let alone a host of them. "Aren't they a bit scrunched with their wings and robes and everything?"

"Mom," Elena said, irritation tinged in her voice, "they're kid angels."

A couple of things occurred to me then. First, sending pint-sized angels to kids in need made perfect sense. Second, Elena was too serious—too certain—to have made this up.

"What are they doing?" I asked, my curiosity winning out.

"Singing," she said.

Singing? "Singing what?"

"*The Little Mermaid. Beauty and the Beast.* Coat of Many Colors."

"Coat of Many Colors" is what Elena called the soundtrack for *Joseph and the Amazing Technicolor Dreamcoat*. It has been her favorite since before she got sick; so it shouldn't have surprised me that it was on her angels' playlist.

"They know your songs," I said. "That's awesome."

"But I'm tired," Elena said, slapping the covers.

Before the aneurysm rupture, Elena was active, adventurous, and energetic. Her goal since coming home was to learn how to walk, talk and be nine again. She had already regained enough strength to stand by herself for nearly five minutes without tiring. But seeing her frustration now reminded me how much more work she had left to do.

"Did you tell them to please be quiet?" I whispered.

She inhaled like she hadn't considered this approach. "Be quiet," she told her visitors. "So I can sleep."

"Please," I said, reminding her to be polite.

"Pul-lease."

"Did it work?" I asked after a while.

She nodded and yawned. I tucked her in. "Sleep tight," I said, like always, before turning out the light. "Dream pleasant dreams."

"G'night," she said amidst another yawn.

"Question," I said before shutting the door. "Did they say why they're here?"

Elena's eyes were closed as she mumbled her answer. "They're staying until I get better."

"Really?" I stared at the corner. I wished I could see Elena's angels. I wanted to thank them, and, honestly, I needed reassurance they were really here.

Elena sighed and snuggled deeper under her covers. I kissed her forehead, inhaled her sweet scent, and paused. Suddenly, it was clear to me. I'd been so invested in Elena's recovery that I had missed the obvious.

Most people die from ruptured aneurysms. Elena survived. Two weeks she had been in a coma. Two long weeks. Doctors prepared us to expect the worst when she awoke—if she awoke. Elena returned to us singing the song, "Any Dream Will Do/Give Me My Colored Coat" from *Joseph and the Amazing Technicolor Dreamcoat*. She knew her name. And ours.

Doctors called Elena's recovery a miracle. In retrospect, it was the first of many.

During her hospitalization, she survived a stroke, multiple neurosurgeries, and a life-threatening infection. Through it all, her trademark perseverance, sense of humor, and spirit remained steadfast.

I may not have seen Elena's angels, but this much I did know—they were as real as the miracles Elena had experienced so far.

What does the future hold? Only God knows. But whatever happens next, I have confidence Elena will face it with grace and grit. After all, she has a heavenly pep squad cheering her on.

~Kim Winters

A Divine Truck Driver

The wings of angels are often found on the backs of the least likely people.
~Eric Honeycutt

"Cutthroat are running! Fishing is great, Dad!" Over the phone, the cheerful voice of our daughter, Katherine, continued. "And Mom... the weather's perfect for hiking in the park without the tourists buzzing on the trails."

Later that morning, my husband and I headed northeast on Interstate 80. At Evanston, Wyoming, we swung off the interstate onto Highway 89 toward Jackson, Wyoming and a week with Katherine and her family. The odometer clicked off miles of unfenced land. Bumps and folds of rocky soil sprouted sparse clumps of grasses and fragrant sagebrush. Like lawn ornaments, small herds of pronghorn posed on the slopes. Angus and Hereford cattle grazed in pastures that hugged the occasional ranch town.

"You could paint a great watercolor of this rugged landscape and the hills beyond," I said.

Grinning, Don tapped his forehead. "I have it right here. It doesn't need to be on paper."

Then, like a Tonka toy in the distance, a pickup truck sped toward us. Just before it passed, the driver whipped his truck in front of us.

"Oh God no-ooo!" My foot pressed hard on the brake pedal. Metal against metal crunched. The passenger side of the other truck crushed inward. The driver's body sprang forward over the steering wheel. His head slammed against the windshield. We wouldn't know for two weeks that he was working in his garden the next day with only a bump on his head.

I looked at my husband, who was gasping for air, his face contorted with pain. Dear Lord, don't let him be having a heart attack. I can only move my right arm.

"Honey, breathe with me." I concentrated on slowing my breathing. Reaching for the CB radio, I turned to channel 9. Dead. We were miles from any town. Antelope were the only nearby residents. I closed my eyes and prayed. Lord, we need your help. A car sped by. I gave a deep sigh. "He didn't even slow down, Why didn't he stop?"

"I don't know, honey. Someone will soon."

"I wish I could hold your hand."

"Ditto."

I didn't see the eighteen-wheeler pull over to the side of the road. When I opened my eyes, a man was bending down until his face was level with mine. He touched my arm and looked into my eyes. The kindness in his gray/blue eyes was a salve to my fear of no one finding us in time.

"Don't worry, I'm here." He undid my seatbelt. "I've had some emergency training. I'm going to get a pillow for your neck." It seemed only a moment before he placed a pillow behind my neck. Then he took hold of my hand. Like the warmth from a blanket, serenity flowed through my body.

"Don?"

"I'm okay, honey."

"I'll stay with you until medical help comes." The man never let go of my hand.

I don't know how much time passed before the ambulance arrived and two women helped Don out of the passenger's seat.

"Is he alright?" I asked.

"He's doing fine."

"How's our black Lab, Lady?"

"She's fine too. We'll take good care of her." One of the women climbed into the truck. "I'm going to secure your neck. Then we'll put you on a board and carry you to the ambulance. You just relax and we'll have you at the hospital in no time at all."

The truck driver squeezed my hand and smiled. "You'll be fine now."

"Thank you for being here."

"I'm glad I could help."

He assisted the EMTs in lifting me onto the board and carrying me to the ambulance. I don't recall the drive to the Montpelier, Idaho hospital. Later, I was transported by ambulance to another hospital, in Salt Lake City. And then, I felt the loving hands of my daughter, Karen, and her soft voice, "I'm here, Mom." The caring eyes and gentle voice of an orthopedic doctor offered comfort as well. ICU and... sleep.

I floated in and out of darkness. Five days slipped away before I saw the flowers in my bedroom. Along with Karen, Katherine and her husband were now a part of my family bedside care. How strange to be fed and bathed by the women who were once the children I fed and bathed.

The second week in the hospital, one of the ambulance nurses brought me flowers. "Do you know the truck driver who was with us after the accident?" I asked.

"No. But I'll check our records and talk with the state police."

No one could come up with his name, trucking company or a license. My husband and I prayed that we could let this person know what his kindness and spiritual presence had meant to us... especially me. Our son-in-law did research on truck companies using the remote route we were traveling. No success. He even contacted and left a message to broadcast on a western music station the eighteen-wheel drivers might listen to... still no luck.

When I first started walking in the hospital corridor, Karen stood on one side of me, Don on the other. I wore a body and neck brace. I looked up at Don. "I'd give you a hug if your ribs weren't cracked."

He grinned. "Hug a tin man? I don't think so."

"Hey, don't knock it until you've tried it."

"Remember Winnie the Pooh," Karen said, "If you can't say something nice..."

"Don't say anything at all," we chimed in unison. Laughter carried us back to my room.

My husband and I flew to Jackson, Wyoming for part of our recovery process in our daughter, Katherine's home. One afternoon, I sat with Don by the window admiring the shadows on the snowfields of the Tetons. "Do you think our truck driver was one of God's angels?"

"I don't know, honey." Don took my hand. "But I'm sure grateful he was there. Not feeling alone meant more to me than he'll ever know."

"I'll never forget his kind eyes and the peace I felt while he held my hand."

Thank you, driver, I murmured softly. May you be there for the next person who needs the comfort of your words... "Don't worry, I'm here."

~Margaret Hevel

Blanketed in Love

A quilt will warm your body and comfort your soul.
~Author Unknown

"Drive safe."

"See you Sunday."

Our church group called out cheerful goodbyes. We had enjoyed a delightful ladies' Christmas party. Now, wrapped in warm coats and holiday joy, we hurried to our cars to escape the bitter cold.

Throughout the early 1990s I worked for a medical staffing agency, and had been on call the night of the party. My beeper had been quiet, an unusual occurrence, and I had relished the uninterrupted evening of fellowship.

I waved and drove off through the dark Nebraska night, thanking God for the evening of carols, cookies, and companionship. I was in an unfamiliar area, so I didn't see the four-way stop sign in the unlit intersection. The driver of a large luxury sedan, assuming I would stop, turned left in front of me. I slammed on my brakes, the tires screeching, but it was too late. My tiny Toyota hatchback smashed into the other car.

Time seemed to shift into slow motion.

I saw the other driver, a middle-aged woman, wide-eyed and open-mouthed. Metal crunched as our vehicles ground together, then spun apart. My head thudded into the windshield.

Stunned and woozy, I tried to get out of my car to check on the other driver, but my door was jammed. "Lord, please let her be okay," I prayed.

Thankfully, several of my friends had been driving behind me. They screeched to a stop, and raced over to help. I unrolled my window, and was inundated with their frantic questions.

"Jeanie, are you okay?"

"What hurts?"

"Can you get out of there?"

I answered, "The door's stuck, but I don't think I can stand right now anyway. Will you check on the other lady?"

They hurried to the other driver. Outrage had replaced her alarm, and she was shrieking curses. My friends stayed with her, trying to calm and comfort her.

As I sat in the sub-freezing temperature, trembling with cold and shock, a woman appeared at my open window. She looked to be in her early thirties. Incredible love shone in her beautiful clear eyes. "Don't worry," she said. "Everything is all right."

The stench of leaking radiator fluid seemed to fade, along with the clouds of profanity floating from the other vehicle.

A feeling of peace flooded me.

"Would you like a blanket?" she asked.

I nodded, teeth chattering. A moment later she laid a light blanket over me. It infused me with a warmth out of proportion to its thin fabric.

"Don't talk. Just rest," the lady said. "I'll be right here."

I was happy to comply until the wail of a police siren pierced my calm. My new friend stepped back when the officer came to assess the situation.

I gave him the highlights. "I didn't see the signs in the dark, and I ran into the other lady's car."

"The rescue squad's on the way," he reassured me. "I'll get a full report at the hospital. Meanwhile, sit tight under that blanket and stay warm." The officer headed toward the other driver, whose river of curses dried up at his approach.

My new friend re-tucked the blanket around me. As the

ambulance arrived in a glare of revolving red light, I asked, "What's your name?"

She smiled, then walked away as the paramedics ran to my car.

The EMTs pried my crumpled door open, and transitioned me to the ambulance.

"Ma'am, I have to remove your blanket to check you over, then I'll wrap you up nice and cozy again," a young paramedic explained as we sped toward the hospital.

My husband and young daughter were already there, anxious for my arrival. The waiting room was filled with our church family, praying.

The hospital staff ran a battery of tests. While waiting for the results, the officer from the accident scene took my statement, wrote out a ticket and handed it to me as I lay on the emergency room table.

Several hours later I was being readied for discharge. The ER nurse lifted the blanket I'd come in with and asked, "Is this yours?"

Muddled from the medications I'd been given, I squinted at it and replied, "Nope."

The nurse handed my purse to my husband, and ushered us into the night. The blanket was left behind.

On our way home I groggily told my husband and daughter about the wreck, and the lady who'd helped me. Then I remembered her blanket.

"Jake, we have to go back for the blanket."

"Sweetie, we'll take care of it tomorrow," my husband replied, "Tonight you need to rest."

The next day I called the hospital, but no one could find the blanket. It wasn't in the ER or the lost and found. "We're sorry, it seems to have disappeared," they apologized.

I felt terrible. The woman had helped me, and now I'd lost her blanket. I hoped that one of my friends who'd been at the accident scene had learned the lady's name.

At church that Sunday I thanked everyone for their prayers and support, then asked my friends if they knew the name of the lady who'd been so kind to me.

They looked at each other, confused. "You mean the woman driving the car you hit? The one swearing up a hot streak?" one of my friends asked.

"No, I'm talking about the woman who brought me the blanket. The one who stayed with me until the ambulance came."

My friends' expressions changed from confused to concerned. "How much medication are you on?"

"None," I replied, "I'm fine. Now come on, you guys were there with me. I need to find the lady to thank her, and give her a new blanket."

Instead of answering me, they huddled together. I could make out a few of their sentences.

"Did you see anyone?"

"No, did you?"

"No, I was busy with Queen Cuss-A-Lot."

Impatient, I interrupted them. "You must have seen her. She stood at my car door the entire time."

My friends turned to me, disconcerted. "Jeanie, we didn't see anyone with you."

I went home perplexed. Days later, while reading my Bible, I came across Psalm 34:7, "The Angel of the Lord encamps around those who fear Him [who revere and worship Him with awe] and each of them He delivers."

The truth of what happened the night of the accident blazed in my mind. Shaken, I sank to my knees, tears of gratitude flowing unchecked.

God had given me a Christmas miracle. He had sent an angel to take care of me.

~Jeanie Jacobson

Glorious Groceries

I am convinced that these heavenly beings exist and that they provide unseen aid on our behalf.
~Billy Graham

I n the summer of 2004, I had moved to a new area in the Colorado Rockies for a change of pace and to enjoy the clean mountain air. I had lived in California for many years and always dreamed of a simple life in the mountains.

Although my new town was beautiful, I had a difficult time finding work. Opportunities were limited for professionals in the resort-like area, and my intended job fell through. I ran out of money trying to find a job after several months. I was alone and stranded.

In October, I became very ill with a rare intestinal infection. It was the beginning of my first winter in central Colorado, and I wasn't accustomed to the harsh weather. I had no job, no health insurance, and few friends in my new town. I was sleeping on the floor of a new friend's vacant rental property. Despite the challenges I faced, I had no choice but to get up every day and pull myself together for job interviews.

Toward Christmastime, I secured a part-time job in a mall store and made enough money to put gas in my car, pay a few bills, and eat at least one meal every day. It was life changing to see people spending money on Christmas gifts when I could barely afford a meal. Some days I didn't eat much at all. Since I needed strength to regain my health, I sat in my car in the parking lot after work one evening and prayed. I prayed deeply and specifically. I asked the angels, my guides, and the loving higher power to hear my request for food. "I need to eat a decent meal, Lord God and Angels on High," I prayed. "I need food so that I can get well and go on with my purpose for being here. I can help no one when I am this low. Please hear me." When I drove back home that night, I was driving on pure faith.

Twenty minutes later, I pulled into the driveway. The snow crunched under my tires, and the wipers strained to push the ice from my windshield. Although the car window was foggy, I noticed something on the porch. I blinked a few times and slowly exited my car, looking all around for any sign of someone who might have paid me a visit. I saw no one, but there on my dimly lit porch sat two brown bags filled with groceries.

My mind raced. Who could have left me this glorious gift of food? I'd been private about the depth of my financial crisis, even to my family back east. No one, including my family, knew where I lived. It could have only been a neighbor or the woman who owned the rental property. There was no other possibility. I knocked on my neighbors' doors to ask about the food. No one had knowledge of it. Then I called the owner of the rental. She said, "I wish it had been me, but it wasn't. I'm stuck here and couldn't have made it down there in this weather."

The most amazing aspect of the mystery groceries is that they included some of my favorite foods. If I had been given fifty dollars to buy myself groceries that night, I'd have purchased many of the same items that were left clandestinely on my porch. To this day, no one has taken credit for the gift. In a way, those two bags of groceries saved my life. I had good food to eat. I became stronger and got better physically. After the gift of the groceries, my faith was strengthened, and my spiritual vigor increased. It was only a few weeks later that I was offered a good job in my profession, and able to move into a healthy environment within two months. You might say that the groceries were a most miraculous Christmas gift, because they were the injection of positive energy I needed to go on.

Of course, many logical explanations went through my mind.

Perhaps someone ordered groceries from a nearby store and they were delivered to my porch by mistake. Maybe an acquaintance left them anonymously, so as to avoid hurting my pride. Or, maybe a local non-profit organization or shelter heard about my plight and sent the groceries. Although I researched these possibilities, I only reached dead ends. I came to accept that there might not be a logical explanation for the gift, and I made peace with the fact that I had received a Christmas miracle.

Who was listening to my prayer on that cold winter night in Colorado? And who was it that had the power to deliver bags of groceries, a tangible gift to my doorstep? I am thankful to the angels for the priceless Christmas gift they quietly gave to me that year.

~Karena D. Bailey

Miracle in the Rain

Don't pray when it rains if you don't pray when the sun shines.
~Satchel Paige

Sometimes miracles are so astonishing they seem to defy the laws of the universe, such as when someone survives a horrific accident without a scratch or a dying person experiences a cure that cannot be explained. And sometimes the miracle comes softly in the rain, and works its magic in a very quiet way.

My mom, brother, sister and I were on our way back from visiting relatives in the country. We didn't have a car of our own, so Mom had borrowed an old truck from a neighbor. The drive to my uncle's farm was a long one, deep in the country and far from any major road. The sun was warm on my face as I sat in the back of the pickup with my sister. I was looking forward to playing with my cousins.

We had such a good time visiting that it was near sunset when we finally got ready for the ride home. Dark clouds had begun to stack up in the sky above us. My aunt hugged my mom and told her to be careful driving home. "Sometimes the storms get pretty fierce out here where there aren't any trees to stop them," she said.

We rode along for a while and I was just beginning to doze off when I felt the first raindrops splash against my face. I scrambled after my sister into the front seat of the truck next to my brother. With night falling and the rain, it was easy to miss a turn on these dirt roads. Soon we were bumping along hard ground that wasn't a road, and I could tell by the look on my mom's face that we were lost.

I watched the rain come down, pierced only a little by the truck's headlights. Mom drove slowly, and for the first time my brother and sister and I sat silently so she could concentrate. The road got muddy, and the truck slowed down even more. All of a sudden we heard a loud pop as the left back tire fell into a hole. The truck shook, and Mom tried to get it to move again, but it wouldn't budge. We were stuck in the middle of nowhere.

"Wait here," Mom told us, as she grabbed a flashlight and stumbled into the torrential rain. She'd left the headlights on and I turned around to watch her struggling with the back tire, kneeling in the mud. She came back after a moment. She was covered in mud and grime. She must have seen how worried we looked, because she smiled and said, "Don't worry, everything will be all right."

"Are we near a farm?" my sister Sandy asked.

"We aren't near anything," Mom said. "I don't even think we're on a road."

"What are we going to do?" my brother Larry asked.

Mom reached over and gave him a hug. "We're going to pray. I'll go back out and see if I can push a rock into the hole so I can drive the wheel out. We don't have a spare tire, but maybe we can drive someplace for help."

I felt a knot of fear in my stomach. Then my mom had us fold our hands and bow our hands while she whispered, "Lord, please help my children and me find a way to get back home. We desperately need your help. Amen."

Then something happened I can't explain. Lights suddenly came on behind us, and I heard footsteps. A large shadow loomed against the driver's window, and a hand gently knocked on the glass. Mom opened it, shining the flashlight into the darkness. A man's face appeared. He was tall, he wore a dark raincoat, and he smiled when he saw us.

"I don't mean to scare you," he said in a voice barely above a whisper. "But I saw you were having trouble. If you all will just sit tight, I'll have you taken care of in a bit."

Then he turned and disappeared back into the darkness. In another moment, I felt the back of the car lifted up. There was some noise I couldn't identify, and more movement of shadows behind us. In what seemed an impossibly short time, the man reappeared at the window. This time he was covered in mud and dirt, but the smile on his face never wavered. He nodded at my mom and said, "I think you're all right to go now."

Mom started the car and it rolled forward. She stopped and leaned out the window. "Thank you so much. I didn't see any farms close by. Do you live near here?"

"I'm from around," he said in that same quiet, friendly voice. "Glad I could be of help. You all have a good trip home." His eyes locked with mine for a second. "Be safe."

Then he was gone again, and the bright lights behind us went out. We waited for him to drive on past us, but nothing happened. Mom put her head out the window and looked back. "He's gone," she said. "I don't see a truck or car anywhere."

Then she turned to us and smiled. She gave us each a hug, and as she did I heard her whisper, "Thank you, God." We drove home in the rain, safe and sound, thanks to a kind soul who came out of the darkness to save us. It was a quiet miracle for which I'll always be grateful.

~John P. Buentello

S'more

Angels are never too distant to hear you.
~Author Unknown

I t was the most beautiful day of that summer—blue sky, billowy clouds, and a dandelion-bright sun. Strange, though, we were the only ones enjoying it at the state park.

My father stood over a campfire roasting hot dogs, while my mother and I pushed marshmallows onto skewers. My two high-strung preschoolers ran amok. We'd arranged the picnic hoping they'd run off some of this energy and go to bed early.

Connor, my five-year-old, grabbed one of the sticks my father had cleaned and sharpened for the marshmallows, raised it over his head, and shouted to his four-year-old brother, "It's morphin' time. Wham. Bam."

Kyle shrieked, sharp like a coach's whistle.

My neck muscles twitched as the boys ran round and round the campsite.

"Stop it," I yelled, trying to hold a skewer of marshmallows over the coals.

Connor poked the stick at his brother. They fell and rolled across the ground.

One of the marshmallows burst into flames. I blew it out.

"Come here and help me!" I shouted, as I turned to see them pulling each other's hair.

When I glanced back at the marshmallows, they'd fallen onto the coals, sizzling in a tar smear.

"That's it," I said, tossing the marshmallows and sticks into the woods.

Connor released a lock of his brother's hair, crestfallen. "But the s'mores, Mommy."

"I don't think so," I snapped and plopped down on the picnic bench next to my parents.

They shot me a look of utter disbelief. A picnic wasn't a picnic without s'mores. It had been our family's tradition ever since my mother was a Brownie troop leader. My sisters and I used to lick the marshmallow-chocolate-graham cracker goo from our fingers, and my mother would wink at us and ask, "You know why they call them s'mores?"

We'd chant back, "Because you always want some more."

Now my mother said, "Why don't you take a break? Dad and I will take the boys to the water. You just sit here and relax."

"The boys can't swim," I said. Then I remembered, neither could my parents.

"They'll just be wading," Mom said. "The water's only this deep at the edge." She pointed to her calf and gave me a you-worry-too-much look.

My parents grabbed their lawn chairs. Also a tradition, they would sit in the shade, let the cool breeze toss their hair, and listen to Hank Williams on the radio, while the kids splashed along the beach.

I waved them off, feeling wickedly happy to have a few minutes to myself.

Still not another boater, swimmer, or picnicker in sight. Strange, I thought.

I saw the boys run on the beach, kick off their sandals, and dunk their toes in the water. Any second Connor would be soaking his brother. I didn't want to watch.

When I looked up the hill, I noticed big tire ruts, now overgrown with weeds, running from the top of the hill down to the water—a path of some kind. Then it hit me—my kids were playing on an old boat launch, a concrete ramp sloping down into deep water.

I ran to the beach just to hear Connor kerplunk into the dark water. His face beamed—but for only a second.

Fingers splayed, he reached to me and screamed, "Help me, Mommy. Help me!"

He slid backwards. I reached, but the tips of my fingers just brushed his. I tried to grab him again, but he slid out of reach.

I kicked off my sandals. My bare feet hit what I thought was going to be concrete. Instead it felt mushy and slick, like Jell-O. I was sliding fast. Long green tendrils of algae covered my feet. I bent my knees, skating down the ramp.

I slid into Connor, grabbed him, and lifted his head. Our weight and the volume of water slowed our glide, but we didn't stop.

I managed to turn us around and tried walking back up the ramp. I fell and fell again. The more I fought, the farther from shore we slid.

Swim. I knew that was our only hope. Between Connor's extra fifty-two pounds and my inability to find a hard, stable surface for my feet, I couldn't lift us to a point of buoyancy. We simply flailed in the water, sliding deeper and deeper.

The water hit my chin. I yelled, "Help!"

My mother wrung her hands. Dad handed my mom his watch. He could barely swim—certainly not enough to save us. He must have figured that he'd rather die than watch us drown.

I wanted to yell at him to stop, but I could only gurgle.

I stood on my tiptoes, the water up to my lips. I knew we were about to drown.

At that point I decided the lake could take me, but it would take not my son—not if I could help it. I would put Connor on my shoulders, hold my breath, and stand like a pillar until he was rescued or until I couldn't stand anymore.

I took one last look at my parents.

To my surprise, they weren't looking at us, but at something in the distance—something moving. Finally I made out a chestnut ponytail bobbing in the water. Then emerged a woman moving towards us with swift, long strides—not slipping at all. Towards Connor and me, she pushed an air mattress.

At the beach, Connor scampered away, but I collapsed, shaking, gasping for air. I looked around to thank this woman, but she was gone.

"Which way did she go?" I asked my parents. They looked around and shrugged. We searched the water, the beach, the park—as before, we were totally alone.

I felt a light tap on my shoulder.

Kyle stood next to me, his hands cupped. He unfurled his fingers to expose a dandelion, no bigger than a lemon drop.

"I picked this for you," he said, blinking back tears.

No stem, just the flower. I pinched the yellow blossom between my thumb and forefinger. My mouth twitched.

Instead of crying, though, a big laugh exploded from within me.

Kyle giggled, which only made me laugh even harder.

Connor joined in, and we laughed, for no reason other than it just felt good being alive and together.

"What about the s'mores, Mommy?" Kyle asked.

"Yeah, Mom," Connor said. "Can we have them… now?"

I saw my children in a way I hadn't for a while—their faces so full of love and life.

"I bet if you look in the edge of the woods, you'll find those marshmallow sticks," I said.

They squealed, which now sounded like music to my ears.

I'd never really believed in miracles. But nothing else explains what happened that day. Since then, though, I thank God every day for giving me a second chance—His own version of s'more.

~Debbie Hagan

Angel on the Highway

People see God every day, they just don't recognize him.
~Pearl Bailey

One of my favorite TV shows was *Touched by an Angel*. Stories about angel encounters always fascinated me, but I never knew if they were real until I had an encounter of my own.

It was a beautiful spring day and crowds gathered along the highway parks, setting up their picnics to celebrate Memorial Day. I drove up to Connecticut for what was to be a quiet family gathering. But in the mid-afternoon the skies opened up, and rain hindered traffic all along I-95. It was dreary, dark and chilly. Traffic was bumper to bumper. At times the rain was so heavy, you couldn't even see one car length ahead.

This was going to be an interesting ride home. Then about twenty minutes into my drive, my car started stalling and making funny noises. It eventually stopped. I managed to pull over to the side of the road, turn on the hazard lights and get out of the way of traffic before the car quit on me.

I got out of the car and into the rain, attempting to flag someone down for help. This was over twenty years ago and before we all had cell phones. A driver stopped to let me know he would stop at the next exit to call for help. About fifteen minutes later, another car stopped and promised the same. Nobody wanted to get out of their car in that torrential downpour. Meanwhile, I was standing on the side of the road, on a major highway, in the rain, wearing my white pants because it was Memorial Day weekend, the unofficial start of summer, and I could finally wear white pants again.

An hour went by and I still waited for help. There were no phone booths along the highway, so I couldn't call anyone, not even AAA. I was at the mercy of a Good Samaritan who might stop and call for help.

So what was a girl to do on a Monday night, in a broken down car on the highway, no way to call anyone, and no help? I got back in my car and prayed for a miracle. I hoped someone might have called for help. I looked in my rearview mirror and saw a tow truck pulling up behind me.

As I got out of my car, a man in his late thirties got out of the truck and approached me. "Are you okay?" he asked.

"I've been waiting for help for about an hour, in my broken-down car in bumper-to-bumper traffic, in the rain. Other than that everything's great!"

The man said he worked for his father's towing company. His name was Tom. He had just come from dropping off a vehicle in Boston and was on his back to Maryland.

"I'll be happy to help you," he said. "I can just imagine what it's like to be stranded here on the side of the road. If my wife's car had broken down I would hope somebody would help her."

I told him that towing my car home would probably add two to three hours to his trip. He didn't mind. I asked him how much he would charge me. "How about $50 to help with gas expenses?" he said.

His generosity and kindness overwhelmed me. For some reason I trusted him. So we went ahead and he put my vehicle on his tow truck. Just as he finished tying down my vehicle, another tow truck came and parked behind Tom's tow truck. A guy stepped out of the truck and approached us.

"We got a call that someone had broken down on the highway," the guy said. "Going to have to let the vehicle down, it's our highway."

Before I knew it, a third tow truck pulled up and parked right in front of Tom's tow truck locking us in between. As I stood there watching the guys from the towing company argue with the Good Samaritan, the police showed up.

The officer called me over to explain that my Good Samaritan was not allowed to tow my vehicle on I-95 because the towing company had an exclusive contract on the highway. Exclusive contract? Really? The officer was concerned about a stranger driving me all the way back to Long Island, so he ran a check on him, just to be safe.

Then we went through the process of taking my vehicle off Tom's truck and putting it on the official tow truck. The Good Samaritan and I followed them less than half a mile off the highway, where they literally dumped my vehicle at the end of the off-ramp, right under the bridge. They billed AAA $42.

By then, I was miserable. Soaking wet, I sat in the truck with the guy from Maryland who was still willing to drive me all the way home. We went through the whole process of putting my vehicle back on his truck, and finally headed to Long Island.

As we drove to my house, he showed me pictures of his wife and kids. He told me that he normally didn't take vehicles out of state, but his trip to Boston was a special request from his father. I was so grateful!

After four long hours, we got to my house. It was still raining and gloomy, and my Good Samaritan had a long trip back to Maryland. I gave him the $50 he'd asked for. He used the restroom, gave me his business card, got back in the truck and left.

The next day I bought a really nice thank you card. I copied the address from the business card onto the envelope and dropped it in the mail. About three weeks later, the card came back, stamped all over with "no such address." I double-checked the business card; it clearly stated Tom's Towing Company and the address that I had written on the envelope. When I called, I never reached anyone.

Some might say that it was a weird coincidence, that maybe the post office made a mistake. But I know for a fact that on the side of that blue tow truck it said Tom's Towing Company with an address in Maryland. Whether Good Samaritan or angel, I know on that day twenty years ago, I experienced a miracle. My prayers were answered by a greater power. Without a doubt, someone out there was watching over me!

~Dr. Karen Jacobson

Highway Rescue

Nurses are angels in comfortable shoes.
~Author Unknown

I t was to be a girls' weekend like none other. My daughters and I loaded the car, happily waving goodbye to my husband Barry, who'd promised to hold the fort down while we were away.

Soon, we were on I-95, leaving Virginia and headed toward sunny Florida where Mom awaited our arrival with great expectation.

We spent the first several hours sharing happy memories and singing "oldies' at the top of our lungs. When my muscles began cramping, my older daughter, Autumn, offered to take her turn behind the wheel.

We'd just entered North Carolina so it was the perfect time to pull over and exchange places at the welcome center. Soon we were heading down I-95 once again.

Suddenly the heavens opened up, sending a torrential downpour to earth. How was anyone supposed to see in this?

"Get off at the next exit," I begged, gripping the door handle with all my might.

Too late.

Trucks barreled by, sending us hydroplaning across several lanes of traffic. We crashed into something parked alongside the road.

I felt my chest being crushed and heard myself screaming.

"Mom," a voice cried from somewhere, "you've got to get out now!"

I stumbled out the door and onto the wet ground. I could see my girls hovering over me. Amber had a bleeding gash over her eye. Autumn was crying into the cell phone begging for an ambulance.

I felt weaker and weaker as my chest continued to throb.

Out of nowhere, a colorful umbrella appeared above my head. A warm afghan was placed over me. A woman took my pulse, reassuring me that she was a nurse. Another woman attended to my daughter's eye. "I am an eye specialist," her calm voice soothed. "Why, I'm a nurse as well," another voice cried.

As an approaching siren sounded in the distance, I attempted to speak.

"Girls, I love you so much. I want you to remember that God is with you always. He's all that matters… "

We arrived at the hospital as the rain ceased, immediately wheeled into the emergency room for various scans and examinations. Miraculously, we were all fine, other than extensive bruising and lacerations.

"Your car slid six feet under a parked motor coach. You're lucky to be alive," an officer explained.

My husband arrived the next morning to take us back home. I spent weeks recuperating from bruised ribs. One afternoon, as I sat in the warm sunshine, a colorful afghan folded across a nearby ottoman caught my eye. Reaching for it, I suddenly envisioned the kind face placing it over me as I lay on the wet highway median. Tenderly, I unfolded the blanket. That's when I spotted it—an enormous angel with outstretched arms.

I'd relived the entire accident countless times over the past few weeks. How had I overlooked that blanket?

I still couldn't comprehend how two nurses and an eye specialist could instantly appear in the middle of a horrific storm. Clutching the afghan a little closer, I closed my eyes. Suddenly it wasn't just the afghan warming me through and through.

"Thank you, Lord, for sending your angels to our rescue," I whispered.

~Mary Z. Whitney

Chapter 10

Miracles Happen

Love that Doesn't Die

The Comforter

It is only with the heart that one can see rightly, what is essential
is invisible to the eye.
~Antoine de Saint-Exupéry

I

t was midnight when I began to rouse from the fog of sleepiness, suddenly aware with my "mother's ear" that one of my children was crying. "Please, God… show me what to do," I prayed as I climbed wearily from my bed and went to the next room.

It was my eleven-year-old daughter Lauren's room. Kneeling at the side of her bed, I tried to soothe and comfort her, knowing full well my daughter's hurt was not one that mere words or hugs from Mommy could heal. For the first time in my fifteen years of parenting, I faced a dilemma for which I had no practical resolution. Neither my husband nor I could solve this problem or "make it all better" and that was a painful (and scary) realization for us. The problem we faced was the death of our oldest child, our three surviving children's big brother.

As I settled myself into Lauren's bed, rubbing her back, speaking what comfort I could, I thought back to four weeks earlier. We had been eagerly preparing to move to our dream home in the country outside our small town in southern Michigan.

During visits to the new property the four children had raced up and down the driveway, kicking up plumes of dust in an old go-cart, or scouted the woods for fort sites. It was truly a five-acre child's paradise, complete with a nearby fishing stream. While our children reveled in the freedom and adventure of their new home, Earl and I had rejoiced watching them. This is what we wanted for our family, a place to experience life outside the crowded confines of our city neighborhood, and away from the roving gangs of boys who'd begun to harass our oldest child, who was fourteen years old. It had all seemed so perfect.

The new house had needed a lot work before we could move in, but we made it an adventure as we enthusiastically filled several dumpsters with the detritus of previous owners and scrubbed the little house inside and out. It was hard work, ripping out old carpeting, gathering up the trash that littered the property and hacking down the weeds that filled the yard. It was truly a labor of love for the whole family. In fact it was because of the hard work we'd all been putting in that Earl and I were glad when Wesley was invited to a sleepover at his best friend's house. It was a much-deserved break for Wes and he was very excited to spend time with his friends.

"See you tomorrow, son, and have a good time!" I called as I waved goodbye to Wes on that sunny June day.

Wesley left home at 3:30 p.m. that Friday afternoon, and it was scarcely 5:30 p.m. when we received the phone call that would change our lives and home forever. Wesley had drowned. While playing in the water at a local lake he'd stepped off an unmarked drop-off and slipped below the surface before anyone could reach him.

The shock and grief of our loss was staggering. It seemed unreal that someone as vital and healthy as Wesley could be gone so abruptly and completely from our lives. The days surrounding the funeral passed in a merciful blur, and soon the crowds of well-wishers were gone and we were left alone to get on with our lives the best we could.

The much-anticipated move to our dream home had felt more like a nightmare in light of our circumstances. Everything seemed to remind us of Wes and his excitement about the move. Earl returned to work and his company began sending him out of town again. Everything seemed to go back to "normal" I thought, except Wesley's place in the family was empty and it hurt us all terribly to have him gone.

That's when these cries in the night first began. One or another of our three surviving children would awaken, terrified, confused and grieving for their older brother. At ages six, eight and eleven, such high concepts as salvation and eternal life were beyond their comprehension. We told them their brother was a believer and had gone to heaven to live with the Lord, but the children simply knew their brother was never to be a part of their lives again, and this knowledge hurt. With Earl gone, the task of helping our children deal with their loss fell more and more to me and I felt wholly inadequate for the task. After all, I was grieving too.

Tonight it was Lauren's turn to grieve and I held her in my arms, rocking her back and forth, trying to comfort her.

"I want Wesley," Lauren sobbed. "Please Mommy, I want Wesley."

"I know, I know," I crooned. "I want Wesley too, but he's in heaven with Jesus now." As I rocked my daughter I felt the familiar pangs of helplessness.

I don't know how long I held Lauren that night but I felt myself falling asleep as she continued to cry restlessly. I laid her down, settled the sheets around her and stroking her hair, prayed out loud for her.

"Dear Lord we pray you will comfort Lauren tonight. You know how much she misses Wes and we ask that You please be with her and help her as only You know how. In Jesus's name we pray, Amen." Then promising Lauren I would continue to pray for her, I returned to my room.

Back in my own bed, my heart aching, and exhausted from yet another night of interrupted sleep, my own tears began to flow. I wanted to beg God to remove this terrible burden of grief from our once happy home but instead I prayed.

"Please God help Lauren, be with her tonight. It hurts me Lord that I can't take away her pain. I don't know if I can ask this of You, but please, please can You send someone to comfort Lauren tonight? And if it's possible Lord, can You please send Wesley to comfort her?" Praying, I fell asleep.

The next morning I slept until 9 a.m. and felt a renewed sense of strength, peace and comfort. It was the first full night's sleep I'd had in a while, though it had come after midnight. Emerging from my bedroom, I found Lauren in the kitchen making toast for her younger siblings. Lauren greeted me with a broad smile, and I was relieved to see her more like her old self.

"Well look at you; good morning, Sunshine," I greeted Lauren as I kissed my two younger children.

"Good morning, Mommy." Lauren beamed. I laughed at the look of joy and mischief on her face and stroked her hair before kissing the top of the head.

"You look cheery this morning. I want you to know I prayed for you last night," I began.

"I know," Lauren exulted, "because someone came and held my hand after you went to bed."

I stopped instantly.

"What do you mean?" I asked, thinking one of the younger children must have wakened in the night and gone to comfort their sister.

"After you went to bed I was still feeling very sad," Lauren said. "And, I was lying there crying when suddenly I felt you take my hand and hold it very gently. I was so glad you'd come back that I squeezed your hand and I felt you squeeze my hand too, but when I opened my eyes there was no one there!" Lauren smiled.

I felt a tingle run the length of my spine, remembering how I'd prayed God would send someone to comfort Lauren.

"You weren't afraid?" I asked.

"Nope, it wasn't scary at all. I just felt happy and safe, and I went to sleep while someone held my hand." Lauren was matter-of-fact about this marvelous revelation and took the toast to her brother and sister at the kitchen table.

I stood a minute, stunned at what my daughter had just told me and wondered… had it been the Lord Jesus who had taken Lauren by the hand or had it been an angel? Or was it even Wesley himself, allowed to return and comfort his grieving little sister? I decided it didn't really matter who took my daughter's hand that night; the miracle had happened.

Lauren and I both firmly believe God sent someone from heaven that night, to hold a little girl's hand and comfort her during one of her life's darkest moments.

~DeVonna R. Allison

A Pink Dress and a Promise

I miss thee, my Mother! Thy image is still
The deepest impressed on my heart.
~Eliza Cook

I was sixteen and more than anything else in the world I wanted my mother to attend my high school graduation the following year. She was suffering from ovarian cancer, and although the expressions on the faces of other family members didn't offer much hope, I firmly believed she would recover and be there.

My mother and I had always enjoyed a special bond, perhaps because I'd been her only child for the first thirteen years of her married life. We shared a passionate love of books and reading. She'd read to me every day until I learned to master the skill myself. Afterwards she continued to share my love of stories by enthusing over my attempts at authorship. An amateur actress, she appeared in numerous local theatre productions. I grew up attending rehearsals and on opening night I was able to mouth every one of her lines.

I especially recall a small party held for the cast and crew one evening after a performance. My mother had bought a new pink dress for the occasion. In my six-year-old eyes, she looked like an angel.

When I was fourteen, my brother was born. Ten months later my mother was diagnosed with cancer. At first I didn't worry. After all, she was my mother. She'd never die and leave me. But as one year stretched to two and she grew thinner and often despondent due to heavy medication, I began to worry.

Two weeks before Christmas the year I was sixteen her condition worsened. I tried to deny the despair I saw in my father's face as we sat by her hospital bed. To strengthen the reality of her recovery I talked to her of the future, a future we'd share.

"And when you come to my graduation, will you wear your pink dress?" I asked her as she lay weak and thin on December 9th.

"Oh, honey, I don't know." She forced a thin smile. "That old thing? Really?"

"Yes, yes, please promise."

"All right, if that's what you really want… I promise." The words were barely above a whisper.

An hour later she passed away.

Somehow I forced myself through the next year and a half of school. My father had drifted away in his own world of grief and my aunt who came to take care of my two-year-old brother had no time for me. When graduation finally rolled around, both declined to attend.

As I sat on the platform with the other graduates, I felt hollow and utterly alone. I'd believed my mother would get well, I'd believed she'd be there for this milestone in my life. No one could possibly feel as bereft of happiness as I did at that moment.

Then the principal was announcing the prize for literature, for outstanding work in creative writing and the student on my right was prodding me. "You won, you won!" she hissed.

Stunned, I remained seated. And then I saw her. Standing at the back right hand corner of the auditorium, my mother was clapping with more vehemence than she'd taught me was ladylike. She was wearing the pink dress.

I stood and made my way to the podium to collect my award, all but staggering under the overwhelming sense of joy. She'd come. She'd promised and she'd come. And she was wearing the pink dress. The moments fluttered wildly in my heart, a beautiful butterfly of joy. In a cloud of happiness so intense I could barely control my movements, I returned to my seat. But when I looked at the back right hand corner of the room she was gone.

Later as I walked home alone in the soft, warm darkness of the spring evening, my award and diploma clasped in my hand, my attitude changed and anger suffused me. Why had she come only for an instant? Why couldn't she have stayed?

I sat down on a park bench by the river and stared at the calm water, and slowly understanding came. She couldn't always be with me, not anymore, but she would be there when I needed her most. She'd kept her promise. She'd come to my graduation and she'd worn the pink dress.

~Gail MacMillan

Hand on My Shoulder

There is no surprise more magical than the surprise of being loved.
It is God's finger on man's shoulder.
~Charles Morgan

It was late summer, smoggy, the daylight slowly fading away. The sun hung low in the western sky, coloring the San Gabriel Mountains a hazy purple. The temperature hovered near 95 degrees. Fortunately, a gentle breeze and some filtered shade from a nearby tree helped to cool the air. From the hillside, I could view the scenery and I felt the peace and quiet in the stillness of the early evening. Green grasses, mixed with clover, carpeted every hill as far as the eye could see. Nearby, on the left, stood a large Aleppo Pine, shading the area around me. The wind blew through its branches. A large bushy-tailed California gray squirrel sat on the lower branch of the old pine, overlooking his kingdom.

Changing my focus to the task at hand, I knelt down in front of the grave marker and cleaned it off. It had been overgrown with weeds and covered with pine needles. I could see the marker clearly now. It read "Raymond Earl Harrel." Dad had always loved the mountain pines. I tried to wipe the tears from my eyes, but that just opened the floodgates. I clutched my Bible, holding it tightly to my chest, and wept uncontrollably.

My dad had worked as a firefighter for the Los Angeles County Fire Department for almost thirty years. He retired early at the age of fifty-five, so he could have time to enjoy his retirement with his family. However, that was not to be. Cancer showed up a few months after he retired; it spread quickly. His death overwhelmed me. I felt lost and alone.

I had never hurt so much in my life. "Oh God, please help me! I don't want to live this way any longer." Self-destructive thoughts poured in like a flood. As I pondered the options of living or dying, the minutes drifted by... then the interruption came.

I felt a tap on my left shoulder. Thinking that pesky squirrel had scampered down the tree and jumped on my shoulder, I swung around, ready to bat him away with my right hand. But I saw nothing. Looking up at the pine tree, I could see the squirrel still perched there, watching me. His tail stood at attention, his glare steady and his posture motionless. Maybe a pinecone had fallen on me. I quickly scanned the area but saw none.

Distracted for a moment, I soon drifted back to memories of Dad. Closing my eyes helped focus my thoughts. Then, I felt it again. This time, however, it wasn't just a touch but a steady pressure across my entire shoulder. Someone was leaning on me from behind; I could feel the weight of a hand, the fingers gently gripping my shoulder. This was not a squirrel!

I could hear the squirrel, who had been quiet the entire time, now chattering up a storm. Not the normal squirrel chatter or warning sounds, but a friendly alert, one of recognition. Did my squirrel companion see or sense something? Maybe.

A warming sensation flowed from my shoulders, down my back, across my legs, and into my toes. Time seemed to stand still. I kept my eyelids closed and dared not open them to look around, lest this mysterious visitor leave. Then I heard the whisper. It sounded like the wind, which had blown through the pine branches earlier. I could feel the breath on my ear. It was cool and warm at the same time. Soon the words were audible in my left ear: "Charles, Charles..." The squirrel chattered on in the background, making those cute little chirps. The voice paused for a moment, and then continued, "Your father is not here. He lives in Heaven now. Go tell your mother." The inflection was deep and gentle—a man's voice.

I felt more pressure on my left shoulder, and then the weight lifted. I stayed kneeling for a second or two. When I opened my eyes and looked around, no one was there. The hillside appeared empty. No cars, no one walking down the pathway or roadway, nothing. Only the squirrel remained, standing erect on two feet, watching me. So, I asked him, "Did you see the angel?" He pointed his bushy tail upright and spun around a couple of times. Smiling, I said to myself, "I'll take that for a yes." Looking down, I noticed three clovers clustered together by the grave marker. I decided to pick them.

The sun had set now, with darkness settling over the cemetery grounds. The park would close soon. As I walked down the hill toward my car, I tucked the shamrocks safely away in my Bible. I turned around to take one last look at the gravesite on the hill and saw the squirrel scampering up the old pine, heading for home. I needed to get back home too. Reflecting on what had just transpired, I drove out the front gate of Glendale's Forest Lawn Memorial Park. For the first time in a year, hope filled my heart. I felt happy inside; life had meaning again. God was real too, really real. And I had a plan.

I waited until Christmas to tell my mother the story. In fact, I wrote the angel's message in a letter and attached one of the clovers from Dad's grave marker. I left it under the Christmas tree at her house. She called me early that morning. She was in tears. "I believe you. You really did encounter an angel of God." Then she told me about the last week of my father's life, something I never heard before: "Every day about evening time, Ray would see a large bushy-tailed squirrel, just like the one you saw at Forest Lawn. At first, I believed he was dreaming or hallucinating. But like clockwork, the squirrel appeared to him at dusk every evening during the final week of his life."

After hearing about my experience, Mom pondered the correlation between the two bushy-tailed squirrels. I really didn't have an explanation for her. Still, I believed God orchestrated it. Mom believed the squirrel appearances were further confirmation that my angel encounter was real and his message true. "This is the best

Christmas gift ever," she said. "Now tell me again, what happened and what did the angel say?"

Later that morning, I gathered my family together and drove to Mom's house in Sandy, Oregon. After dinner and opening presents, Mom and I visited for several hours. That was the last time we talked intimately about spiritual matters.

I felt that warm, weighty hand on my shoulder one other time. It happened the morning my mother passed away. I didn't hear a voice of encouragement or see a heavenly visitor that day. I didn't need to—his simple touch was more than enough.

~Charles Earl Harrel

81

Anne and Bill

Clouds on clouds, in volumes driven,
Curtain round the vault of heaven.
~Thomas Love Peacock

bout eleven years ago, my mother was diagnosed with lung cancer. After two years of fighting hard to stay alive, she was hospitalized for pain management. We all thought she would be in the hospital for a week or so; but she took a turn for the worse and it looked like she was coming to the end of her life.

She talked to me about life after death. She believed very strongly that she would be able to come back and somehow let me know she was okay.

She told me the story of her own mother. My grandmother went into the hospital after my uncle was born. Mom was never sure if it was pneumonia or cancer. My mother was only eight years old at the time. One night she was awakened by something that literally sat her up in bed, and her arm went up as if someone was pulling on it. She immediately knew her mother had died. She was sure it was her mother coming to say goodbye to her. Mom told me to watch for lights going on and off—that would be her sign to let me know she was safely on the other side.

I believed her completely, as I had my own experiences when I was younger and my son died.

My mother passed away on October 1, 2002 in the middle of

the night. We all rushed to the hospital to say our goodbyes and then wearily drove back home.

I lay down in my bed and closed my eyes. Within minutes, the lamp in my room went on by itself.

I jumped up and looked at the lamp. It went off again. This began to happen quite often.

I was not the only one experiencing these things. During the first month following my mother's death, lights went on and off everywhere. I had not mentioned this to my sister until she said she was having this odd problem at her house... lights were going on outside her house by themselves and the electrician could not figure out what was wrong.

Needless to say, I knew immediately.

That was not the end of it. One day I was having a pretty serious disagreement with my brothers and sister when, all of a sudden, all the lights in the house went out. We all stood there for a minute, and they came back on. We all looked at each other and said that was Mom telling us to stop fighting.

To be honest, the most incredible sign my mother gave me was about a month after she died. My husband took me away for a weekend trip to Quebec. We went to visit the Cathedral of St Anne, for whom my mother was named. It was a dark, rainy day, and when we got to the church it was pouring so hard even the umbrella was useless.

We stepped inside, said some prayers and lit a candle for Mom. When we stepped outside onto the front porch of the church, I looked at my husband and said, "Mom would be so happy right now that we are here."

At that very moment, the pitch-black sky parted and a huge ball of sun emerged, almost blinding us. The only way to describe it is like the Good Witch in *The Wizard of Oz* when she first appeared in the movie. As quickly as the sun came toward us, it retreated. The sky closed up, turned dark again and began to pour. I turned to my husband and said, "Oh my god, that was my mother." He looked at me and said, "If I was not here with you, I would never have believed this."

I knew that Mom was okay.

Over the course of the last decade, Mom has come and gone many times. Always lights going on or off without any reason, or something falling off a wall at an odd time.

She came again recently as my father was preparing to leave us. Dad had lived with us for the last four years after his stroke. He began to decline and we knew he was going to die shortly. I was sitting with him most of the day and decided to go into the kitchen to check on my daughter.

I sat down at the table, right under the skylight. It was a rainy, gray day. All of a sudden, I felt heat coming from the skylight. I looked up and saw the sun coming through the clouds much like the day at St Anne's. I could not believe my eyes and I asked my daughter if she was seeing what I was… she was also shocked. Once again, the sun came and went in a matter of minutes and then it began to rain again.

My first thought was that my father must have died, so I ran to his room. He was still alive, but I knew in my heart that my mother was here and had come to get him.

That same afternoon, my father's caregiver felt a presence when walking toward his room. She turned to see who was behind her. Out of the corner of her eye, she saw someone walking into the room. The trouble was that no one was in there. As she entered my father's room, she walked into what she described as a ball of heat. She thought that perhaps the air conditioning was not working. But as she walked a bit further into the room, it felt very cold. She was not going to mention it, but my daughter walked in shortly after and asked her if she felt the heat at the doorway. Both of them believed some kind of spirit was there to take him.

He died shortly thereafter that day.

My father has been gone for a month now. So far I have woken up in the middle of the night to my computer going on for no apparent reason, and, out of the blue, my husband's alarm clock started going off at five in the morning. I am still trying to figure Dad out. I am hopeful this is his way of letting us know he is okay.

~Debbie Rouhana Lane

82

Divine Dream

*Miracles occur naturally as expressions of love. The real miracle is the love
that inspires them. In this sense everything that comes from love is a miracle.*
~Marianne Williamson

M indy was my best friend growing up. When I was
six years old, my mother went to the animal shelter
to get a hunting companion dog for my brother,
Kevin. Lo and behold, she came back with this
shaggy black and white mutt! Kevin sputtered, "Mom, what the
heck? This dog is clearly not a hunting dog!" Mom replied, "She was
the cutest one there and the only one that looked quietly into my
eyes and told me to take her home, so I did." I couldn't have been
more thrilled.

Mindy and I had a connection immediately and I knew we
would be great pals forever. She let me dress her up as a baby and
take her for walks in the stroller. She became the friend I needed so
desperately growing up as an introverted child.

As I grew into an awkward teenager, our bond grew even stronger. Mindy's coat was gray now instead of black. I knew she was
aging, but did not want to admit that to myself.

When I was sixteen, I lost my dearest Aunt Laurel to emphy-
sema. She was an inspiration in my life and treated me like her own
child. As long as I had my Aunt Laurel and Mindy, I was happy. Aunt
Laurel lived in Missouri but would often drive up to Minnesota for
long visits. She took the time to listen and get to know me. She

made me feel important and loved in so many ways. I worshipped the ground she walked on and cherished the time we spent together. I was not prepared to lose Aunt Laurel, and Mindy comforted me greatly in the grieving process.

About three months after Aunt Laurel passed away, Mindy developed a large tumor above her right eye. My parents knew they had to try to save her life because I still needed her dearly. The surgery was complicated and expensive, but it bought her a little time. Sadly, about three months later we had to help her to let her go.

Losing both Aunt Laurel and Mindy in the same year devastated me. I cried each night for two weeks and asked God to bring them both back to me to say goodbye. Then one night, I had the most comforting dream. It didn't feel like a dream at all, but something miraculous and extraordinary. I stood by a beautiful hillside with glorious flowers and tall grass all around me. A gentle breeze swayed at my back and it smelled of fresh cotton. A fast flowing river ran through the hillside, which was covered by lush oak trees. I took it all in before I realized that I was there to see Mindy. Suddenly, panic set in because I could not find her. I called and called for her, yet she was not coming to me.

Then I saw Aunt Laurel walking slowly up the hillside with a drenched Mindy. I knew immediately that Aunt Laurel saved Mindy from the river by pulling her to safety. Now they walked up the hill toward me! Aunt Laurel smiled serenely at me as she guided Mindy over the hillside to a small path that led up to heaven. I could see that Mindy's tail was wagging joyfully and she was no longer in pain. Aunt Laurel could now breathe easily and no longer need her oxygen tank. I was not allowed to interact with them and they could not stop and greet me. The sky opened up and the light radiated toward them as they walked into heaven and just disappeared. I felt the warmth of the light enter my body, which filled me with peace and love.

I woke up in tears. What I had just witnessed was a true miracle sent to me by God. For the first time since I had lost my two best friends, I was at peace.

The next morning at breakfast, I excitedly explained my dream to my mother. She looked at me in astonishment and said, "I had the very same dream last night." We both knew we had witnessed something magnificent and life altering, and we were grateful.

~Rita Kaye Vetsch

83

Password

May the wings of the butterfly kiss the sun
And find your shoulder to light on,
To bring you luck, happiness and riches
Today, tomorrow and beyond.
~Irish Blessing

I was nothing less than devastated by the news that my beloved black Labrador, Lady, had a cancerous tumor in her lung, and was so enlarged it had literally pushed her heart to the other side of her chest. Fortunately, Lady didn't even look ill, and certainly failed to exhibit any outward signs of pain. The veterinarian explained that surgery was an option, we decided surgery was pointless and cruel and would not extend her life.

So, Lady was expected to live another three or four weeks.

It was decided that putting Lady on a high-protein diet of "people food" was the best choice under the circumstances. She loved scrambled eggs, baked turkey and chicken breasts, cheeses, and her favorite — prime rib cooked just to her liking. I snuck her a few pieces of pizza too.

I spent many long hours talking with my brother about Lady and the great joy she brought me over a decade. A month passed, then two, then three and four. Lady was holding her own and I treasured every single day she lived.

The veterinarian came to the house regularly to check on Lady.

She was amazed at how well she appeared, and the remarkable fact she was clearly not declining.

Nevertheless, I continued to break down and my brother continued to comfort me. Another couple of months passed and soon we reached an unbelievable marker of ten months! Lady continued to feast on her high-protein foods and although her weight stayed the same, she exhibited absolutely no signs of discomfort. By Christmas, I wondered if the diagnosis had been a horrible mistake.

That was not to be the case. After the holidays, Lady suddenly lost weight at an accelerated rate, and I could no longer postpone a very important decision about euthanasia. I knew the day would come when I would be forced to call the veterinarian and ask her to come to the house to see Lady one final time. I agonized over that decision, and even worse was choosing "when" that exact day would be. I started losing my courage to make that final decision, and I discussed this at length with my dear brother. He suggested that I "talk" to Lady about the issue. I took his advice.

I sat on the floor with Lady, looked into those incredibly loving brown eyes, hugged her closely to me, and cried myself to sleep at her side—for two days and two nights. Yes, Lady gave me a sign that she was ready, an unmistakable body language message distinctly hers, and I made the dreaded call to the vet.

The inevitable day of Lady's passing was a serene moment in my life and one of a true blessing. I was so privileged to have had her love, and I held her as she took her last breath. The impression of her soul leaving her body and soaring to lofty heights nearly overtook me. I told her, "Run like the wind, my precious Lady, run like the wind!"

Strangely, I cried no more tears that day and again my brother offered words of comfort, acknowledging and honoring the profound love we share with our pets. He reassured me that one day I would have another dog. He reiterated this on many occasions.

Several years came and went, and there was no talk of getting another dog.

Another inevitable day presented itself; my dear brother was gravely ill and not expected to live. I was devastated. Nevertheless, my brother was upbeat and in total acceptance. He reassured me that once he had passed, he would somehow relay a message to me from the other side, or wherever he was destined to be. We decided on a password and he vowed to contact me.

Several weeks later, I asked my brother if he remembered what his message or password was; he laughed loudly and answered that he'd forgotten it too! He then suggested a new password, evidently a word chosen at random, and one that I felt had no significance for either of us. The password was "butterfly." I agreed to this and promised my brother I would remember his password and he vowed to do the same.

Although my brother passed away very soon after this conversation, I felt so blessed to have had the opportunity to say goodbye, and to thank him for his genuine sweetness, his love and all his words of comfort throughout my dark days. He winked at me and said, "Don't forget the password, Sis."

Several months later, my husband brought home an unexpected early birthday present for me, and something totally out of character. After parking his truck, I watched my husband walk along our sidewalk as he approached the house, and trailing behind him was a bouncing white and brown puppy with a long snout and impossibly large floppy ears. He was the cutest puppy in the world!

"Whatever possessed you to bring a puppy home?"

My husband smiled. "Just waiting for the right time, I guess."

"That's so... unlike you."

"True enough. I just felt a strong compulsion, and well, who could resist that face?"

I kissed and cuddled and played with my new puppy; my heart overjoyed. That evening I called a few friends to tell them of our new puppy. On one such call, I looked at my calendar as I spoke. I suddenly realized it would have been my brother's birthday and mentioned this to my friend on the phone.

"My brother would have been so happy for me to get this new

puppy. I only wish he could have lived long enough to see him," I said.

"Have you picked out a name? What breed of dog is the new puppy?"

"Well, his name is Pappy, and he's a Toy Spaniel, a Papillon."

I stopped speaking, and I think I stopped breathing for a long moment as my mind raced back to the promise my brother had made before he died.

"Oh!" I said, as the realization hit. "Yes, he's a Papillon, which is the French word for butterfly!"

The long anticipated message from my brother finally came through loud and clear. Tears of joy covered my face and the small puppy licked them away. Butterfly... butterfly... butterfly!

This was a miraculous confirmation sent with love from my brother, and I do believe perhaps my precious Lady too.

~Louetta Jensen

84

Kiss Me Goodbye

'Twas not my lips you kissed
But my soul.
~Judy Garland

The Thursday progressed like any other. Newly retired, I awoke early, ready for a day filled with my art and writing. My semi-retired husband Paul had already left. He was semi-retired but still working despite several health issues—none of which were life threatening.

He was usually home by five o'clock. We had a new ritual of meeting on the couch for appetizers and to watch the news. It was our new routine as leisurely happy empty nesters.

That evening, about fifteen minutes into the show, Paul got up from the couch to refill our chips and salsa while I went for more cola.

Crash!

I turned to see Paul stumble back with a surprised look on his face, the dish flying through the air and smashing against the coffee table. He fell lifeless onto the couch.

"Paul, Paul, answer me!" I yelled running to his side. "Can you hear me?"

I ran back and forth from Paul to the phone trying to dial 911 with trembling hands.

"My husband, you gotta help my husband!" I yelled to the emergency operator.

"Okay ma'am, calm down, we're sending someone."

"Can you get him on the floor?" she asked after I explained the situation.

I took the phone with me and put it on speaker.

"Talk to me," she said. "Is he on the floor?"

"No, I can't move him. He's like dead weight!" I said. How prophetic those words would be.

"Can you get a neighbor to help?"

With that I ran out my side porch. As luck would have it, my neighbor was at her kitchen sink. I could see her from my stoop.

"Help me!" I screamed, jumping up and down waving my arms. Within three seconds she and her husband came in my side door.

He helped me get Paul on the floor and I started CPR.

One, two, three, four, five. Breathe. One, two, three, four, five. Breathe.

That was the last time my lips would touch Paul's.

The rest of the evening was a blur: paramedics, calling my children from a screaming ambulance.

"I'm sorry Mrs. Rodman, we shocked him four times."

The priest and my children arrived. A week later we had his funeral and then a reception at the house. Our children and I buried him in the pouring rain a week before Christmas.

My life evolved into a nightmare of putting one foot in front of the other. Doing what I had to. Eating because my kids said eat. Lonely days, anxiety-ridden nights. I cried every day. I turned his pictures over. I couldn't bear to think of life without him. I gave away his clothes. I worked hard every day to keep moving through the darkness.

Year one turned to year two and I always lamented the same thing: he never got to kiss me goodbye.

By the third year I started to let in my memoires of him without falling apart. The pictures I had turned over now lined my mantel; I saw him in my kid's eyes. He was larger than life and I sought him everywhere. I didn't want to forget him and now I was ready to reach out to him. I talked to him daily.

About this time, a friend told me of a show on Internet radio that a reputable medium hosted. I was intrigued and eager to connect with Paul. Enough time had passed that I knew it wouldn't shatter me. I decided to give it a try.

The first week the phone lines were jammed and I couldn't get through. The next week was Paul's birthday so I asked him to send me a message of healing.

The night of the show came. I debated trying to call again. "Oh what the heck are you doing that's so important?" I asked myself. I turned on my computer and tuned in. I started calling early. No answer but I kept at it, hitting redial over and over.

All of a sudden I heard, "Hi, what's your name and where are you calling from?"

I almost stuttered I was so surprised, but managed to answer.

The medium asked, "What can I do for you?"

"Do you have a message for me from the other side?" I asked.

"Well, your mother is stepping forward with a man. Oh my," she told her co-hosts, "did you see that bright flash of light? The man is your husband. This person really wants to be heard. Now he's showing me his wallet. It's important to him. He's trying to show me his name and social security number. Do you still have his wallet?"

"Yes, I do. I just had it out last week for the first time since his death to fill out some legal papers related to his work." I always had trouble remembering Paul's social security number so I was looking for his Medicare card and his driver's license.

"He died suddenly of his heart," she stated. "He says he was sick. He died in your home."

"Yes," I said, starting to cry.

"He's glad you're still living in the house and he likes what you've done to it, he's happy you're comfortable there," she continued.

Paul was always so proud of our home. I have tried to keep it up just like he did and I was also in the middle of a bathroom remodel.

She said, "This is strange. I have never gotten this message before, but he says he can't wait to kiss your lips."

With that I totally lost it. The one thing I had cried, raved and ranted about for three years was that missing kiss.

"Yes, I didn't get to kiss him goodbye," I said through tears. "And he was a good kisser!" I kind of laughed, trying to pull myself together.

She laughed too. "Well, that's good."

"You guys didn't get to Hawaii?" she asked.

"Oh God," I said sucking in my breath. "We were planning a trip to Hawaii for our anniversary when he died."

The medium continued, "This is kind of embarrassing but he said to tell you, 'Honey, don't worry, it's not your time but when you come, we'll take that trip. They have beautiful exotic places here. But it's not your time yet. You have things to do yet. I'll be waiting for you and can't wait to kiss your beautiful lips.' He just told me that kissing you was his favorite thing to do!"

I was blown away and sobbing. I would get my long overdue kiss and more after all!

The medium ended the session with wishing me well and saying everyone in my family who had passed on—my mom, dad, sister and my sweet Paul—was with me every day; they watched over and protected me. I thanked her for her truly precious gift.

I believe heaven is closer than we think. I was so happy to know my loved ones, especially Paul, were with me. My heart was light with the promise of a reunion someday. I would have to wait, but knowing Paul and I would be together again in heaven makes the journey here easier. I found peace that night and can smile now and get on with my life knowing he is with me.

~Sallie A. Rodman

From Heaven, With Love

My heart leaps up when I behold
A rainbow in the sky...
~William Wordsworth

"Watch for it," said my friend Joani on her deathbed. "Not one, but two rainbows, exactly three days after I die. Got it?"

"Got it," I choked out, squeezing her hand tight.

"You go out on the beach, walk the boardwalk, and wait for it, you hear me?"

I nodded mutely.

It had been hard for me to accept that Joani was about to leave us. When she'd been diagnosed with stage IV melanoma, she fought to beat the odds, outliving the doctor's prediction of three months by more than three years.

Some friends come into your life by sheer accident, or coincidence, if you believe in such things. When others arrive, you know in your heart it must have been divine intervention.

That was the case with Joani. I was the new kid on the block, and I knew no one at all when I entered the huge conference center to attend my first community college faculty gathering. I was an adjunct professor, and I taught only one off-campus class, but I'd driven over 100 miles to attend the back-to-school orientation anyway.

After I picked up my nametag at the "New Staff" registration table, I turned and looked around for a place to sit.

"Yoo-hoo!" a voice called out. "Over here!" A woman was motioning for me to join her.

I looked to the right and left, and even turned and looked behind me to see who she was calling. Then I turned back to face her and pointed to my chest. "Me?"

She nodded enthusiastically and waved me over, pointing to the seat next to her. "I was saving this seat for you!"

I had never met this woman, and yet within minutes we became friends for life—which in this case turned out to be six and a half more years.

Joani took me under her wing, encouraged me, inspired me, and mentored me through my first year. Her zest and gusto for all things "illiterary," as she called it, were contagious, and I learned more about teaching English from an afternoon with her than I did in four years of college.

"Those dumb doctors don't know me," she said when she first told me about her diagnosis. "I can't die in three months—I have wine to drink!"

So when she told me to look for double rainbows three days after she passed, I had no doubt they'd be there. And they were—both vividly bright and arcing across the sky, a fitting tribute to the colorful life she'd lived.

~Jan Bono

Chapter 11

Miracles Happen

Everyday Miracles

86

Chariots of Fire Was Not Luck

Attempt something so impossible that unless God is in it,
it's doomed to failure.
~John Hagee

I n the early 1980s, my husband Darryl and his brother Frank started a film production company that specialized in comedy films with a light Christian message. Kuntz Brothers' films garnered a number of awards and were among the most popular films offered by the Christian Film Distributors Association, which distributed films to churches and other Christian organizations all over the world.

But by 1987, Darryl had a new vision. He wanted to make a full-length family feature to be distributed in mainstream theaters in cities across America. It wouldn't have an overt Christian message, but it would have a wholesome and uplifting story, something to make the whole family feel good.

Frank was not so sure. He loved kids and shared Darryl's conviction that there was a desperate need for wholesome family features. But producing one? It seemed too risky a proposition. At that time, family movies, especially those made by independents, were usually commercial disasters, seldom making enough money to pay back all the expenses incurred in production and distribution. The concept of home video rentals, which is now by far the biggest source of income for family films, was brand new and entirely unproven.

"No," Frank said. "A full-length theatrical release is too big a step, too chancy."

Soon after, the brothers attended the USA Film Festival in Dallas to accept an award for one of their films and to attend several seminars on filmmaking. The final seminar addressed the making of feature films. As they left the building, Darryl again warmed up to the topic of producing a feature.

"We can do this, Frank. I know we can."

"I agree there's a need for it. But somebody else will have to do it," Frank countered. "Sure, lots of people say they want wholesome family films. But unfortunately they just don't support them at the box office anymore."

"Wait a minute. What about *Chariots of Fire*?" Darryl asked, referring to a hugely successful inspirational film about a Scottish missionary, which was awarded the 1981 Academy Award for Best Picture.

"*Chariots of Fire*?" Frank scoffed, as they drove out of the parking lot into downtown Dallas rush hour traffic. "That was a fluke. *Chariots of Fire* was just luck."

At that moment a dark, new model Mercedes with tinted windows zipped into the lane in front of them. Frank's mouth dropped open when he saw its bumper sticker. "Chariots of Fire was not luck," it read. The brothers had just enough time to read it before the car switched lanes again and disappeared into the traffic.

"Well, shut my mouth," Frank said.

Kuntz Brothers' family feature film *Dakota*, starring Lou Diamond Phillips and distributed by Miramax, released to theaters nationwide in 1988. While not a runaway hit, it did receive favorable reviews and paved the way for future family films. *Los Angeles Times* critic Gary Franklin referred to then-President George Bush's call for a kinder and gentler America and rated *Dakota* "a kinder and gentler 8 on Franklin's scale of 1 to 10." NBC critic David Sheehan called it "a film filled with high ideals and a very big heart." *Good Housekeeping* magazine labeled it "one of the year's best choices for youngsters of all ages." Ted Baehr, author of *The Christian Family Guide to Movies & Video*, named it "a fine film the whole family can enjoy," and Bob Briner, author of *Roaring Lambs*, cited it as a breakthrough for producers of wholesome family films. By the standards Frank and Darryl valued, *Dakota* was, indeed, successful.

As for the bumper sticker: neither Frank nor Darryl nor anyone they know has ever seen or heard of another like it. It was, perhaps, one of a kind, appearing in just the right place at just the right time to convince Frank and Darryl Kuntz that they would have all the help they needed to buck the system and produce a successful feature family film.

~Sara Lynn Worley Kuntz

87

The Brush of a Wing

Hope is faith holding out its hand in the dark.
~George Iles

I'm a Boy Scout Venturing Crew Leader, so I have been trained to prepare for any challenge encountered while camping. I will never forget one early autumn campout when I did everything wrong despite my training, leaving me desperate for a miracle.

Our camp was 300 acres of heavily wooded hills. A rural road, little more than a lane, bisected it. The boys were camped in and around the farthest cabin and the girls were in the building closest to the parking lot, yet across the road. The dining hall, the only building with plumbing, sat atop a high hill behind the lot. There was a small winding drive on one side, but most campers took the direct route over a stream and straight up the hill.

We arrived Friday evening and had activities until late Saturday night. I'm an early riser and always the first one awake on Sunday to make coffee and start cleanup. This particular weekend I awoke just a few minutes past 3 a.m. with an urgent need for a bathroom.

I often lectured the youth on safety procedures, such as never wandering alone, always having a flashlight and letting someone know where you are going. I reached down for my shoes and the small flashlight I leave in one of them for quick access. My shoe was empty. I sighed remembering the small boy who had borrowed it. I pulled on my shoes and slipped out of the building without waking anyone. After all, I was only going to the port-a-potty a few yards from the cabin. On my way there I changed my mind and decided to go to the dining hall to use a real bathroom.

I stumbled down the steep rutted drive and walked along the road. This was the long way, but easier to follow in the dark. I trudged up the stony drive, used the bathroom, and then fixed a cup of tea and sat on the porch enjoying the peace. The cloud cover was heavy and I couldn't find a single star in the heavens. As I sipped I pondered the silence. No crickets, frogs, not even a scurrying mouse made a sound. I felt completely alone, and it wasn't all that bad. I returned my mug to the kitchen and went back outside.

I looked down the rocky drive, contemplating the long walk back to my cabin. I was exhausted. It had been a busy weekend and I'd only had a few hours sleep. Plus it was frustrating to know my cabin was directly across from where I stood atop the hill. Returning the same way I had come was about four times longer. Yes, it was dark, but I had walked the shortcut hundreds of times. Chiding myself for being too cautious, I headed straight down the grassy hill toward the stream.

The parking lot has lights, so I found the footbridge over the stream and made my way across the sandy field filled with a few dozen cars. I was at the far left end of the lot. A thicket hid the road beyond, but this end had a small set of steps up to the road.

I found the first steps and crossed the road. The brush on the other side was heavy and it took several minutes to find the other set of stairs. They were overgrown and when I reached what should have been a small clearing with at least four paths leading out like wheel spokes, it seemed the brush and trees enveloped me. I stumbled along in what I hoped was the right direction, but there was no light and the path was so covered with wild brush I was no longer sure. After several minutes of fighting the branches I decided to backtrack and take the longer, but more sure, route. But now I couldn't see where I'd just come from. I felt the branches, hoping to find a bent or broken one to testify of my passage but found nothing.

I started to panic. I was lost within a football field's length of my cabin! What kind of example would that be? Then I realized all the safety rules I had ignored. I didn't want to wake anyone to go to the bathroom with me, so not only did I go alone, I had left no note nor told anyone where I was going. I had no flashlight, which would have prevented my blind rambling, and I had followed a poorly marked trail. I had been over-confident, and I was lost in the dark.

Unsure what to do, cold and frightened, I sat down and tried to regain my composure. In my mind I spoke a prayer, asking for literal guidance. I even chuckled at the ludicrousness of my situation: a BSA crew leader lost within sight of her cabin. Sight that is, once the sun came up. Still sunrise was several hours away and I really didn't want to sit on the cold ground that long.

The silence was no longer restful, but now oppressive. I stopped looking up at the blackness and lowered my head into my hands. As I fought back tears of frustration a velvet touch brushed down my cheek. Startled, I opened my eyes to see a pure white feather a foot long, lying on the ground a few inches away. It resembled an arrow and I stretched out to pick it up. From this point, with my eyes at ground level, I could see the path beneath the overgrowth. I was only a few yards from the cabin and that single white feather had pointed me in the right direction.

In a moment I was lying on my bunk, the feather tucked in my pillow. It is my reminder that miracles can arrive in silence, and without any witness. I was saved from cold and fright, but most of all embarrassment. Now I always carry a spare flashlight and my feather!

~Anna M. Lowther

A Home of Our Own

Home, the spot of earth supremely blest,
A dearer, sweeter spot than all the rest.
~Robert Montgomery

I dreaded telling him. "Ryan, we're going to have to move again."

My nine-year-old son just stared at me. "Mom, why? You said we'd live here a long time."

Since his dad and I divorced, Ryan and I had moved three times already, and he'd been to four different schools. We were both frustrated with renting.

"Do we have to?" Ryan asked. I knew he was deeply disappointed. So was I.

"Unfortunately, the landlord is going to sell this house. I'm sorry, honey. There's nothing I can do."

We had been in the house for a year, and we loved it. It was in a quiet—though low-income—neighborhood in the town of Anderson, a few miles south of the city where I worked. Living in Anderson was ideal for us. A good elementary school was close by and we liked our neighbors.

The street we lived on was actually a circular block, made up of 120 similar homes. Some of the houses were owner-occupied and some—like ours—were renter-occupied. Some were well cared for and some... not so much. But we were happy there.

Sometimes in the early evening we'd walk around the entire

circle and talk about the day and things we noticed about the other houses.

"This one needs paint," Ryan said quietly.

"Yeah, but it has a nice fenced yard in front, and a great dog."

Then one evening, we both noticed one particular house. It was as if it had appeared out of nowhere.

"Look at that one, Mom!"

We paused a moment. "I like the color," I said. "This house looks loved. Why haven't we noticed it before?"

He shrugged. "I like the apple tree."

From then on it became the apple tree house, and we took special notice of it whenever we passed.

After the landlord broke the news to us, I looked for a rental in Anderson but found nothing suitable. With no other choice, we moved back to the city, about twelve miles north. Our house in the city was newer and bigger than our Anderson house, but somehow it didn't feel right. We never settled in and always felt restless there.

I knew I had to find us a place we could stay indefinitely, a place where Ryan could make friends and continue in one school. I'd heard about a program in our area that helped low-income people make a down payment and buy a home. As far as anyone knew, the program had run out of money and wasn't active. Yet somehow, I found a phone number for the program director and wasted no time in calling.

"This is Lisa," a woman said. I breathed a silent prayer, and introduced myself.

"Lisa, I don't have much money, but I can pay a mortgage if I can get one. Can you help me?"

Lisa shrieked with a loud laugh, and my heart sank. Evidently, everyone was right. The program was toast.

"I cannot believe you called me today of all days!" Lisa said. "We ran out of money ages ago. We didn't even keep a waiting list because we had no idea when we'd see more funds. Then last night, out of nowhere, I got new funding, and you are the first caller."

It was my turn to shriek. As I listened to her instructions, I prayed quietly, "Please God, please God, please God." One thing I knew, this funding was not "out of nowhere." It was from God.

Then we talked money and what I could afford.

Again, Lisa laughed. "You're not going to believe this. I just got a listing in your price range. The only thing is, it's not in the city. It's down in Anderson."

My heart leaped. "Are you kidding me? We love Anderson!"

"A pastor owns the house. His family has been transferred already, so it's sitting empty. They need to sell it fast. Can you meet me there tomorrow?"

I agreed, and then she told me the address. I didn't recognize the house number, but I sure knew the street name. It was on the same circular block we'd lived on before. I knew none of this was coincidental. The next day Ryan and I drove to Anderson to meet Lisa.

"You be the navigator," I said, handing him a paper. "We're looking for number 1935."

We drove up the circle, past our old house, and Ryan began calling out addresses. "There's 1889." A few houses later, "1909, we're getting closer, Mom."

Then a thought occurred to me. "Ryan, wouldn't it be amazing if this house turns out to be the apple tree house?"

No sooner did I say those words then we saw it, number 1935. Out of 120 houses on the block and all the houses in Anderson, the one we were going to see was indeed our apple tree house.

"Ryan," I said solemnly, "this is a God thing."

Minutes later, we were inside. It needed a few minor fixes, but Ryan and I both knew this was our new home. Standing in our future kitchen, Lisa started the paperwork, including a check of my finances.

With Lisa's help, the process went smoothly. My offer was accepted, and in no time the house was ours. It was everything I'd prayed for—big trees, affordable payments, a school Ryan liked, and a fenced yard for a dog. The day we moved in, I promised Ryan we would not move again until he finished high school… and we didn't.

That was twenty years ago. Ryan is a grown man, but I'm still here in my apple tree house. I could have moved to a newer, fancier place by now. But this is my miracle house. With the economy in turmoil, I've watched as numerous friends and family members have lost their big, beautiful homes to foreclosure. Each time I shared their heartbreak, and quietly thanked God for my humble but affordable home.

My dad always told me, "God's not often early, but He's never late." This house and the funding to buy it seemed to come out of nowhere. But I believe when the house came on the market, God covered it with His hand, till we were ready.

Oh, and there's one more important thing about this house, which it took me a long time to notice. Our house number is 1935, which just happens to be a combination of my birthday (January 9th or 1/9) and Ryan's birthday (March 5th or 3/5). I believe God stamped this house with our special number, a sign that He'd set it aside just for us.

Whenever I see our number on the front of the house, 1935, I smile. And I hear God's voice say to me, "You're welcome."

~Teresa Ambord

89

He Forgets Me Not

Silently, one by one, in the infinite meadows of heaven,
Blossomed the lovely stars, the forget-me-nots of the angels.
~Henry Wadsworth Longfellow, "Evangeline"

I felt discouraged. For the last two years my husband and I had tried to respond to a call to minister in Canada. Our visas had been declined and we questioned our call to Canada. We always sensed we were meant for something more, but felt frustrated our life lacked any physical evidence of this.

On the second attempt, our visas were approved and I finally prepared to leave my workplace. The months of dealing with the unknown had left me desperate for God to reach into my life in a tangible way. One spring evening, as our days in England were coming to an end, I stepped off the train on my way home from work. It was a beautiful day and I took a deep breath, breathing in the fresh spring air. As I crossed the bridge to meet my husband, something blue caught my eye. My eyes rested upon forget-me-not flowers growing by the side of the road. Doesn't it say somewhere in the Bible that God will not forget us? From that point on I decided I would see these flowers as a reminder God hadn't forgotten me.

I continued with the final weeks of my work. The last days of farewell lunches, heartfelt conversations, gifts and cards touched my heart deeply. It was a bittersweet time. On my last day at work a colleague called me over to her desk. She said she had a gift for me from her mother who wouldn't be able to see me before I left. Her mother was a special person and I'd enjoyed our connection at work. It saddened me that I wouldn't have the chance to say goodbye to her, but grateful she had thought of me. I took the gift from her daughter's hands and decided to open it later when I was alone. With all the goodbyes and sense of loss from closing this chapter in my life, I needed time away to process. That was until my colleague said these words: "My mom asked me to tell you that it's made with real forget-me-nots."

I asked her to repeat herself because I couldn't believe what I heard. As she repeated the message I felt like time had stopped. Those words travelled straight into that deep place within my soul that had been so desperate for God. No one knew what I had thought that day about the forget-me-nots, not even my husband. Only God knew. I thanked the girl and quickly returned to my desk, clasping the gift in my hand. I unwrapped it, revealing a dark blue box with "made with real flowers" embossed in silver on the lid. I slowly opened the box to reveal a small cross on a silver chain. As I lifted the necklace, I could see that inside the cross were real forget-me-not flowers.

I could have burst into tears. I had been so desperate for God's encouragement, for Him to reach into my world and reassure me after so much uncertainty. I knew this was God telling me, "I have not forgotten you." He knows just how to drop something into your life — a simple word someone says, a gift, a card, a sunrise, a forget-me-not — to reach into your heart and remind you that you are loved and He has not forgotten you.

~Zoe Ayrton

90

The Peach Tree

Grow flowers of gratitude in the soil of prayer.
~Terri Guillemets

When I was twenty-two, I volunteered for my church's home fellowship program and left Pennsylvania for a year. I drove across the country to Edwardsville, Illinois with my two enthusiastic roommates, George, a college boy, and Michael, a seminary student. Four of us were supposed to go, but the other girl chickened out.

We pooled our money and rented a small house. We did odd jobs, ran a Friday night fellowship, and made friends. Unfortunately, we didn't make a lot of money. SIU students had apparently snagged all of the coveted jobs at the beginning of summer. The guys and I stretched every penny, but our meals barely fed us. My family didn't approve of my adventure, so there was no way I'd ask them for help.

I poked around the yard one day, wondering if I could grow vegetables. One of my neighbors, Mrs. Norris, leaned over the fence. Her garden was in perfect condition. A daisy bobbed in her silvery bun. She waved a powdered jelly doughnut as she talked.

"You got nothing but weeds and grass, dearie. This here's August. The growing season is almost over. Besides, you don't get enough sun."

I had to agree. Her enormous oaks shaded our small yard, where a few shrubs and a tree struggled to survive. We kept the lawn mowed.

Sometimes, I'd sit outside, writing and trying not to be homesick, missing my large, noisy family.

Powder from the doughnut floated in the air like sugary snow. My stomach rumbled. I hadn't had sweets in ages. I swallowed and leaned against the tree, dislodging a few leaves. A small, hard ball bounced off my foot. I picked it up.

"Hey, isn't this fruit?" It smelled mossy and old, not like a juicy apple or pear.

"Nothing to get excited about." Mrs. Norris chewed the last bite. A bee settled on her daisy. I stifled my giggles. She continued.

"That peach tree's been coming up green for the last ten years, but it never ripens." She nodded her head and the bee zoomed off to bother another flower.

"I imagine crows and squirrels get a bellyache just thinking about it." After a few more discouraging comments, she hobbled back into her house.

I sat down, back against the tree, tempted to have a long cry. Michael and George were wonderful, big brothers who made me laugh even though they didn't share my love of books. None of us really knew how to cook; peanut butter and jelly sandwiches and oatmeal weren't going to keep us full in the winter. Maybe we hadn't been practical, running off for a year of service, but didn't it count that our hearts were in the right place?

I peered up through the leaves, squinting at the faint patch of blue sky.

"God, we need a break. I could also use a chocolate chip cookie and a Big Mac. Maybe this seems stupid to You, but I've got a craving for pie topped with vanilla ice cream." I waited for thunder to roar at my impudence, but only a bird cheeped in the branches. Tossing the shrunken fruit aside, I headed to town. Time to sweep the library floors.

The next week was a turning point.

Michael challenged the owner of the local grocery store to let him work for free. After two days, he was offered a full-time job. George made friends wherever he went, and got a job at the local factory. A happy mistake landed me a job as a waitress.

Me a waitress? I was terrified, but soon learned that a smile went a long way. My tips weren't big, but for the first night in a long time we all had Big Macs and French fries for dinner. After the dishes were done, the guys visited friends.

I went outside and spread a sheet under the tree. A few yards over, kids were playing baseball, calling out the plays in shrill, excited voices. The smell of barbecue drifted on the breeze. I flopped on my stomach and something soft squished under my T-shirt. Sticky wetness seeped over my chest.

"Aw, man!" I cautiously peered under the blanket then, disbelievingly, scooped up a pulpy, squished mess.

"You've got to be kidding me." Juice dripped through my fingers. I licked a drop. Peaches didn't get any sweeter! I stared at the tree. The gnarled trunk didn't seem any different, but several peaches nestled in the branches.

"Peaches! We've got real live peaches!" Whooping like a little kid, I danced around the yard, gathering the fruit in the sheet and almost fighting over the last one with a squirrel. I hurried into the house and washed them. I arranged the eight peaches in a cracked blue bowl and placed it on the kitchen table. They were beautiful, gold and softly blushing, just like at the store.

We had a peach tree.

"God, ain't you something, as my grandma Velma would say." My voice choked up and I wiped away a happy tear. Wait until I told George and Michael. Getting jobs was wonderful, but a peach tree returning to life was amazing. I suddenly knew that this year wasn't going to be a waste.

I'd see God's heart.

Tomorrow, I'd make pie. While it was still warm, I'd take Mrs. Norris a piece. Then, I was going to sit outside and eat a slice of peach pie topped with vanilla ice cream.

~Karla Brown

One of Those Days

I cannot imagine how the clockwork of the universe can exist without a clockmaker.

~Voltaire

It was one of those days when nothing seemed to line up right. I'd woken up late and then rushed out of the house to a doctor's appointment only to spend way too much time in the waiting room. Then, during what I expected to be a routine examination, I was advised that I needed minor surgery. I walked out of the appointment and straight into the beginnings of a January snowstorm. I wondered if anything would go right that day.

Later, at home, more irritations piled up: dinner burned in the oven, the kitchen sink clogged, and the cat coughed up a hairball the size of a small gerbil. No way was I going to that book discussion at the library. Instead, I decided to surrender to the bad karma of the day.

"I'm taking a long, hot bubble bath and I'm locking the bathroom door," I told my husband. "Do not come knocking."

He nodded knowingly and I escaped behind the door. I ran the water and poured an extra dose of my favorite orange-scented bubble bath into the tub. I submerged myself and closed my eyes. Then the phone rang.

"Uh, Monica. Please call me back right away. Your brother passed out at the bowling alley and someone is taking him to the hospital right now."

My brother Louis had gone bowling with a group of friends that evening. They were preparing to leave the lanes when he passed out cold on the floor and appeared to have stopped breathing. His friends stood around, stunned, until one woman in his group grabbed him and started shaking him until he regained consciousness. Louis appeared alert but woozy, and complained of feeling tired. Since the nearest hospital was only a short distance down the road, another friend drove Louis directly to the emergency room.

I towel-dried my hair and threw on the nearest pair of jeans and sweatshirt I could grab before I ran out the door. I was Louis's next of kin, his only sibling, and I was on my way to him. I'd always been a praying woman, but at that moment words seemed to elude me. All I could think to utter at that moment was a simple phrase, "Lord, please be present in this situation."

A few minutes and a few miles later, I was at my brother's bedside. Pale and solemn-faced, he was hooked up to monitors and IVs. We spoke briefly. Exhausted from the day's events, he dozed and I allowed him to sleep. Every few minutes, though, Louis appeared to have a spasm. When questioned, his nurse told me that meant the external pacemaker attached across his chest was engaging.

My eyes went wide. "External pacemaker?"

Enter the cardiologist with the rest of the details. Louis and his friend had just been seated in the emergency room as the cardiologist was walking through. Suddenly, Louis lost consciousness again, slumped forward from his chair and fell to the ground. Alerted by the thud, the doctor turned and went to my brother's side to assess the situation and begin treatment. Louis was then taken directly into the Intensive Care Unit.

As I understood the cardiologist's explanation, my brother's heart was no longer responding to his body's electrical impulse to beat on a regular basis. Treatment, in the doctor's terms, was simple: implant a pacemaker and all would be well. A routine procedure, he assured.

I, on the other hand, wasn't so certain. Any type of cardiac surgery, no matter how routine, frightened me. "Are you sure my brother needs a pacemaker?" I asked.

"You know," he began, "if your brother had come into the ER and explained the details of what happened tonight, we might have started with neurological testing, or written the episode off as fatigue due to a recent virus he had. But, your brother collapsed right in front of me. As a cardiologist, I could see what he was experiencing right away."

I nodded.

"It's funny," the doctor added as he turned to leave, "I usually never walk through the emergency room waiting area, but tonight I brought some paperwork down to the ER receptionist as a favor to another doctor."

I sat at my brother's side as he continued to doze. In those stolen moments of peace, I examined my thoughts from earlier that day. Just that afternoon, I had wondered whether anything would go right that day. Now, in some odd way, it seemed as though everything had gone right. Then and there I started to play a game of "what if." What if my brother had not gone bowling that night and instead collapsed at home, alone? What if his friend had not shaken him awake at the lanes? What if he had not just happened to be down the road from one of the best hospitals in the county? What if the cardiologist had not passed through the ER when he did? What if Louis's heart condition had been written off as fainting from fatigue and he had been sent home with nothing more than instructions to rest? What if?

There are many different names for what I sometimes like to call "the powers that be." Call it the work of God, Jesus, Jehovah, Allah, fate, or kismet, but as far as I was concerned some force of divine providence had intervened on my brother's behalf. Now in hindsight, it seems to me my prayer had been answered before it had even been spoken. All the day's happenings, one by one, had built upon each other and led to my brother's quick diagnosis, treatment, and speedy recovery. Even the frustrations of my day had kept me at home where I was able to receive that important phone call in a timely manner. Clearly, the Lord had been present all along.

And the Lord continues to be present because four years later Louis remains happy and healthy. That snowy January night the stars aligned and my forty-four-year-old brother was given what he considers a second chance at life. We both agree there is no greater miracle than that.

~Monica A. Andermann

92

Miracle in the Bushes

Peace is not the absence of affliction, but the presence of God.
~Author Unknown

Lost! Is there a more frightening word to a parent? Our two-year-old daughter, Alanna, was lost. We had gone out to eat in an unfamiliar area and now we couldn't find her, no matter how hard my husband and I looked.

In the midst of my fear, I turned to prayer. "Please, dear Father, help us find our baby."

The words stuck in my heart. "Father, we need thee as we've never needed thee before. Alanna is lost. We can't find her on our own." A sob caught in my throat.

Despite the noise and shouts and cries around me, I felt a measure of peace.

"All is well."

Where had the words come from? The voice was quiet, but, at the same time, unmistakable.

Calm overtook me, and I started from the point where we had last seen Alanna. Once more, words appeared in my mind. "Look down."

I did as instructed and looked down. There, among the bushes flanking the restaurant was Alanna, curled up and fast asleep.

Laughing, crying, I knelt and picked her up, holding her close.

Would I have seen Alanna in the darkness if I hadn't looked down as the voice had directed me? I doubt it.

A miracle? To be sure.

Sometimes, when a voice comes from above, it helps to look down.

~Jane McBride Choate

93

Mysterious Ways

Every happening, great and small, is a parable whereby God speaks to us,
and the art of life is to get the message.
~Malcolm Muggeridge

August is a bad month for restaurants. And as a single mom working as a server, it was hard to make enough to pay my bills. My two children were holding me to the promise that I'd take them to a water park as the park had lowered its prices for a month. All I needed was $105 for three passes and we could all have a great day. Even better, if you bought your passes on Wednesday, you could get them stamped for a free return visit on Thursday.

Try as I did, I just could not come up with the money. I did, however, manage to get the $70 needed for two tickets and was on my way to a friend's house to see if she was going and could take my two as well. I was grouchy with God. I had prayed and prayed, still managed to tithe, and yet He hadn't answered my prayers for the $105 so I could have a fun day with my kids. Just then, I heard a bang and then a swoosh that turned into a flub-flub-flub. Pulling over to the side of the road, I got out to see a very flat right rear tire. "Now what?" I looked up at the sky. "You couldn't even make sure my kids got to the park?"

Soon a truck pulled over and two young men got out. After making fun of my predicament, one of them said, "Hey, we were just on the way to the dump. I got this tire in back that would fit your car."

Things were starting to look up. "How much do you want for it?" I asked cautiously.

"Oh, that thing," he answered. "It's okay... it'll last you a month or two. You can just have it. I won't charge you for the tire."

Before I could thank him and praise God, he added, "But you gotta pay us something for our trouble unless you got somebody else who could change your flat for you."

I didn't. They told me they each wanted twenty dollars to change it. It didn't take long for me to think it over. Ten minutes later, the two young men were happily on their way and I was left with two whining kids and $30, not enough for even one of them to go the water park.

I broke the news to them. My son was so upset that he took off a shoe and threw it into the tall weeds. Searching through the bushes and weeds, I apologized silently to God as I remembered all the many blessings He had bestowed on me already.

"Thank you, God, and I'm so sorry. I know you love us and I'm going to look forward to whatever you have in store for us this day, even if it's not the water park."

It took several minutes of searching through tall weeds but I finally found the shoe and reached down to grab it. Something crinkly came up with it. It was covered with mud, but I could see that it was a hundred-dollar bill. I looked it over carefully. It was real all right. How it ended up in those weeds I'll never know. That section of brush was just outside the reach of the road mower.

With that found money, we had $130, enough to go to the park and enough for refreshments for that day, and the free Thursday. I explained to my kids that evening how badly I had behaved, how I had asked God for this day and then thought He had let me down. It was a wonderful lesson, not just for them but even more so for me.

I believe God was trying to teach us all that miracles still happen today. I've always heard that God works in mysterious ways. This was a perfect example.

~Diana Perry

Chapter 12

Miracles Happen

Count Your Blessings

A Necessary Break

*Miracles happen every day, change your perception of what a miracle is
and you'll see them all around you.*

~Jon Bon Jovi

O n January 27, 2011, a massive nor'easter swept
through the D.C. metro area and blanketed the city
in heavy, wet snow that downed trees, caused power
outages, and closed schools. The ambulatory surgery
center where I worked was also closed; therefore I too was home
with the children. Excitedly, they looked at the glistening white snow
from our fifteenth-floor condo window. "Mama! Can we please go out
sledding today? Please!" they squealed as they jumped on my bed,
rumpling the blankets.

It had been two years since my daughters had experienced any
snow. They had just moved back to the States from the Sunshine
Coast of Australia, where they lived with their father for the past
eighteen months. Our difficult divorce left the children leading an
intercontinental life, spending half their time in the U.S. amongst
the concrete high-rises and congested city life with their overworked,
stressed, single mother, and half in the peaceful, luxurious Australian
bush on a twenty-eight-acre resort property, complete with kanga-
roos, kookaburras, and goannas. There, they attended private country
schools and lived a leisurely slow-paced life with their nurseryman
father.

For a year and a half, I had tried creating a new life for my children in the U.S., but they never adjusted to having a nanny and missed the beauty and simplicity of their idyllic life Down Under. So I made the heart-wrenching decision, à la *Sophie's Choice*, to part from my daughters and send them back to live with their father.

While they were away, I spent my hours writing songs with my electric keyboard in the middle of my sleepless nights; worked at multiple different surgery centers as a contracting anesthesiologist three months at a time; planned and financed a citywide health and wellness conference for women that would be held the next week—anything to fill my time, anything to keep me from thinking about how much I missed them.

Back home for only three weeks when the storm hit D.C., my girls were ecstatic about having a "snow day" and couldn't wait to slide down the great hill on Massachusetts Avenue. Before I had completely parked the car, they were opening the doors, grabbing their sleds and running up the side of the hill. By the time I had reached the foot of the hill my elder daughter, Cedar, and two friends had already taken their first exhilarating sled ride down the icy, fast-paced hill. Nikki, however, was not so adventurous and remained tentative at the top of the hill, the three girls beckoning and calling loudly from below, encouraging her to take off now!

Suddenly, on her little orange saucer, she flew down the hill, holding on for dear life, spinning and zooming, smiling, laughing, and completely unaware of the massive oak tree in her path. I saw it all flash before my eyes—my baby girl about to collide with this immovable tree trunk—and my heart skipped a beat as I instinctively leapt in front of her rocketing sled. I just barely grabbed onto her down jacket, trying to pull her off the sled before the imminent crash. But the force and velocity of her on the sled was too great for me, and I went smashing into that tree with the sled and my little girl.

Thank God my body provided enough of a cushion for her and she bounced onto the snow without injury. But I heard a loud "crack" as we made impact, and felt an excruciating pain in my right ankle. Tears came pouring down my face as I lay on the snow, barely breathing, as pain swept through my battered body. The girls and several bystanders immediately rushed to my aid.

"Mama! Are you alright? You need ice!" my baby cried, as she piled snow on top of my rapidly swelling, throbbing ankle. Through her tears I could see the worry, fear, and guilt on her little cherubic rosy-cheeked face.

As I endured the pain and looked into those sad eyes, I couldn't help but think, "What if I had stayed in the car for one instant longer? What if I hadn't reached the tree in time? What if I had turned away as she raced down the hill? What if I was talking with another worried parent? What if I slipped on the snow before reaching her?" One thousand and one alternate scenarios flooded my brain.

One week later, in a Percocet haze, I was laying face up on my sofa, staring at the living room walls with my right leg elevated, post-surgical ankle fixed with several titanium screws and a fluorescent pink knee-high cast, immobilized, non-weight bearing, and alone. My citywide conference for women had been cancelled. My children had grown up tremendously, learning to cook, clean, do homework, and pawn rides from friend's parents, and become Mama's caretaker.

I, on the other hand, spent hours each day contemplating my life, wondering WHY this had happened to me.

It wasn't enough I'd recently lost both my parents, divorced, moved back and forth between the U.S. and Australia, struggled finding steady employment, went through several nannies who thought my children were challenging, gone into debt, overburdened with medical bills, and had the expenses of raising two children on my own in an extremely high-cost area? Now I had to deal with this!

I was burning the candle at both ends. I wasn't sleeping and nearly running on empty. Somehow, He knew this. I had plenty of warning signs and indications that I needed to slow down, take a breather, regroup and find stability again; but still I carried on. It took divine intervention to literally stop me in my tracks, and save not only my daughter's life, but mine too.

In my months of disability that followed, I finally had the time to find me again, to absorb and process the events of the past several years, to take the time to grieve and feel my losses, and at last to create a plan for me, and for my girls' future. Frightening and overwhelming as it seemed, I was thankful for this "break," and no longer felt alone.

I wrote a song, which will appear on my next album, and talks about how thankful I am that God intervened and gave me the "necessary break" that allowed me to reorient my life and find the right path for myself and my girls.

THANKFUL

When I was younger I always thought there had to be
    something in it for me
Some kind of reward that I could hold to prove my worth to
    all the world.
It's taken this long for me to believe in something I cannot
    touch or see
But now that I know, there's no other way for me to make it
    through each day.

CHORUS
And so I'm THANKFUL that you've shown me
That Your love can be the answer to my mystery if I'd just let
    it be.
And I'm THANKFUL for this moment 'cause
Livin' in the present when You're here with me is all that I
    need.

I'm listening hard to all that You're tryin to say to me in so
    many different ways
It's not always clear, and thoughts in my head often confuse
    the words You've said.
I analyze and try to make sense of everything but all I really
    need to do

Is take time to breathe, accept how I feel and know that this
feeling comes from You.

Repeat CHORUS

It's not so easy to hear Your voice when I close the door
And think that my way's the only choice
Then I realize that You have a plan
And I begin to understand

I can't analyze and try to make sense of everything
'Cause all I really need to do
Is take time to breathe, accept how I feel
And know that this feeling comes from You.

Repeat CHORUS last time.

©2011 Shari Hall

~Dr. Shari Hall

95

Not Before She Graduates

He performs wonders that cannot be fathomed,
miracles that cannot be counted.
~Job 9:10

In thirty years of practicing medicine, no patient affected me like Doris Baxter. Through Doris, I witnessed God's grace and power—and a bona fide miracle.

Doris, a pleasant forty-seven-year-old librarian, took great pleasure in mothering her bubbly, fifteen-year-old daughter, Julie. Since Doris and her husband had waited years to conceive Julie, they savored every moment with their daughter. At her annual check-ups, Doris displayed photos of Julie singing in the church choir, or kicking the winning soccer goal, or decorating a lopsided birthday cake she had baked for her father. In fact, Doris was more interested in talking about her daughter than complaining about a creaky knee or ten-pound weight gain like so many women her age.

One year, however, Doris complained of severe fatigue, nosebleeds, easy bruising, and chronic sinus infections. A battery of tests confirmed my suspicion: acute leukemia. The leukemia cells, called blasts, had crowded out the healthy cells in her bone marrow, causing bleeding, anemia, and fatigue.

I referred her to a top oncologist and she began the first of five cycles of chemotherapy. Hair loss, nausea, worsening fatigue, and frequent blood transfusions became Doris's constant nemesis.

Because of Julie, Doris was desperate to live. So desperate, she probably would have snuck into Mexico in the bottom of an avocado truck to obtain illegal Laetrile, if she'd thought it would cure her leukemia. She and Julie did everything together—Girl Scouts, shopping, cooking, and you-name-it. Thus, they had never suffered the "you've-ruined-my-life, I-hate-you, Mom," drama that so many teenaged girls and mothers weather on the rocky path to adulthood. Leaving Julie to fend for herself during her tumultuous teen years was unthinkable.

One day, after a rough cycle of chemotherapy, Doris gripped my hand and pleaded, "Please pray for me—that this chemotherapy works, and God allows me to see Julie graduate from high school. I don't need to grow old; I just don't want to abandon Julie when she's still in high school. Is three years too much to ask?"

Tears filled my eyes. As a mother of two children myself, I could only imagine her drive to usher her daughter into adulthood. What if my little girl had to face life with no mommy? With a hand on Doris's shoulder, I promised, "I will pray for you every day, and I'll get my weekly prayer group to pray also."

The creases in her face relaxed. "Thank you," she whispered, squeezing my hand. "All we can do is pray. The rest is in God's hands."

We thought our prayers were answered when the blasts disappeared and her blood counts normalized. She was responding to the chemotherapy! But after her fifth cycle, the blasts returned and her blood counts plummeted; her leukemia had grown resistant to the chemotherapy.

"We'll try a different drug," her oncologist said. But it, too, proved a failure. Doris then agreed to an experimental drug in a leukemia drug trial, but it caused a rash and painful mouth sores. Worse yet, it didn't work either. Unfortunately, no one in her family was a match for a bone marrow transplant. Doris was out of luck.

With leukemia hogging her bone marrow, she required blood and platelet transfusions almost daily. But then she developed antibodies to the transfused platelets, thus destroying them within hours.

Her prognosis looked bleak. But Doris had unwavering faith. She, along with her family, church, friends, and doctors prayed for a miracle. Her one persistent prayer? "Let me see Julie graduate from high school."

Infections and nosebleeds necessitating trips to the hospital now plagued her. One night, disaster struck: she hemorrhaged into her lungs and brain. Paramedics rushed her to the ER. She was already comatose and required a ventilator to breathe for her. Things looked so hopeless the hematologist called in her family to say their final goodbyes. "She won't survive the night," he told them sadly and advised a "Do Not Resuscitate" order.

Later that night, I came by her room wishing, praying, there was something I could do. I pored over her medical record and shook my head. I placed a hand on Doris's shoulder and offered up a heartfelt plea. "God, I pray for a miracle. Doris just wants to see her daughter finish high school. If it is your will, please grant her that." I exited her room suspecting this would be the last time I'd see her this side of heaven. My eyes pooled, as I'd grown fond of Doris and her family. Her family needed her, and she was such a nice lady.

Amazingly, Doris survived the night, and over the next few days, with no treatment whatsoever, her blood counts unexplainably improved. Soon, the blasts were gone. Then, her breathing improved enough to come off the ventilator. What was going on? Everyone's unspoken fear was that she would still remain in a coma and have brain damage.

Several days later, Doris bolted up singing along to the praise music playing in the background! She moved all four extremities, swallowed water, talked, walked, and acted normal. We doctors scratched out heads. How could she have sustained such a massive bleed into her brain and come out unscathed? And why had the blasts just disappeared? It made no sense.

It made no sense until Doris shared her near death experience. Doris told me that while she was comatose Jesus appeared to her in a translucent white robe and told her He had heard her prayers and would heal her long enough to see her daughter graduate from high school. I stared at Doris in disbelief, barely able to breathe. God had granted her a miracle!

Just as promised, for the next three years, Doris suffered no serious infections or bleeds, and her blood remained leukemia-free. She cheered for Julie at soccer games, helped her select a luscious fuchsia prom dress, and snapped countless pictures of Julie in her graduation cap and gown. Julie headed off to college to begin a four-year nursing program.

Unfortunately, within three months of Julie starting college, the leukemia returned with a vengeance, and this time nothing stopped it. Doris died of an overwhelming infection shortly after receiving a bone marrow transplant from an anonymous donor.

Why didn't God heal Doris permanently? Was it because we had only prayed for her to live long enough to see her daughter graduate?

Julie, not surprisingly, became an oncology nurse. While sad about her mother's early death, she still marvels that God allowed her mother to survive a massive brain and lung hemorrhage so Julie could have her mother around another three years. Julie carries pictures in her wallet of her mother styling her hair for the homecoming dance, and standing in front of Old Faithful, and riding a mule to the bottom of the Grand Canyon.

"She was here on borrowed time," Julie told me. "Those extra years with Mom mean everything to me because they were a gift from God. I know where Mom is, and someday I'll be with her again."

~Sally Willard Burbank

96

A New Life

If you don't know what's meant by God, watch a forsythia branch
or a lettuce leaf sprout.
~Martin H. Fischer

Fifty years old! Other women dread turning fifty, but I was joyful. I wanted to sing and dance and celebrate life. Fifty was my age, but I was really celebrating thirteen years of actual living. The doctor had said, "You have cancer," on my thirty-seventh birthday. I looked at Rick, my husband, who looked frightened. I reached out and took his hand. The doctor told us I had a grapefruit-size tumor. The doctor's assistant scheduled appointments for me to see a radiation oncologist and chemo oncologist.

The doctor advised me to quit work. The store I managed was also a redemption center. It was dirty and involved physical labor. He said I couldn't be in that environment since I would have a weakened immune system. I didn't like this particular job, but when I accepted it we still had two teenaged children to support and the money was good. I was a workaholic. What was I going to do if I wasn't working? I couldn't just sit and do nothing. Little did I know this illness would eventually teach me to sit and relax.

Both oncologists told me the type of cancer I had was "unusual for someone as young as you, and a cancer we don't know much about." The prognosis wasn't positive, but positives did result from the cancer.

One positive was realizing just how much Rick loved me. Prior to surgery, the doctor made me an appointment with a colostomy specialist. I didn't want a bag hanging from my side. The thought of it upset me more than having cancer, treatment and surgery. Rick took my shoulders, looked directly into my eyes and said, "I don't care if you have a colostomy. I don't care about any scars you may have. I just want you with me."

Another positive result is harder to explain. It was a rebirth. I had always been a perfectionist who had to control every aspect of my life. I was a take-charge, independent person. I never asked anyone for help nor did I expect help from anyone. I constantly worried, since no one can actually control everything. I was working, married and plugging along with day-to-day life. I was going through the motions more than actually living, but I didn't realize it. I felt like I was constantly searching, but didn't know what I was looking for.

Rick planted flower seeds in a window box so I could see it from the couch. Neither of us had taken time to plant flowers before. After I saw green sprouts grow through the brown dirt, I began going outside every day to check their growth.

One sunny day I was home alone. I opened the front door, stepped out and stopped in my tracks. Beside our driveway stood a towering, full green tree. It looked so beautiful, I said, "Wow!" We had lived in this house five years, but I had been too busy, too preoccupied, to see this tree. It was exciting and fresh.

We began buying peanuts for a blue jay that appeared at our house. Perhaps he was always nearby, I just hadn't noticed. Life became joy! Mentally and emotionally, I felt at peace and ready to face whatever came my way. I didn't want to leave Rick but accepted the fact earthly death could be soon. Daily, I thanked God for opening my eyes to see and for opening my heart to feel pure joy. Feeling this new joy made my life complete. I no longer searched. All burdens were lifted from my soul. I had received a treasure, love and joy, which made life peaceful and beautiful.

I became weak. My weight dropped from 125 pounds to 99 pounds. As I lay on the couch too weak to move, I prayed to God, "Your will be done." Sometimes I would add, "If it be your will, please just let me live to our tenth wedding anniversary." It was eight months away.

It was difficult at times, but I made the best of the situation. I talked to the nurses and doctors in the oncologists' offices as if making new friends. Due to the newfound joy inside me, I tried to have a smile for everyone. This baffled the nurses and doctors. I heard comments such as "You are always smiling." It was said more like a question than a statement.

Prior to surgery, the doctor told Rick and my sister it would take about four hours. They became worried when four hours turned into five hours and then six hours. We discovered later the surgery took longer because the cancer had spread to the corner of my liver and lymph nodes of the liver and stomach.

The prognosis wasn't good even after the chemo, radiation and surgery (no colostomy needed). The doctors all believed the cancer would reappear within a year, but it only took a short time.

Three weeks after surgery, I had a complication and was readmitted to the hospital. During this stay, a CAT scan showed four new metastases on the liver. The doctor wrote in his report, "Outlook for extended survival is not great in view of the progressive liver disease."

Rick took me down south to see all our family members. We stopped to see sights along the way, and I held onto his arm to walk. The six weeks of traveling were full of love and laughter, but we both knew this might be our last adventure together.

Then, with no treatments or medications, the liver disease disappeared. It no longer showed on any tests. One of the oncologists began calling me "a walking miracle."

Yes, I am fifty years old, and we celebrated our twenty-second wedding anniversary last month. I've had thirteen years of experiencing joy now. Despite gray hairs, wrinkles, scars and some flab, life is beautiful! I no longer simply live, no longer search, but see the beauty all around me.

~Sara Schafer

Check Is in the Mail

You can tell the size of your God by looking at the size of your worry list.
The longer your list, the smaller your God.
~Author Unknown

The columns didn't balance, so I ran them again. Same result. I wanted to blame the bank, but I knew the error was mine. No matter how I analyzed the numbers, I didn't have enough money to make it through the rest of the month.

I suppose everyone has had the sinking feeling that swept over me that day. It's a part of financial life to balance the accounts, and find that a simple error in addition or subtraction had left us short. We deal with it, but I was nineteen years old and 6,000 miles from home in a foreign country with an overdrawn budget, a missionary companion with his own financial struggles, rent due and an unsympathetic landlord.

Six months earlier I had worked as a "hoddy," tending the needs of a handful of brick masons in the hot August sun. The work was hard, but the pay would help me sock away some extra money before leaving on a church mission. At the moment, that hard work and August sun seemed pretty enticing.

The opportunity to donate two years in the service of the Lord was both an honor and a challenge. The mission was voluntary and self-funded with help from my family, if necessary. Since my father was a schoolteacher nine months out of the year and a driving instructor during the summer, we had always had sufficient funds for our needs but not enough for surprises. It would be no different during my missionary experience. Faith was certainly going to be an ongoing part of my service in faraway Germany.

My companion and I shared expenses and we were both out of money. We put the matter to prayer, seeking divine intervention without a clue as to how the Lord would help us resolve our problem. We retired for the evening, with faith in our hearts and zeros in our bankbooks.

This was pre-Internet, pre-Skype, back in the 1970s. Our only communication was the postal system. A letter took eight to ten days from Munich to home and the same in return. So as I mailed my letter home asking for $60, I knew it was a futile effort, since I needed the rent money the very next day.

That night, we tried to avoid the building manager, who would insist on receiving the rent on time. He wasn't a bad sort—he was just doing the job he was paid to do. As we crept past his apartment, his door opened.

"Sie haben eilpost," he said without emotion. That means, "You have express mail." I took the envelope from his outstretched hand. Then he reminded us that the rent was due.

We went inside and I used a butter knife to open the priority mail envelope. Unfolding a single sheet letter within, a check for $60 fell out. My father's letter was three words long. "You need this."

It is difficult to express the thoughts that rushed through my mind. For that check, in the exact amount needed, to have arrived within twenty-four hours of our mailed request, my father would have to have known our specific need and mailed the funds almost two weeks before we even knew we had a problem.

Many months later I expressed my gratitude as I related this experience to my father. He told me he arose one morning and knew that I needed $60. Without knowing why, he rushed to the post office and mailed the check, by express mail. Many people would write such things off as coincidence, but I recognized then and have often since, that miracles happen.

~Edwin F. Smith

The Real Superman

God is faithful...
~1 Corinthians 1:9

I was sipping my morning coffee when the front door opened and my husband, James, walked in. I had sent him off to work an hour earlier and didn't expect him until lunchtime.

"Chris, get dressed," he said. "We have to go see Bradley."

He continued as I dressed. "I got a call saying there was an explosion at work and all I know is that his eyes were injured."

"No, no, no... please no, God! His eyes? Oh nooo..." I began to cry. "What other injuries?"

"That's all I know. It will take a couple of hours. Are you ready?" We walked toward the door. Just as one would reach for a lifeline, I instinctively reached for my Bible.

James drove in silence. I began to picture my son lying in a hospital bed, blinded... burned... internal injuries.... Stop! Desperately, I searched my memory for verses I could speak to calm myself. "I will not leave you or forsake you." "I will not give you more than you can bear." As I called one after another to mind, it didn't matter that I didn't know the scriptures word for word or even where they could be found. I spoke them aloud, interspersed with partial prayers for mercy and comfort.

"Please, God, comfort my son. Do not let him be afraid. Let him feel Your presence." I continued to sob even as I prayed. James remained silent. We each had to handle this in our own way.

"If it be in your divine will, God, I ask you to heal my son's eyes. Let him see." I could not imagine my son not being able to see, to work, to support his family.

"Whatever happens, God… I ask You to give us peace, comfort and strength."

I reached for my Bible. My hands shook, my body trembled, and my heart raced. I opened it and a slip of blue paper fell out. My four-year-old granddaughter had colored a picture on one side. On the opposite side was a scripture reference written by her Sunday school teacher along with the words, "I can talk to God." I quickly found the scripture in my Bible and read it and those that followed. Amazing! God was telling me that he hears my prayers.

A peace came over me. The panic and fear, the trembling and accelerated heartbeat all faded. God had given me assurance through a child's long-forgotten lesson stuck within the pages of His Word!

As James and I drew closer to the hospital we received a phone call telling us that our son had been released! We took a detour and headed to his home instead. He was on his couch propped up with pillows.

Wanting badly to embrace my son, I examined him for visible injuries. His face was burned, but not as badly as I had pictured. His hair was singed and he had no eyebrows. Both eyes were bandaged as well. Besides a problem hearing in one ear, he seemed to have no other injuries. I breathed a grateful sigh of relief. "Thank You, God!"

"Can you tell us what happened?" his dad asked.

Bradley is an electrician. When the accident occurred he and a co-worker were inside a large walk-in closet.

Bradley explained. "The foreman arrived and checked first to make sure all power was off using his voltage meter. Then I checked, using my own voltage meter. My co-worker did the same. We always follow this procedure before work begins. A red flag is then placed to notify other workers that voltage must remain off. We all pronounced 'all clear' and began work." He spoke as though he were examining each detail for a flaw, something left undone.

"My co-worker stepped outside the closet to get a tool as I began to pull new wire into the closet. I needed to cut a couple of inches off a conduit pipe. The pipe hit the high voltage buss bar, which would have been no problem had the power actually been off. Someone had removed the red tag and turned power back on without clearing it with the work crew first. The pipe exploded in my hand and became red-hot flying shrapnel. My full body was facing the explosion." He gave a slight shudder as he relived that moment.

"I saw a bright light and one minute I was standing there, the next I was face down on the floor about six feet back. I remember everything on me hurting. Then I remember trying to get up, trying to open my eyes and being extremely frustrated that I could do neither." Bradley's voice now held a sense of urgency.

"Alarms and sirens were blaring. I smelled singed hair and thick smoke. I heard voices but they seemed off in a distance and distorted... except for one." Brad's voice softened when he shared what he remembered next.

"Another co-worker and good friend had come running and knelt beside me. 'Just stay down. Stay down, buddy. You'll be okay. Take it easy.' He kept speaking to me calmly. 'Just stay there. Help's coming, buddy. You're okay. Help's coming.' I listened and stilled.

"Then the paramedics came and put me onto a gurney and loaded me into an ambulance. I should have been scared witless by now but wasn't. I felt frustration," Brad recalled. "I wanted to open my eyes but couldn't.

"Doctor said my eyelids were melted shut. It hurt like heck when he peeled them apart and applied drops. That numbed the pain, then the drops felt cool and wonderful in my eyes. All I could see was super bright light. Then he closed my eyes, slathered them with a medicated ointment, and applied bandages." Bradley stopped here and we thought he had shared all he wanted. We waited.

He reached blindly for his wife's hand and found it, turned to his other side and found his sister's before he finished. "Next I heard my sister's voice beside me. Then I heard my wife. No one can imagine how comforting a familiar voice can be."

Brad was off for a month then returned to work. At work they call him Superman. He is quick to tell them, "There is only one real Superman and without Him I wouldn't be here!"

Though his eyesight returned, he had to use eye drops daily and wear sunglasses even on cloudy days when outdoors. He still has a slight hearing loss in one ear and also has to deal with frequent, chronic headaches. "I've only complained once and Dad set me straight." He laughs. "Dad says, 'Brad, you are here... you're playing golf!'"

The closet where Bradley had worked had shrapnel embedded in all four walls. On one wall shrapnel outlined Bradley's silhouette. Holes randomly formed where the shrapnel had blown through the wall. Bradley's Superman cap had blown off his head.

Not one piece, not even a small piece of shrapnel embedded in my son or his cap! Though his clothing had scattered burn holes, all his burns were superficial and he had no internal injuries! We've seen pictures of victims in similar electrical explosions and are simply amazed. Only divine intervention can explain Bradley's miraculous protection!

~Christine M. Smith

My Mother's Ring

The deepest wishes of the heart find expression in secret prayer.
~George E. Rees

N o, it couldn't be! But it was—my mother's ring! My head was reeling, my thoughts jumbled. The familiar gold ring glistened and gleamed in my palm, but how? I had lost it two and a half years ago and 1,500 miles away.

My mum had given me the ring in August 2006. After twenty years watching my children grow in Jamaica she had moved back to her "home," so my son and I had visited her in England. We spent a fabulous three weeks together. At the end of our visit, Mum took the ring off her finger and gave it to me saying it was to remember her by.

I wasn't surprised by the gesture; my mum loved rings. Her elegant fingers were usually adorned with some jeweler's delight of gold and precious stones. On my eldest daughter's twenty-first birthday, my mother gave my daughter her favorite ring, a custom-made emerald and diamond creation. My second daughter was not disappointed either; she received mum's broad gold and silver Greek filigree designer piece on her twenty-first birthday. So I accepted the band that had decorated mum's finger for the past twenty years. Twelve small diamonds set in two rows of six across, a thin vertical gold bar separating each set of two. I placed it above my own wedding ring; they looked good together. I would cherish it as much as I cherished our relationship.

Four years later, November 2010, I was visiting my favorite aunt in New Jersey. It was a crisp fall evening. As the family drove to dinner, I rubbed hand lotion on my cold, shriveled fingers and noticed my mum's ring had slipped off. We searched the car—no ring. Maybe it had fallen off in the house. We searched the bedroom, the bathroom, the kitchen, high and low—no ring. I was really upset. Mom and I spoke every day and I looked at the ring often. Hadn't it had just been on my finger?

May 5, 2011, my mum passed away. Now I really noticed the space on my finger where her ring had been for such a short time. I had been privileged to spend the last eight weeks of mum's life with her, but hadn't stayed in England for her funeral. I wanted the comfort of my husband and children, so I made the sad journey back to Jamaica alone and we watched the funeral service via satellite.

Two and a half years after Mum's passing, I was sitting on the verandah of our beach house in Silver Sands. We had so many fond memories here: Mum making coffee at the crack of dawn and setting her towel on the nearest beach chair, claiming the cabana as our own. Mum making sand castles with my kids. All of us going for walks to collect shells. Mum hiding Easter eggs in the garden, hoping the kids would find them before the ants did. This was where mum was happiest and where she wanted her ashes sprinkled.

I needed to make an effort for my family to have closure. It was difficult to get everyone together these days. My oldest daughter was married and my second daughter didn't live at home anymore. But we had a big family reunion at Silver Sands that week, so both girls had planned their vacation to be here. My son had just started a new job, but it was his twenty-first birthday and a holiday weekend, so he planned to come after work to reunite with our overseas family for a few days too. I had an important church function, so would leave the reunion to drive into Kingston for the event and then return to Silver Sands. We would eventually have precious family time together.

But as I sat on the verandah watching my friend and her daughter enjoying an early morning swim, I cried. I knew I still wasn't ready to let Mum go. Nope, I wasn't ready to sprinkle her ashes yet. Her ashes sat in my cupboard at home in a beautiful wooden box. Her name, Marie Marchand, was engraved on a brass plaque on the top. Saturday evening came and I drove to Kingston. I saw my son for his birthday in the morning before he drove to Silver Sands to be with his dad and sisters for birthday cake. That evening I looked at Mum's box, but quickly closed my cupboard. Maybe next year at Easter. We always spend Easter together at Silver Sands, maybe then.

I got up early Monday morning, eager get back to Silver Sands, back to my family and my vacation. As I walked through the kitchen to water the orchids before I left home, I bent down to pick up something sparkly from the ground.

No it couldn't be! But it was—my mother's ring. My head was reeling, my thoughts jumbled, I had lost it two and a half years ago and 1,500 miles away.

It hadn't been on the floor when I was ironing my church dress the day before. I had been standing right here, I would have seen it—but here it was—my mother's ring, the familiar circle glistening and gleaming in my hand. My heart was pounding, my stomach was queasy, I counted them: twelve small diamonds set in two rows of six across, a thin vertical gold bar separating each set of two. I slipped my wedding band off and put my mother's ring on below it.

Explain it? God is good. He knows the desires of our heart. He is rich in grace and mercy. Other than that, I can't explain it. So if you find yourself in Silver Sands, Jamaica on Easter 2014, come down the beach at the crack of dawn and meet my family as we sprinkle Mum's ashes and say our final farewell, and I will show you my mother's ring.

~Nandi Stewart

Divine Connection

The telephone rang as my family wearily stumbled into our home after a five-hour drive from my grandmother's house. I still remember my disbelief, four days earlier, when my parents told me she was dying. We left Winston-Salem, North Carolina where my father was finishing his residency at Wake Forest Medical School to travel to my grandmother's house. After staying for four days, she seemed to rally. Since she seemed better and my father needed to get back to the hospital, we went home.

My grandmother had been in a wheelchair for as long as I could remember, but I never thought of her as ill. Instead I remembered her as someone who always had a big laugh, stories and rhymes that would have us glued to the edge of our seats, and someone who always had ice pops, homemade from Kool-Aid, waiting for us. She had a mischievous grin and the smell of gardenias permeated the air around her house.

I now know, however, that she was sick and had been for a long time. She had an autoimmune disease that affected her arteries and caused her to lose the use of both legs and one arm. Even so, she would play tag with us as we darted around her wheelchair and she reached out to touch us. Now as an adult, I believe she did not seem sick because I, along with my siblings, had spent our childhood in

West Africa where our parents helped run a hospital. We were accustomed to seeing people impaired by both war and disease. However, during this last visit I studied my paternal grandmother's pale face as she lay in her bed and I knew that my beloved Ma was indeed dying.

My father answered the phone as my older brother lifted the last piece of luggage from the trunk. A woman on the other end said, "I have the person on the line that you have been trying to reach." My father was totally confused. The person he was trying to reach? He had been driving for five hours, and this was long before cell phones. What was she talking about? He was just about to hang up when he heard his sister's voice.

"Oh! Keith!" she said urgently. "I am so glad you called! Ma has taken a turn for the worse and she is not expected to make it through the night; you need to hurry back as fast as you can." My father did not take the time to tell her that he had not called; the phone had just rung at our house. My parents hustled the luggage and us four tired children back into the car and rushed back to South Carolina.

We arrived back at my grandmother's house in time for my father and his sister to sit together holding their mother's hands and talk to her one last time. Loving memories were shared and precious goodbyes said. Goodbyes that would not have been possible if the phone had not rung at our house with the strange message that connected my father to his sister. But who made the phone ring and who was the other woman on the line?

What happened that day? The phone rang simultaneously at both our house and my aunt's house. When my aunt answered her phone, her brother—my father—was on the line. My aunt had not attempted to call my father, knowing that it would take at least five hours for us to get home. My father had left South Carolina thinking his mother was doing much better, but someone, somewhere knew differently. Someone, an angel perhaps, knew he needed to speak to his sister to learn about his mother's sudden decline. And if he wanted to say goodbye to his mother, he would need to immediately drive back to her bedside.

My family went back to Africa for many more years. And as life progressed with its times of troubles and times of triumph, I am certain my father thought of the night the angel called. Called to allow him to say goodbye to the mother he loved.

~Alisa Edwards Smith

Heaven Can Wait

The feeling remains that God is on the journey, too.
~Teresa of Avila

I am a forty-six-year-old mom with young kids. Due to my family history, I proactively got annual mammograms. My mammogram results in January of 2013 showed I was healthy, with no abnormalities. However, there was a voice inside me that was unsettled, telling me to look closer.

I went to see my doctor and he reassuringly said, "Sit back, let me take a look." Then I heard him say, "What's this?"

A mere three weeks after my original mammogram, six tumors were found between my two breasts by ultrasound and MRI. The mammogram did not show a single tumor because I happen to have dense breast tissue. Yes, I was scared. But also enraged to learn that, in women with dense breast tissue, a mammogram will miss 40 percent of potentially cancerous growths. Within two weeks, I underwent a double mastectomy where it was found that the cancer had in fact spread to my lymph nodes. Chemotherapy treatments were to follow along with the sad reality of hair loss, mouth sores and severe bone pain.

Even when I felt my worst, I always felt in God's favor. I felt that my toil was His toil. I believe that God shows himself to us every single day of our lives. He speaks through friends and family, nature, strangers and mysteries unexplained. There is just one secret—you must be open to hear and see His messages, truly open in your heart of hearts.

I have always had a strong faith but I experienced astonishing events that felt like a frying pan to the head, with the message: "I am here. You are not alone."

During chemotherapy and feeling my worst, I would force myself to walk to the corner of my street. One day, I found a little hummingbird on the sidewalk. She was very small and the same color as the pavement—I could have easily missed her. But she just lay there, looking up at me. We named her Lucky. She never left my side or flew away—even outside in the yard. When I kissed her, she would stick her beak up my nose. When she flew around the kitchen, she always landed right on my shoulder. I would wake up a couple times a night to feed her the sugar water she loved. One night, I woke up worrying about her. I went over to her and noticed she looked terrible. I held her in my hand as she looked up at me and then she just fell on her side. She died there in my hand. I believe that Lucky was sent to me from Heaven to help me through the worst and to remind me that I am never, ever alone.

In the weeks after my diagnosis I prayed to the Catholic saint Padre Pio, as he was a beloved saint of my mother whom I had lost to breast cancer when I was young. The day after my mastectomy, I asked the nurse to send the hospital's priest to my room so that we could pray. When the priest arrived, he introduced himself, looked at me and said, "Padre Pio." Then he said, "I don't know why I just said that." I told him that I had been praying to Padre Pio and he told me, "This is an external message that your prayers have been heard."

I had another little miracle during chemotherapy. I was scheduled to get what little hair I had left shaved off. I woke that morning feeling low. I took a couple of photos for posterity and was shocked to see that the hair on the back of my head had fallen out in the shape of a heart—truly.

My journey inspired me to create a necklace bearing the words "Heaven Can Wait" because of the many magical blessings that had been bestowed upon me while ill. For me, the loveliest part of my necklace is that the first chord it hits is humor, which is so meaning-ful because there is joy in humor, and my story is about the journey of survival. Beyond my necklace, I will work diligently to raise aware-ness on the limitations of mammograms for women with dense breast tissue. A portion of all sales will go to this effort.

~Christine Miller

Miracles Happen

Meet Our Contributors
Meet Our Authors
Thank You
About Chicken Soup for the Soul

Meet Our Contributors

DeVonna R. Allison is a freelance writer/speaker who has published work in various Christian periodicals and educational materials. Though her children are all grown, she and her husband, Earl, still live in their dream house in the country. E-mail her at devonna. allison@gmail.com.

Teresa Ambord is a full-time business writer/editor, working from her home in far Northern California. When she's not writing about business she enjoys writing about her family, her friends, and her faith. She also loves raising her posse of small dogs who inspire her writing and decorate her life.

Monica A. Andermann lives on Long Island where she shares a home with her husband Bill and their most recent addition, a kitten named Samson. Her work has been included in such publications as *The Secret Place*, *Sasee*, *His Mysterious Ways*, and *Woman's World*, as well as many titles in the Chicken Soup for the Soul series.

Gloria Ashby is a writer, speaker, and funny lady. She publishes her weekly blog "Glimpses of God," and writes inspirational stories about God encounters. Living in Texas with husband Jim, Gloria enjoys reading and digging in her butterfly garden. E-mail her at GA@ GloriaAshby.com and read her blog at www.gloriaashby.com.

Zoe Ayrton is a fellow journeyer in life. She lives to inspire others to enjoy a transforming connection with God. After thirty years in England, Zoe now lives in northern Canada where she enjoys negotiating life as a wife, mother, shepherd, trainer and musician. E-mail her at simonandzoeayrton@gmail.com.

Karena Delite Bailey received her B.S. degree in Journalism, with honors, from Illinois State University. She is a published writer and speaker, with a background in technology. A believer in miracles, Karena meditates to create inner peace and a closer connection to the divine within us. E-mail her at karenadbailey@gmail.com.

Francine L. Baldwin-Billingslea has been published in over twenty-five anthologies including several in the Chicken Soup for the Soul series, Whispering Angel, Thin Threads, and Silver Boomers books, and many others as well as authoring an inspirational memoir titled, *Through It All and Out On the Other Side.*

Joan McClure Beck is a retired teacher with a master's degree. She has been published in many anthologies, including several in the Chicken Soup for the Soul series. Besides being a writer, she tutors privately, paints in watercolors, delivers Mobile Meals, helps with church mission projects, and volunteers with community charities.

Lisa Benkert shares her story to honor her son, Jordan Mackinder, who she loves and misses so much, as well as to bring awareness to the Gift of Life Program. Her son giving four people a second chance at life brings comfort to her, knowing that he has helped four other families from feeling the pain of losing a loved one.

Long Beach, WA author **Jan Bono's** specialty is humorous personal experience. She has published several such collections, two poetry chapbooks, nine one-act plays, and a dinner theater mystery play. She's written for *Guideposts*, *Star*, and *Woman's World*, and is currently writing a mystery series set on the southwest Washington coast. Learn more at www.JanBonoBooks.com.

Karla Brown lives on the outskirts of Philadelphia and is a flight attendant. She loves gardening, spending time with her family and sports. Her current work-in-progress is a paranormal romantic suspense novel. E-mail her at karlab612@yahoo.com.

John P. Buentello writes essays, short stories, poems and nonfiction. His books include the novel *Reproduction Rights* and the short story collections *Binary Tales* and *The Night Rose of the Mountain*. He is currently at work on a mystery novel and a collection of essays. E-mail him at jakkhakk@yahoo.com.

Sally Willard Burbank is a practicing internist in Nashville. She is the married mother of two college students. She has been published in two other Chicken Soup for the Soul books. She enjoys gardening, cycling, reading, and writing. She has written three novels. Check out her blog of humorous doctor stories: www.patientswewillneverforget. wordpress.com.

Jill Burns lives in the mountains of West Virginia with her family. She is a retired piano teacher and performer. She enjoys writing, music, gardening and nature.

Christianna Capra, Co-Founder, Spring Reins of Life (501c3), which provides EAP services to PTSD veterans, at-risk youth and bereaved children in central New Jersey. CC lives in New York City and has fifteen-plus years in the publicity industry, yet EAP work and horses like Straw are her life's true passion. For information/donations, visit www.springreinsoflife.org.

Margaret Chandler was a legal secretary in Los Angeles for thirty-five years. After moving to a senior retirement community in Arizona, she volunteers her time helping those in need of assistance. She also enjoys exercising, reading and walking with her little Yorkie, Bella.

Jane McBride Choate is the proud mother of five, the even prouder grandmother of four, and the beleaguered staff of a cat who thinks she is of royal lineage.

Peggy A. Cloninger is a wife and mother of two. She lives in both Seldovia, AK and Nampa, ID. She homeschooled her daughters, invented a new art form using animal hides, plays drums at her church, and is writing a cookbook. Peggy thanks C. Ellen Watts for writing her miracle story.

Chrissy Conner is a wife, mother, runner, recruiter, author, and certified life/career coach and is currently working on her first inspirational book series! Chrissy lives in Oklahoma City, OK with her husband and two children. E-mail her at cconner@connerintl. com or follow her on Twitter @Chrissy_Conner.

Linda J. Cooper writes songs, poems and speeches that enable people to creatively deliver tributes at parties and special events. She has been published in *Hilton Head Monthly* magazine and is pleased to be included once again in the Chicken Soup for the Soul series. E-mail her at ljcooper@ix.netcom.com.

Heather Davis is a momma, a writer and drives in the funny lane. She's the author of *TMI Mom: Oversharing My Life* and *TMI Mom: Getting Lucky*. She and her husband have two daughters and live in Bartlesville, OK. She blogs at www.Minivan-Momma.com.

Amy McCoy Dees is a member of the Society of Children's Book Writers and Illustrators. She has written numerous articles for children and educators. She currently holds the District One seat on the Coweta County Board of Education. She enjoys reading and laughing along with her family. E-mail her at adees@hughes.net.

Teresa DeLeon-Cook is a military wife, mother and grandmother. She has spent twenty years in civil service, passionate about her work, her staff and her agency's mission. She is a native Texan, an avid reader, and a tireless traveler. She plans to continue writing. E-mail her at tdeleoncook@gmail.com.

Michele Dellapenta has been writing since childhood. This is her second publication in the Chicken Soup for the Soul series. She credits her sister, Jodi L. Severson, a writer, as her inspiration. Married since 1982 to Lou, Michele lives in Ohio and enjoys reading, writing, scrapbooking and cooking. E-mail her at mdellapenta@earthlink.net.

Lynn Dove calls herself a breast cancer "thriver" rather than "survivor." An award-winning author and writer, she has been married to her best friend, Charles, for thirty-five years and she is the proud mom of three brilliant children and grandmother to two adorable grandbabies. Learn more at http://lynndove.com or on Twitter @LynnIDove.

Annette M. Eckart founded Bridge for Peace with her husband Edward. She brings healing to the nations through Jesus Christ. A dynamic speaker, Annette inspires as she teaches and prays with people worldwide. Visit her website at bridgeforpeace.org.

Logan Eliasen is a theology student who enjoys spending time with his family and friends. A few of his favorite things are acoustic songs, chai tea, and classic books. E-mail him loganrocks@frontiernet.net.

Shawnelle Eliasen and her husband Lonny raise their brood of boys in Illinois. Her stories have been published in *Guideposts*, *MomSense*, *Marriage Partnership*, *Thriving Family*, Cup of Comfort books, numerous Chicken Soup for the Soul books, and more. Visit her blog "Family Grace with My Five Sons" at shawnellewrites.blogspot.com.

Suzie Farthing, RN, has over eighteen years of experience in adult hospital and emergency nursing. In 2006, Suzie founded One Love for Nurses and since then has pursued many activities to encourage other nurses. She hosts the One Love for Nurses podcast (available on iTunes). E-mail her at suzie.onelovefornurses@gmail.com.

Yvonne Fogarty was born with a natural gift of healing and her life's work has been that of an intuitive healer/teacher. She is writing her first book, sharing personal real-life experiences and that of clients she has helped and treated. Now permanently residing in Tasmania, Yvonne is still actively healing.

Jess Forte is a sophomore in college studying creative writing. When she is not sitting at her laptop working on one of her novels or at a meeting for one of the many campus organizations she is involved in, she enjoys spending time with friends. Follow her on Twitter @ authorjessforte.

Jay Fox, born in Bermuda, has been in the music business for many years. Jay began writing stories at St. David's Primary School. He was awarded first in class for his adventure story "The Last Hope." Later, Jay began writing songs and became a recording artist and entertainer. E-mail him at jayfox.fox290@gmail.com.

Carolyn Bennett Fraiser is a freelance writer, teacher and publications specialist for several non-profit organizations in Asheville, NC. In addition to writing, Carolyn enjoys photography, music, cooking, and hiking. Visit her blog at carolynbfraiser.wordpress.com or follow her on Twitter @carolynbfraiser.

Jody Fuller was born and raised in Opelika, AL. He is a comedian, speaker, writer, and soldier with three tours of duty in Iraq. He is also a lifetime stutterer. Jody enjoys Auburn football and spending time with Ruby, his chocolate Labrador Retriever. E-mail him at jody@ jodyfuller.com.

Carmen Goldthwaite, an author, teacher and storyteller, writes about Texas history and sailing, her favorite hobby. She teaches creative writing at SMU. Her book, *Texas Dames: Sassy and Savvy Women Throughout Lone Star History*, was published October 2012 by The History Press. Learn more at www.carmengoldthwaite.com.

Karen Goltz earned her MDiv from Wartburg Theological Seminary in Dubuque, IA, in 2004. She is a homeschooling mom of two children and the owner and editor-in-chief of Quiet Publications. She enjoys reading, writing, and spending quiet moments with her husband.

Debbie Hagan received her MFA degree in creative nonfiction from Goucher College. She is a full-time writer and adjunct writing instructor at New Hampshire Institute of Art, in addition to book reviews editor for *Brevity* literary magazine. Her writing has appeared in *Brain, Child* and elsewhere. E-mail her at debhagan@aol.com.

Dr. Shari Hall, a Yale and Columbia graduate, has worked internationally in Australian Aboriginal communities, underserved pediatric populations of Guatemala, and with wounded warriors at Walter Reed. A Top 40 Adult Contemporary recording artist, a mother, and motivational speaker, she inspires others to live a healthy, passionate life. E-mail her at sharihallinfo@gmail.com.

Gloria Jean Hansen has penned columns and articles for local newspapers and magazines and written books for many years. She is a nurse educator/writer/bluegrass musician and hopes one day to retire to a cabin by the river to write full-time. Contact her at glowin@persona.ca or http://arielgroup.ca/index.php/gloria-hansen.

Charles Earl Harrel pastored for thirty years before stepping aside to pursue writing. He has 465 published works. His stories and devotionals have appeared in thirty anthologies, including *Chicken Soup for the Father & Son Soul* and *Chicken Soup for the Soul: Thanks Dad*. Charles enjoys photography and playing 12-string guitar.

Carol Goodman Heizer, M.Ed., resides in Louisville, KY. She is a six-time published author whose books have sold in the U.S. and overseas. Her work has previously appeared in the Chicken Soup for the Soul series. Her latest book (and accompanying workbook) is *Losing Your Child — Finding Your Way*. E-mail her at cgheizer@twc.com.

Christine Henderson is a Realtor by day and writer by night. Hidden Brook Press and Write Integrity Press have published her life-inspired stories about family in their anthologies. You can also find her writing in *Ruminate Magazine*, *The Secret Place* and *Berry Blue Haiku*.

Margaret Hevel's professional background includes: Professor of Nursing, Nurse Health Educator, Founder and Director of a child abuse prevention program, NARAH-certified to teach equine driving for those with special needs. She coauthored *Parenting with Pets*. Margaret is the mother of four daughters raised in the companionship of animals.

Thomas Ann Hines holds a BS degree in criminal justice; loves "going to prison" to share her experiences with inmates in hopes of helping them understand the never-ending pain of their victims. She also speaks in churches of her journey to forgiveness. E-mail her at tahines@aol.com.

Jeanie Jacobson has enjoyed varied careers—everything from computer programming to educating students about exotic pets. She loves Jesus, and is a joyful wife, mother, and grandma. She loves spending time with family and friends, reading, hiking, horseback riding, and praise dancing. She's currently writing a Christian-fantasy series for young people.

Dr. Karen Jacobson started her private practice in 1992 as a family chiropractor and is currently a success coach and professional speaker. Her passions include Latin ballroom dancing, health, fitness and music. She is a member of the Flying Samaritans, providing services in Mexico. E-mail her at drj@drkarenjacobson.com.

As a member of the International Women's Writing Guild, **Louetta Jensen** has authored four novels and three screenplays. Her novel, *Bittersweet Serenity*, was a winner in the North American Fiction Writer Awards, and also received a Certificate of Merit in the 9th Annual Writer's Digest National Book Awards.

Ms. Jones is retired and lives in Wisconsin. E-mail her at lightworker.9912@yahoo.com.

Janet Sheppard Kelleher is honored to win a 2013 Carrie McCray Literary Award for Nonfiction. She's a newspaper columnist whose collection of Southern stories, *Havin' My Cotton-Pickin' Say*, and her humorous memoir, *Big C, little ta-tas*, about kicking breast cancer's rear end, debut this year. E-mail her at gop53her@gmail.com.

Jean Thompson Kinsey lives in Brooks, KY, near her three adult children. She likes to read, write, travel, and be involved in church. Jean writes inspirational fiction and nonfiction. Her fourth novel was recently released. E-mail her at kystorywriter@yahoo.com.

Vicki Kitchner recently retired after teaching Exceptional Student Education for thirty years. She and her husband divide their time between North Carolina and Florida, unless they're off on an adventure, such as backpacking around Mont Blanc or floating down the Colorado River in a dory. E-mail at her at Vicki@hikersrest.com.

Jennifer Knickerbocker is a mother of four boys. In her spare time, she runs a non-profit educational organization in Spokane, WA. Jennifer is passionate about her family and her children, but that doesn't mean it is easy. "Motherhood is the best hard work."

Sharon Knopic is an artist and author, educated in Pennsylvania as an X-ray technologist. She currently works for the Pennsylvania Bureau of Child Support. Enjoying all kinds of artistic venues, she has taught scrapbooking nationwide as well as publishing other biographical stories. E-mail her at sheerly@hotmail.com.

Sara Lynn Worley Kuntz is an award-winning writer whose credits include children's books, numerous newspaper and magazine articles, and a feature family film. Her stories have appeared in several titles in the Chicken Soup for the Soul series. She teaches writing workshops in the Fort Lewis College Continuing Education program.

Debbie Rouhana Lane, born in Brooklyn, grew up in the late '50s and '60s, a "hippie" some would say. She married at 19 and endured some real tragedy and hardships. She is a mother, grandmother, and business owner whose joy in life revolves around family and caring for those around her. She is a hard worker and runs Testa Wines, a wine importing business in New York.

Colleen Leftheris received her Bachelor of Science degree in Elementary Education with honors in 1997. She has taught third and fifth grades. She has been writing stories and poems since a teenager. She loves children, animals, traveling and writing, but mostly to make learning fun. E-mail her at irishrock17@gmail.com.

Anna Lowther resides in Ohio. She is a wife, mother, editor and writer. Her husband, Eric, is an accomplished author and they hope to start their own publishing house in the near future. Anna's interests are varied and include alternate history, fairy tales, dark fantasy and horror.

Susan Lugli is a Christian speaker and author. Her stories have appeared in several Chicken Soup for the Soul anthologies. She is an advocate for burn survivors and speaks on their behalf. E-mail her at suenrusty@aol.com.

Lisa Mackinder received her Bachelor of Arts degree at Western Michigan University. A freelance writer, she lives in Portage, MI, with her husband and rescue animals. Besides writing, Lisa enjoys photography, traveling, reading, running, hiking, biking, climbing, camping and fishing. E-mail her at mackinder.lisa@yahoo.com.

A graduate of Queen's University, **Gail MacMillan** has had her work published throughout North American and Western Europe. Recently she has signed the contract for her thirtieth book. Gail lives in New Brunswick, Canada with her husband and two dogs. She is the award-winning author of two books and several short stories.

Elaine Olelo Masters has had eighteen books published. Available are *What the Witch Doctor Taught Me* for adults and *The Dragon Who Stole the Holidays* for kids 7-11. This is her second story in the Chicken Soup for the Soul series. Elaine lives in Waikiki, a ten-minute walk from the ocean. E-mail her elaineomasters@gmail.com.

Tina Wagner Mattern is a Portland, OR writer/hairstylist, married to a wonderful man and is mother to two great kids. She has been blessed beyond measure with miracles her whole life. This is her seventh story published in the Chicken Soup for the Soul series. E-mail her at tinamattern@earthlink.net.

Anne Merrigan is a therapist by trade, working in the field of trauma. Her personal experiences on "earth school" motivates her to assist others in discovering their own inner light. Anne enjoys painting, gardening, friends and family. She is currently working on a YA novel. E-mail her at creative13us@yahoo.com.

Christine Miller is healthy and living in California. Her Heaven Can Wait Necklace was inspired by her spiritual journey through breast cancer. If you would like to see a video and photos of Lucky the Hummingbird or the photo of the heart on her head, please visit her website at heavencanwaitnecklace.com.

Sarah Mitchell believes in living life to the fullest. As a mother of three, she divides her passion between her family and writing. Sarah is revising her novel-length manuscript to submit for publication with the hope that when her children are young adults, they'll read it and be proud.

Kacey Morabito-Grean wakes up New York's Hudson Valley weekdays on 100.7 WHUD. Her health and happiness show is on

Sunday mornings and at www.kaceyontheradio.com. Kacey and her husband Mike are living happily ever after with three Pugs, a Beagle and two barn cats in Cold Spring.

Marya Morin is a freelance writer. Her stories and poems have appeared in publications such as *Woman's World* and Hallmark. Marya also penned a weekly humorous column for an online newsletter, and writes custom poetry on request. She lives in the country with her husband. E-mail her at akushla514@hotmail.com.

Linda Newton is an "Empowerment Educator," helping people find healing and strength for a better life. View her blog at www.youtube.com/user/answersfrommomanddad. She has written three books: *Better Than Jewels*, *Sapphires from Psalms*, and *12 Ways to Turn Your Pain Into Praise*. An international speaker, learn more at www.LindaNewtonSpeaks.com.

Linda Nichols is a former 911 dispatcher and full-time mother to Abbie, Alex, and AJ. She owns a small contracting business with her husband, Garren, and is an accomplished professional singer. She enjoys music, traveling, riding motorcycles, and studying all things supernatural and spiritual.

Shirley M. Oakes has been a co-owner, with her daughter, in Family Affair Day Care/Preschool for over fifteen years. She has written several short stories for magazines and has had a children's book titled *No Bed for Mommy* published. Her hobbies include family history, gardening, sewing and painting.

Jeanne Pallos has several stories in the Chicken Soup for the Soul series and is the author of stories for adults and children. She is passionate about writing family stories and preserving the memories of loved ones for future generations. She lives in Laguna Niguel, CA. E-mail her at jlpallos@cox.net.

Diana Perry lives in Columbus, OH and writes for magazines and newspapers as well as writing juvenile books, teen novels, mysteries and action adventures. Currently she is on tour with *The Weather by Heather* and working on her next book, *The Fairyland Pet Show*. Contact her at info@bibliopublishing.com or dianaperryenterprises@yahoo.com.

Pam Phree is a full-time Certified Nursing Assistant but her true passion is writing. The co-author of *Betrayal, Murder and Greed: The True Story of a Bounty Hunter and a Bail Bond Agent*, she lives in Puyallup, WA and is currently working on a novel about heaven and the afterlife.

Delena Richeson is a Licensed Professional Counselor holding an MS degree from Lee University. She enjoys travelling with family and friends. Her passion is writing about her life challenges to help others. Her first novel will be released later this year. To discover more, visit http://nolongerwounded.wordpress.com or www.facebook.com/wounded.minister.

Jeannette Richter lives on a farm on the short-grass prairie of Alberta with her husband John. She is currently working on a novel about the loss of language rights and confessional schools in Manitoba after the Riel Uprising of 1870.

Sallie A. Rodman has written for numerous Chicken Soup for the Soul anthologies. She received her Certificate in Professional Writing at California State University, Long Beach. Sallie believes heaven is all around us if we just stop and listen. E-mail her at sa.rodman@verizon.net.

Tammy Ruggles is a legally blind freelance writer, finger painter, and photographer based in Kentucky. Faith, family, and friends are important to her. She also writes screenplays and poetry, and welcomes e-mail at tammyruggles@yahoo.com.

Theresa Sanders loves writing for the Chicken Soup for the Soul series. She also writes fiction, and is now pursuing publication for her soon-to-be-complete third novel. A previous novel placed as a finalist in a national competition, and before her creative endeavors, she was an award-winning technical writer.

Sara Schafer is a two-time cancer survivor who is married with two children and a grandson. She cross-stitches bookmarks and writes nonfiction inspirational stories and daily devotionals. E-mail her at sara757s@aol.com.

Dayle Allen Shockley is an award-winning writer whose byline has appeared in dozens of publications. She is the author of three books and a contributor to many other works. She and her husband (a retired fire captain) enjoy traveling RV-style, enjoying God's handiwork.

As the daughter of a missionary doctor, **Alisa Edwards Smith** spent her childhood in Nigeria. She has written articles for *Guideposts* magazine and several other publications. Alisa graduated from Duke University and currently lives in Chapel Hill, NC with her husband and children.

Christine Smith is a mother, grandmother, and great-grandmother who lives with her husband of forty-five years in Oklahoma. Sharing stories of family memories has become a fun and rewarding experience. Christine enjoys reading, writing, and staying busy with family, church, and friends.

A past president and board member of the League of Utah Writers, **Edwin F. Smith** has written articles for the Chicken Soup for the Soul series, *The Ensign*, *Deseret News* and *The Davis County Clipper*. He resides in Kaysville, UT with his wife Ann. E-mail him at efsmithwrites@gmail.com.

Jenny Sokol received her Bachelor of Science degree from the U.S. Naval

Academy in 1994. She writes a weekly column for the *Orange County Register*. Jenny is a military spouse and loves traveling, running, and the adventures of motherhood. E-mail her at SokolOCR@yahoo.com.

Gary Stein co-founded an NYSE-member investment banking division. He has been an advisor to many entertainment firms and helped build a thirty-time Emmy-winning kids' TV company. A previous contributor to Chicken Soup for the Soul, Gary has authored the book, *Confessions of an Unfiltered Mind*. E-mail him at gm.stein@verizon.net.

Nandi Stewart is a Christian, wife and mother of three adult children. Nandi is the librarian at a preparatory school in Jamaica. She loves reading and putting on voices as she reads aloud to her students. Nandi loves paper; she makes beautiful handmade cards.

Genie Stoker graduated from The University of Arizona. She is the mother of three grown children and grandmother of two. Genie has taught parenting classes and has mentored children in reading and science. She's published articles on community service and child development. E-mail Genie at GEStoker@aol.com.

R. Stone is now a global professional in the field of energy and faith healing for people and animals. She practices an interfaith model. She strongly prefers to not receive advice about her own health or beliefs. She may be reached for healing at faithlightheals@gmail.com.

Kamia Taylor has been writing stories since she was six years old, winning her first essay contest in third grade. Since then she has been published in several magazines, and continues to write on the environment, spirituality, business and money tips while playing with her five rescue dogs.

Connie Hyde Thurber grew up on a farm on Prince Edward Island, Canada. She graduated from university in Greenville, SC. She and her husband have two married children. Connie is director of a nonprofit organization in Moncton, NB and enjoys cottage life, reading, biking, and skiing.

Award-winning author **Susan Traugh** has been writing essays, educational and nonfiction books for over twenty-five years. Susan just finished her first young adult novel and a book of essays. She lives in San Diego, CA with her husband Steven. They have two daughters, a son, and an "extra daughter." E-mail her at kiducation@cox.net.

Arlene Uslander received her Bachelor of Arts degree from Northwestern University. She has published sixteen nonfiction books and over 400 newspaper and magazine articles. She is an award-winning journalist and a freelance editor, helping writers polish their manuscripts before they send them to publishers and/or agents.

Rita Kaye Vetsch resides in central Minnesota with her loving family and her quirky pets. She has a passion for writing and recently had her first children's book, *The Many Colors of Friendship*, published by Eloquent Books. Rita enjoys photography, taking care of children and spending time with family.

Marlene Wallach, President, Wilhelmina Kids, takes pride in nurturing young people with a message to become your dream. Marlene has published books promoting the message of empowerment for young teens. She received her MBA degree from Pace University where she gives a series of talks. E-mail her at mwall@wilhelmina.com.

Brenda Warneka has a B.A. degree in history from Oakland University, Rochester, MI, and a JD degree from Wayne State University Law School. She practiced law for twenty-five years. She enjoys travel and researching and writing nonfiction. She lives in Laughlin, NV with her husband, Dick. E-mail her at warneka@cox.net.

Mary Z. Whitney is a regular contributor to the Chicken Soup for the Soul series as well as *Guideposts* and *Angels on Earth* magazines. When not penning praises to her heavenly Father, she can be found gardening or walking her little dog Max with her Marine husband, John, in their country surroundings of Leavittsburg, OH.

Kim Winters leads monthly writing workshops for teens. Her short stories have been published in several anthologies. She eagerly awaits the release of her first young adult fantasy novel *Keeper's Mark*. Follow Kim at Kat's Eye Journal (www.kimwinters.blogspot.com). E-mail her at kwinters16@sbcglobal.net.

Melissa Wootan enjoys refurbishing furniture alongside her husband Joey, but is most passionate about writing. Her stories have appeared in the Chicken Soup for the Soul series and *Guideposts*. She is currently working on her first young adult novel. You may contact her through Facebook at www.facebook.com/chicvintique.

Amy Wyatt is a Jesus-following, Southern-talking, recovering perfectionist, wife and mom who advocates for those living with epilepsy by speaking, writing and spreading awareness. Amy is the founder of Seizing Opportunities, an organization that encourages those affected by epilepsy to enjoy every moment and live life to its fullest.

Jamie White Wyatt is a Bible teacher, speaker, retreat planner, writer, former business owner, and ballroom dancer. Jamie loves encouraging traditions and joy-filled living. Originally from Florida, Jamie, husband Ed, and their grown children, live in Georgia. E-mail her at rockhavenw@gmail.com, or read her blog at www.dancingonthejourney.blogspot.com.

Meet Our Authors

Jack Canfield and **Mark Victor Hansen** are the co-founders of Chicken Soup for the Soul. Jack is the author of many bestselling books and is CEO of the Canfield Training Group. Mark is a prolific writer and has had a profound influence in the field of human potential through his library of audios, videos, and articles. Jack and Mark have received many awards and honors, including a Guinness World Records Certificate for having seven books from the Chicken Soup for the Soul series on the New York Times bestseller list on May 24, 1998. You can reach them at www.jackcanfield.com and www.markvictorhansen.com.

Amy Newmark has been Chicken Soup for the Soul's publisher, coauthor, and editor-in-chief for the last six years, after a 30-year career as a writer, speaker, financial analyst, and business executive in the worlds of finance and telecommunications. Amy is a Chartered Financial Analyst and a *magna cum laude* graduate of Harvard College, where she majored in Portuguese, minored in French, and traveled extensively. She and her husband have four grown children.

After a long career writing books on telecommunications, voluminous financial reports, business plans, and corporate press releases, Chicken Soup for the Soul is a breath of fresh air for Amy. She loves creating these life-changing books for Chicken Soup for the Soul's wonderful readers. She has coauthored and/or edited more than 100 Chicken Soup for the Soul books.

You can reach Amy with any questions or comments through webmaster@chickensoupforthesoul.com and you can follow her on Twitter @amynewmark or @chickensoupsoul.

Thank You

We owe huge thanks to all of our contributors. We know that you poured your hearts and souls into the thousands of stories that you shared with us, and ultimately with each other. As we read and edited these stories, we were truly amazed by your experiences. We appreciate your willingness to share these inspiring and encouraging stories with our readers.

We could only publish a small percentage of the stories that were submitted, but we read every single one and even the ones that do not appear in the book had an influence on us and on the final manuscript. We owe special thanks to our college intern Madeleine Feinberg who read all the stories submitted for this book and helped us narrow the field. Our managing editor and production coordinator Kristiana Pastir narrowed the list down to a more manageable number of finalists for my consideration and helped me create the chapters and the initial manuscript. Our assistant publisher D'ette Corona did her normal masterful job of working with the contributors to approve our edits and answer any questions we had, as well as helping select many stories. And Barbara LoMonaco ran our story database to get the stories in, and then did the final proofreading as we went into production.

We also owe a special thanks to our creative director and book producer, Brian Taylor at Pneuma Books, for his brilliant vision for our covers and interiors.

~Amy Newmark

Sharing Happiness, Inspiration, and Wellness

Real people sharing real stories, every day, all over the world. In 2007, *USA Today* named *Chicken Soup for the Soul* one of the five most memorable books in the last quarter-century. With over 100 million books sold to date in the U.S. and Canada alone, more than 200 titles in print, and translations into more than 40 languages, "chicken soup for the soul" is one of the world's best-known phrases.

Today, 20 years after we first began sharing happiness, inspiration and wellness through our books, we continue to delight our readers with new titles, but have also evolved beyond the bookstore, with wholesome and balanced pet food, delicious nutritious comfort food, and a major motion picture in development. Whatever you're doing, wherever you are, Chicken Soup for the Soul is "always there for you™." Thanks for reading!

Share with Us

We all have had Chicken Soup for the Soul moments in our lives. If you would like to share your story or poem with millions of people around the world, go to chickensoup.com and click on "Submit Your Story." You may be able to help another reader, and become a published author at the same time. Some of our past contributors have launched writing and speaking careers from the publication of their stories in our books!

Our submission volume has been increasing steadily—the quality and quantity of your submissions has been fabulous. We only accept story submissions via our website. They are no longer accepted via mail or fax.

To contact us regarding other matters, please send us an e-mail through webmaster@chickensoupforthesoul.com, or fax or write us at:

Chicken Soup for the Soul
P.O. Box 700
Cos Cob, CT 06807-0700
Fax: 203-861-7194

One more note from your friends at Chicken Soup for the Soul: Occasionally, we receive an unsolicited book manuscript from one of our readers, and we would like to respectfully inform you that we do not accept unsolicited manuscripts and we must discard the ones that appear.

www.chickensoup.com